THE EVERYDAY GUIDE TO CANADIAN FAMILY LAW

"Access to justice" are the call words of aggrieved family members who believe they have been wronged in the emotional rupturing of their family unit. "Why does it take so long?" "Nobody understood me!" "It costs so much."

This book provides the answers. Judges, lawyers, paralegals, law clerks, legal secretaries, court administrators, social workers, mediators, arbitrators, doctors, teachers, friends and all persons interested in the breakup of families will benefit from this book although it is not written especially for them. It is aimed at spouses. It is information which de-mystifies a process almost as complex as life itself.

The Everyday Guide to Canadian Family Law will save the reader countless hours of worry and frustration. And its by-product may very well produce a far happier reconstituted family, the benefit of which will be gratefully felt by the innocent children I represent.

-Willson A. McTavish, Q.C.
Official Guardian (Ontario)

The best lawyers are happy to save their clients substantial sums of money in legal fees. This volume will achieve just that by assisting the client who seeks to become knowledgeable of his or her rights and responsibilities and of the legal processes leading to their determination.

-Chief Judge H.T.G. Andrews
Provincial Court of Ontario (Family Division)

Michael Cochrane's credentials as a lecturer, private practitioner and family law policy analyst for government not only permit him to write this book, they require that he should do so. Its goal is to make the reader an informed consumer of legal services in the family law area. The book is not intended to replace a lawyer's critical and essential function (that is impossible); it is intended to give a consumer some knowledge of the territory and a guide to reading the signposts.

No Canadian should turn to the law for a resolution of his or her matrimonial problems without reading this straightforward and useful book.

-Ian Scott, M.P.P. St. George—St. David
former Attorney General of Ontario

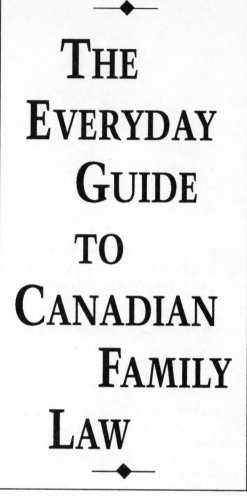

THE EVERYDAY GUIDE TO CANADIAN FAMILY LAW

Michael G. Cochrane, LL.B.

Prentice-Hall Canada Inc., Scarborough, Ontario

Canadian Cataloguing in Publication Data

Cochrane, Michael G. (Michael George), 1953--
The everyday guide to Canadian family law

ISBN 0-13-298894-1

1. Domestic relations - Canada - Popular works.
I. Title.
KE539.2.C63 1991   346.7101'5   C91-093170-4

Prentice-Hall Inc., *Englewood Cliffs, New Jersey*
Prentice-Hall International, Inc., *London*
Prentice-Hall of Australia, Pty., *Sydney*
Prentice-Hall of India Pvt. Ltd., *New Delhi*
Prentice-Hall of Southeast Asia (Pte.) Ltd., *Singapore*
Editora Prentice-Hall do Brasil Ltda., *Rio de Janeiro*
Prentice-Hall Hispanoamericana, S.A., *Mexico*

Editor: Cyril Strom
Design: Monica Kompter
Manufacturing Buyer: Lisa Kreuch

ISBN 0-13-298894-1

Printed and bound in the U.S.A. by R.R. Donnelley &
Sons Company

1 2 3 4 5   RRD   95 94 93 92 91

Acknowledgements

I would like to acknowledge the help of all those family law clients who, over the years, have shared their experiences with me. Your need for information encouraged me to write this book.

I would also like to acknowledge the assistance of the Federal/Provincial/ Territorial Committee on Family Law Policy, whose members made sure the book was up-to-date.

The Helen Heller Agency was responsible for my introduction to Prentice-Hall Canada who recognized this book's potential. I thank them both for their support.

Yasmin Poplata, my faithful word processor operator, deserves special thanks for helping me "do it again."

Cy Strom provided some very helpful editorial comments and polish.

The Law Foundation of Ontario generously provided a grant to assist in preparing this manuscript.

My most important acknowledgement is of my one true inspiration, my daughter Emma. Thanks, sweetie.

Michael G. Cochrane

Author's Note

It is a goal of this book to make the reader a more informed consumer of legal services in the family law area. It is designed as an overview and guide to Canadian family law.

Each family law case is different and the law varies from province to province, so the book's applicability to individual cases is limited. We cannot warrant that the laws described will apply to your particular case. If you have a family law problem, consult a lawyer to determine how your circumstances may be affected by the law of your province.

My goal is not to help you to avoid lawyers—it is to help you to deal with them.

A considerable amount of my family law knowledge and experience has been derived from my position as a Senior Policy Counsel with the Ministry of the Attorney General of Ontario, for which I am extremely grateful. However, the opinions ex-pressed in this book are mine alone and should in no way be interpreted as having been endorsed by either the Ministry of the Attorney General or the Government of Ontario.

In this book I have used factual situations to illustrate some of the problems people encounter. While all of the circumstances described are real, the names, places and some facts have been changed to protect clients' privacy and the confidentiality clients enjoy with their lawyers.

Table of Contents

Introduction

Over the last ten years family law in Canada has undergone some very dramatic reform in order to keep pace with the many changes occurring in our society. The increasing number of marriage breakdowns, common-law relationships, single-parent families, the recognition of domestic violence and the mobility of families have all contributed to the growing complexity in family relations. Newspapers, magazines and television provide us with the most intimate details of family disputes—"grandparent seeks access to grandchild," "mother loses custody of children," "father refuses to pay support," "wealthy couple fights over family business" and so on. Yet little of the relevant law is understood.

As complex as family law has become, little if any material is available to help families or individuals undergoing family crises to understand for themselves exactly what is happening to them. What little information they gain is picked up second hand from the experiences of friends who have "gone through the mill." The only alternative is to go directly to a lawyer and pay for a potentially expensive lesson in basic family law.

This lack of information means that families in crisis are among the least informed of consumers. They head into the marketplace of legal services without the foggiest idea about our family law system. They are powerless and because of it they are taken advantage of by the system.

On the basis of my experiences as a lawyer in private practice, as a lecturer at universities and law schools, as a policy advisor in the Attorney General's Office and as someone who has talked directly to consumers about this issue I believe that ordinary people want more than gossip and often require less than a lawyer's advice before they make informed decisions about their personal lives and the lives of their children.

This book is designed as a handbook for those people and for anyone who wants to know more about Canadian family law. Who will benefit from reading it?

- people who are separated and involved in legal proceedings—or may become involved
- people who are thinking about separating
- people who are living common law—or thinking about it

1

- people who are thinking about getting married
- people who want marriage contracts
- people who are involved in violent marriages or relationships
- people who have been through the legal mill and are still wondering what happened

A quick glance at the Table of Contents will give you an idea of some of the areas that I try to demystify for you, areas like

- the emotional stages of marriage breakdown
- domestic violence
- hiring and firing lawyers
- the family law court system
- the division of family property
- support
- custody and access
- the rights of common-law spouses
- marriage contracts

and more.

When I described this project to a family law lawyer friend of mine he told me, "You're giving away all the secrets." He was right.

Take a quick look at the Appendices. They contain examples of the paperwork that you face in a family dispute and a glossary of legal terms to guide you through the legal mumbo jumbo.

All this information is provided in a way that makes it useful in all provinces (except Quebec) and the territories. While the specific names of documents and courts and procedures can vary from jurisdiction to jurisdiction, the broad principles and guidelines are similar. I have tried to organize these guidelines by subject area, and in the way that most people actually ask for such information.

My goals in writing the book are fairly straightforward: I want you to become an informed consumer of family law legal services. If you do, you will save thousands of dollars in legal fees, you will have a great deal more control over your life and you will make better decisions for yourself and your family.

Will reading this book save you a thousand dollars in legal fees? The promise isn't an idle one. If you read this book and digest some of the advice before going to a lawyer about a family law matter, you could save at least that amount. In some cases you may save much more. The reason is very simple: After reading this book you will be a much better informed consumer. You will know how to pick the right lawyer for your needs and how to tell the lawyer what you want for yourself and your children. You will have a good understanding of what our laws actually say about family problems and how "the system" works. You will even learn when not to see your lawyer—a significant saving in itself.

The best way to illustrate the potential savings in being an informed consumer is through some examples. The following situations are all drawn from cases of which I was personally aware while in private practice or while participating in the reform of our family laws.

The Battered Client

An older woman arrived in a lawyer's office early one Monday morning still bearing the marks of a beating she had received over a week earlier. She was accompanied by three lovely children who had finally persuaded her to leave their father, her abusive husband of thirty years. She had finally had enough and had left him the previous week. Where had she been? The first lawyer she had consulted was the real estate lawyer who had helped with the purchase of their home and occasional refinancing. He didn't "do family law" but agreed to see her. After two interviews, the collection of some of her important documents such as her marriage certificate, after telephone calls to the husband who was holed up in the family home on an alcoholic binge and after taking care of some other clients' real estate deals, he gave his advice: He suggested she try to "work things out," especially since legal proceedings would be slow and expensive. A court order, he said, couldn't be obtained for over a month. With this priceless advice she received a bill for $1,000.

She nearly took the advice until her eldest daughter prevailed on her to get a second opinion from a family law lawyer. Twenty-four hours after she arrived in that lawyer's office she had an order for exclusive possession of the home, a restraining order against the husband, custody of the youngest child and a support order. The first thousand dollars would have been better spent on the children.

The Client in the Dark

A thirty-six-year-old man who had divorced two years earlier consulted a lawyer about enforcing an order which gave him access to his eight-year-old son on specific days of each week. He had started a new relationship recently and brought this woman when he went to pick up his son one Friday evening. His former spouse didn't approve of this new development and denied him access. His lawyer said, "Leave it with me." A court proceeding was started involving a sworn affidavit from the man setting out what had occurred. The proceeding asked that the wife be found in contempt of court and that she be jailed or fined. It was served on the former wife and was scheduled to be in court three weeks later (the first available court date). When the day arrived the case was adjourned to allow her to file a sworn affidavit, too. Then it was adjourned to allow both lawyers to ask the clients questions under oath in front of a court reporter. Then they waited for the transcript to be prepared. Then it was adjourned because the lawyers were detained in other courts on other cases.

Finally, nine weeks after the proceeding was started, the matter was actually going to be dealt with by a judge. The former wife's lawyer suggested that it be settled by giving the child's father an extra weekend with the son sometime to make up for the time lost. It was also suggested that both clients pay their own lawyers' fees. The husband's lawyer recommended that the offer be accepted because contempt motions *are rarely if ever successful anyway*.

The client wanted to know why he hadn't been told that in the first place. Cost? No less than $3,500, and he hadn't seen his child regularly during those nine weeks.

The Angry Client

When this older childless couple separated, the wife was beside herself with anger. After years of devotion to her husband he had become distant and then suddenly left her for another woman. She retained the "toughest" family law lawyer in Toronto. Property division and support were the only issues and even those were not very difficult. Her instructions? She wanted to get what she was entitled to by law and to teach him a lesson. The lawyer took her instructions seriously and a battle began that allowed the lawyers to show each other just how good they were in court.

Two years and over a dozen court appearances later she got what she wanted, a judgment for half the family's property in the amount of $185,000 and spousal support. She did not "get her costs"; in other words, the court did not order the husband to pay all or even part of her legal fees, which were $50,000. The court didn't make such an order because her judgment was *equal to that for which the husband had offered to settle the case.* She instructed her lawyer to take steps to collect the $185,000 and he said he would be happy to do so—once the balance of his account, $25,000, was paid. She explained that she would pay him out of the money collected. His answer? Sorry, he had invested enough time and money in the case and would not take any further steps until paid. And remember, she was entitled to the $185,000 by law.

The Blindsided Client

A young couple went to their respective lawyers to get a separation agreement. They were on relatively friendly terms and knew what they wanted except for a couple of small concerns about their two children. Both suddenly found themselves being told not to discuss the matter with each other—to avoid "confusion" during the settlement discussions.

His lawyer suggested that legal proceedings be commenced, as a precaution, and held in the file. If negotiations didn't go well, they could serve the proceedings and gain strategic advantage. Discussions continued, but suddenly the proceedings were served on her at work in front of her friends. The papers said that her husband wanted custody, so she instructed her lawyer to file for custody, too. They were in court before they knew what hit them. The matter was adjourned to allow everybody to cool off. Cost? $2,500—each.

She heard from a friend that mediation (where an objective third person facilitates settlement discussions between the couple directly) should be tried. With a little help they found a mediator, the original problem was solved and an agreement reached for joint custody of the children.

The mediator's fees were $900. The clients wanted to know why the lawyers had not told them about mediation. His lawyer's answer? "You didn't ask about it." Her lawyer's answer? She didn't "believe" in mediation.

The $5,000 in lawyers' fees was a waste, particularly in a year when finances were tight due to the separation and the new expense of maintaining two households.

The Surprised Bride

Late one Friday afternoon, which is one of the busiest times in a law office, my secretary informed me that a young woman and her parents had just arrived in need of "emergency advice." They were escorted into my office where the father plunked down a marriage contract which had been presented to his daughter by her fiancé the night before. The emergency? She had been given the contract at the wedding rehearsal! The wedding was scheduled for Saturday. The bride-to-be had been told to take the marriage contract to a lawyer and sign it if the wedding was to go ahead as planned.

Her mother explained that the church had been booked a year in advance, the caterers five months in advance, guests were coming from across the country—what choice did they have?

I decided to see the daughter alone. She wanted to sign. They were in love, she said, and would never separate anyway, so who cared what the contract said? As we talked, she explained that it wasn't really the groom's idea, it was his parents' idea because they were giving the couple such a large wedding present—a down payment on a house. In fact, the parents' lawyer had drafted it.

I spent a few minutes reviewing the contract and determined that it went a little further than her husband-to-be thought. It took a few more hours that afternoon and most of the evening to get the contract straightened out—which we did with a little imagination and a lot of bluff. The wedding went ahead and the couple, as far as I know, is as happy as can be. But between Friday and Saturday afternoon the bride-to-be got the education of a lifetime. I'll tell you how we resolved that one in a later chapter that deals with marriage contracts.

I could probably fill a book with similar examples of uninformed clients seeing things slip away once in the lawyer's office or in the legal system. My point is that this would be less likely to occur if people had a good idea about what awaited them and if they played a role in deciding what was going to happen to them or their children or their hard-earned property. The aforementioned clients could have saved a lot more than the thousand dollars I cited earlier if, for example, they had gone to a family law specialist, if they had asked for written retainers and opinions before proceeding, if they had understood that instructions given in anger are invitations for disaster, if they had understood that the "toughest" lawyer may not be the best, and that there is more to family law than what is thrashed out in the courtroom.

Read the book. Save a thousand dollars—maybe more. But more importantly, gain some control over what will be a difficult time.

WHAT'S WRONG WITH FAMILY LAW?

I've been asked this question a few dozen times, especially when speaking to the public about family law issues. In trying to explain what I think is wrong I divide our system of family law into three general components: the people in the system with problems; the process of family law—the rules and methods of problem solving; and finally, the other key players who are responsible for guiding people through the process—the lawyers. Each component is a part of the larger problem, but all share the blame.

Let's consider for a moment the people who must use the family law process—people undergoing separation and divorce. This group is largely uninformed (or worse, misinformed) about what is about to happen and the decisions that will be expected of them. To make matters worse, at the time they are expected to make these decisions, they may be angry, broken hearted, victims of violence, despairing and frequently unaware of their future needs.

We then take these poor souls and make them resolve their problems in a process that is adversarial, slow and often illogical. It is expensive, not flexible enough, and sometimes controlled by judges who do not have an interest in family law cases. At the same time there is no emotional support in the system itself for the people who are looking for help.

Who is best placed to help people through this maze? Lawyers, of course. But even the important decision of selecting a personal guide to family law is left to chance.

With all of the above in mind we can now turn to an examination of each of these three components. My goal is to enable you to exercise control over yourselves as users of the system, control over the lawyers and finally control over the process itself. Lawyers should not just listen to your opinion, they should respect it.

It is not a goal of this book to convince you to go it alone without a lawyer. There is too much at stake to tinker with your own case. Support, property division and most importantly, the best interests of your children, are all at risk. You should understand that by informing yourself, you are doing your part, but there is still a part for your lawyer. You are helping your lawyer do a better job for you. Your knowledge and confidence will undoubtedly speed up the process, save time and expenses, narrow the issues in dispute and facilitate a solution.

1

The Emotional Stages
of Marriage Breakdown

Lawyers love to go to court. That's where all the real drama is played out: witnesses cross-examined, exhibits shown, legal argument presented and, almost anti-climactically, a judgment or some order handed down by the court. But as dramatic as that setting may be, lawyers also love to settle cases, and they can often be found around courthouses leaning against the walls and talking with pride about "the one they just settled" as if it were some trophy they had just mounted.

I had a chance to eavesdrop before a meeting one day as a couple of family law lawyers, one senior, one very junior, traded banter about their recent settlements. The junior lawyer was bemoaning the fact that his client had just accepted a settlement that was, in his opinion, satisfactory. That's right—satisfactory, and the lawyer was unhappy.

"I can't figure it," he said. "I could have got her that settlement six months ago. Suddenly one morning my client waltzes into my office and instructs me to accept the offer of settlement that had been made months earlier. I couldn't believe my ears. After six months of vicious motions and real testy discoveries, six months of bloodletting, she wants to settle. She was like a different person.... The same settlement was available six months ago ..." The lawyer's voice trailed off in disbelief. He was totally baffled by the about-face of his client.

The senior lawyer nodded knowingly but added an observation. "Maybe she was a different person."

"No, it was her, all right," the junior lawyer added somewhat facetiously.

"I'm serious, maybe she was a different person, maybe she had changed." The senior lawyer bore down a little on her pupil. "Maybe she had moved into that stage at which she felt comfortable restructuring her life."

"Stage? What stage?" The junior looked uncomfortable.

I sat there pretending as best I could to be reading a thick report for my meeting, thinking to myself: "Oh my God, this lawyer is out there trying to help people involved in family problems and does not understand the first thing about the emotional stages that most people move through at marriage breakdown."

7

Not only must lawyers themselves understand these stages, but I believe they have an obligation to explain them to their clients at the very outset. I believe lawyers have an obligation to provide their clients with some perspective on where they are and where they may be headed emotionally.

This poor young lawyer was destined to a never-ending string of family law clients who would be surprising him constantly with seemingly unpredictable mood changes and apparently conflicting opinions and instructions. The lawyer's only explanation? "Wow, clients in family disputes are crazy!" His clients probably went away feeling that he was right, not knowing how or why their feelings could change so dramatically over a relatively short period of time.

Well, they are not crazy at all. They are simply being asked to make some of the most important decisions of their lives under the most painful and stressful of circumstances. Would that we could all shine and be reasonable and sensible under such pressure. However, with a little help and perspective on the emotional changes that accompany them, these difficult times can be made considerably smoother.

Understanding a person undergoing family breakdown is possible if one understands some general stages or phases through which that person may pass. I say that a person *may* pass through them because there are no guarantees that everyone will do so. I still have vivid memories of clients who never quite got on with their lives. Some stayed stalled for five, even ten years after the separation, not really wanting or needing to reconcile with their spouse, sometimes seething with a vague anger, but at the same time not knowing what to do next.

Others, of course, move quickly and smoothly through all the emotional stages and emerge in a few months ready for career changes, new loves and new families. I can't help but wonder whether they had an "emotional perspective" on the family breakdown that contributed in some way to their having a sense of direction and control.

In 1969, Elisabeth Kübler-Ross, then Medical Director of the Family Service and Mental Health Center of South Cook County in Illinois, published a book entitled *On Death and Dying*. *Life* magazine described it as a "profound lesson for the living." Her observations on death and dying were formed on the basis of her experiences with terminally ill patients. She identified a number of distinct phases through which the terminally ill will pass.

Many experienced family law practitioners and mental health professionals have been struck by the parallels between the experiences of those who are dying and those undergoing a marriage or family breakdown. While these stages will not apply to every case, they provide a useful framework to understand where a person may be in emotional terms. This understanding is invaluable because it may, for example, act as a rare clue to a person's motivation when instructing his or her lawyer.

Kübler-Ross identified the following stages:

1. Denial and isolation
2. Anger

3. Bargaining
4. Depression
5. Acceptance

What follows is a modest attempt to adapt her analysis of terminally ill patients to those undergoing the breakdown of a relationship or family.

1. DENIAL AND ISOLATION ("It's not happening to me ... Something else is wrong.")

In the context of learning that one is terminally ill, Kübler-Ross identified a tendency to deny the fact of the illness. This, she speculated, is meant to be a buffer after the shock of unexpected news. It allows the patient to collect himself or herself and to mobilize defences.

Our expectations of our marriages are not unlike our expectations about life—that is, that we will be immortal in both. These expectations are not unreasonable given the rather spectacular pledges made at weddings. This is not for a moment to suggest that we should be more cynical about wedding vows, but rather that we should recognize the extremely high expectations with which couples begin their marriages and live in relationships. It is these expectations that come crashing down at separation. This appears to be true regardless of the number of marriages the individual enters into. Time and time again I have encountered people who have married three and four times, each time with renewed confidence that "this one is the right one."

It is not surprising, therefore, that the first reaction to marital strain, marriage breakdown or many other problems in a family is a denial of what is occurring. Something ("his job's too much lately") or someone else ("her family") must be to blame. A typical response would be: "If I ignore this problem, it will blow over or go away on its own." This denial more likely than not occurs (or begins to occur) well in advance of the actual separation. Some spouses report knowing "something was wrong" months or even years before they separate. Commonly, they admit denying there was a problem—"Please let it be something else," "He'll change," "She promised it would never happen again," "He has been working hard lately," "She's just depressed," and so on and so on. Sometimes it works and the problem appears to blow over. In fact, sometimes it is "something else." But many times it is just plain old denial of a fundamental challenge to the relationship or family.

If the marriage has indeed "ended" for one partner but not the other (as is often the case), denial can be a powerful obstacle to a lawyer attempting to assist in the orderly severing of the knot. "Denying clients" may move from lawyer to lawyer in search of someone who will share their view, someone who will keep them in the marriage, who will keep the family together. It is not unlike the terminally ill patient who seeks a second, a third, even a fourth medical opinion. They search for someone who will keep their original expectation of immortality alive.

So we should understand that for those experiencing marital difficulties or other family problems, a likely first response from one or both individuals—out of self-defence—is to deny, deny, deny. This can be tragic and painful for the people involved. Imagine the difficulty in resolving any issue between spouses in such a predicament. One person is not ready to discuss a settlement because that person doesn't even know or agree that there is a major problem. I remember one client who asked me to delay a divorce so that his wife would have time to "snap out of it." She was remarried by the time he clued in.

2. ANGER ("It *is* happening to me ... and I hate it.")

The denial stage is often followed by a partial acceptance of what has occurred. The issue or problem between the partners can no longer be avoided, perhaps because the other partner has taken unmistakable steps to confront the issue—like moving out or starting divorce proceedings. The "patient" finally accepts the diagnosis, perhaps after multiple consultations with other "doctors." However, while the diagnosis is finally accepted, denial is often replaced with anger because the client doesn't like what he or she hears. The anger may be directed against the other spouse, family members, oneself (the harshest, perhaps) or the lawyers who may now be involved. These angry clients often talk of being made to look foolish, of being blind or stupid. Suddenly the other spouse has been taking advantage of him or her, apparently laughing all the while.

Once the awful truth is accepted, a spouse may be left with little else but his or her anger at a frustrating, possibly humiliating, predicament. It is at this stage that people often consult their lawyers. The other spouse may have forced the issue into the open by consulting a lawyer, letters are sent and the truth comes home to roost for the denying spouse.

It is also at this stage that lawyers frequently receive their instructions to start legal proceedings, to bring motions, to be tough and, in short, to vent the angry client's venom in legal proceedings. They are proceedings that the lawyer and client can ill afford to institute because they are not designed to advance the client's interests, nor will they make the client happy. If anything, such proceedings may produce only regrets. The client who offers instructions to a lawyer while in such a state of mind will never be happy, and will later blame his or her lawyer for wasting time and money. At this stage we may be left with a person who no longer denies that there is a problem but now confronts the issue with what is never a scarce resource—unproductive anger.

Beware: this stage has been known to last a long time.

3. BARGAINING ("If I do this, maybe you will do that.")

Kübler-Ross describes this next phase as an attempt to postpone the inevitable. The anger, which has not produced anything, subsides partially. But now promises, often unrealistic, are made in the hope of gaining "more time." The patient has accepted what is happening but now negotiates to postpone it. Again the same is often true of people in family breakdown. Unrealistic promises are made to extend the marriage or the bond between the partners.

The bargaining may manifest itself in overly generous settlement proposals: "She can have everything." Sometimes the offer is no more than a weak attempt to ease guilt or to prove to the other spouse that "I'm not so bad after all": "I'm the one who left, he can keep the house." Unfortunately, but not surprisingly, such promises are rarely wise—and rarely kept—and the day of reckoning arrives. The client's interests have not been advanced; in fact, they may have been harmed.

At this stage we have a client whose anger may be subsiding but whose instructions are nonetheless tainted by unreal feelings. Lawyers and clients alike must be alert to these motivations and recognize that instructions during this phase of false bargaining are unlikely to produce lasting settlements. They will, however, produce a legal bill—and you will later wonder what you are paying for.

4. DEPRESSION   ("I'm losing my past and I have no future.")

This next phase is identified by Kübler-Ross as one in which the terminally ill patient's sense of anger subsides, the false bargaining has ended unsuccessfully (as it had to) and a sense of great loss sets in. She identifies this depression as being two-edged—a *reactive* depression and a *preparatory* depression.

The first depression is in reaction to the past loss. What the patient once had is now gone or is slipping away. The second depression is one that results from taking into account impending losses.

For the couple undergoing marriage breakdown this "double depression" is understandable. Their reactive depression may be in response to the loss of such things as "their best friend," "their life partner," a sense of family, time with their children, the family home, valued possessions and so on. At the same time they must face the losses yet to come—the companionship of the spouse, the old network of friends and acquaintances, the plans that were made but will never materialize. The future is suddenly tainted. In many cases both spouses must lower their financial expectations. A standard of living once taken for granted is gone.

Few clients in this state of mind are equipped to provide balanced instructions to their lawyer. Not only does the past generate feelings of sadness, but prospects for the future seem bleak as well. Sadness and loss of hope suddenly overwhelm everything. Negotiating on behalf of this client is of course pointless for a lawyer. The client does not care what happens.

5. ACCEPTANCE   ("I've got things I want to do.")

It may appear from all of the above that people are virtually never able to provide instructions to their lawyers. If they are not denying the problem, angry or depressed, they are engaged in false bargaining. As we shall see, there *is* a time when clients are best equipped to make decisions. Lawyers may not always have the luxury of awaiting that moment (if it actually arrives), but there is a recognizable moment. This stage is described by

Kübler-Ross as a time when the patient is neither depressed nor angry about his fate. It is a time of contemplation and almost void of feelings. The dying patient at this time has found some peace and acceptance.

In the case of marriage breakdown, the spouse at this stage will have accepted the end of the marriage and will no longer see the dispute or court process as a means of prolonging any link with the other spouse. It is as if everything has suddenly become clearer. Settlement proposals suddenly seem worthy of consideration. If the marriage is truly over, then the final loose ends should be tied up. The chapter of life that was the marriage must be closed as best it can be. Suddenly, planning seems worthwhile, new events have meaning and the past is just that—past. What is also important at this stage is what I call the client's willingness to reconstruct or start again. What is ahead is what is important. As corny as it sounds, what is past truly is prologue.

It is at this stage of acceptance that clients are best equipped emotionally to settle. (Please understand that by "settle" I do not mean "give up.") For the first time, perhaps in months or years, emotions are not obstructing their powers of reason. They are able to describe what is best for their children, what they need and what they want.

This is the stage at which, in my anecdote, the junior lawyer's client had "suddenly" arrived. She had denied, she had been angry, she had been depressed. She had even tried a little false bargaining to buy time. But she ultimately accepted what had occurred and found herself ready to move on.

No one should be embarrassed about this experience, because it is a natural evolution of feelings. I would be more embarrassed (or worried) if it didn't occur. Of course you should be angry and depressed—you are going through something that is awful. The best you can do sometimes is just to understand it, roll with it and recognize that it will all pass and you will move on.

A final note concerns two invitations to any lawyers who might be reading this book. First, look back on the family law files that you have closed. Virtually everyone has a file that settled late in the proceedings on terms that were similar, if not identical, to a proposal made earlier in the proceedings. If the client's acceptance of the final settlement was considered as simply the client's whim or wish to avoid an impending trial, consider that the client may have been in two different phases when the offers were presented.

The second invitation is the more important one. Pull out each and every active file and give some consideration to where your client—and the other spouse—might be emotionally, and then act accordingly. Start by talking to your client about which emotional stage he or she may have reached.

CONCLUSIONS

We have seen the five emotional stages of marriage breakdown (denial, anger, bargaining, depression and acceptance), but knowing of them is of little use unless you apply them to your own circumstances. Read the following questions. You might not be able to answer them all immediately, but if you work through them, you may gain some valuable insights.

1. How do you feel about the predicament in which you find yourself?
2. Are you in any of these stages?
3. What has been your motivation in retaining a lawyer?
4. Have you provided instructions to your lawyer out of anger?
5. Out of guilt?
6. Out of fear?
7. Have you been trying to bargain for time?
8. Why?
9. What do you really want?
10. Can you realistically have that?
11. Why not?
12. What can you have, realistically?
13. Would you be happy with that?
14. Are you unhappy with what occurred?
15. Are you anxious about the future?
16. Are you filled with second thoughts?
17. Secretly relieved that it may be over?
18. Are you ready to start living again?
19. Are you making plans?

If you have asked yourself any or all of these questions—you are like thousands of others. You are a person with a family problem.

Thousands of people are in the same position, but what makes you different is that you are one of the very few who have taken a look at themselves from an emotional point of view in the context of their legal problems. You are on the way to becoming an informed consumer of legal services and a very powerful client.

2

Domestic Violence

As I sat here organizing the material for this chapter, the local radio news featured an item concerning a woman and child who had been abducted. With great relief the announcer reported that the two, who had been abducted the previous evening, had in fact been taken hostage by the woman's husband, who was upset over their recent separation. He had beaten her with a brick and apparently driven around the city all night. "But," the reporter said, "everything is fine now and the woman does not wish to press charges." I think what struck me most about this story was that the announcer related this last fact as if to say, "Well there's another typical husband and wife spat that has settled back down." On to the next news item.

I thought about that woman and child for a few moments and about what they had really returned to in that home. Why didn't she press charges? I think I have a good idea about why she didn't. In this chapter, we shall examine the ugly secret of violence that affects thousands of women and children every day in Canada. Perhaps it has occurred in your neighbour's home, in your family's, or even in your own home.

What do we mean by "domestic violence"? Other terms are used from time to time—"wife beating," "wife battering," "wife assault" and "wife abuse." I have used the term "domestic violence" because it captures two important aspects of this issue: it generally occurs in the home and the term does not leave the impression that it only happens to "married women." We are talking about violence by men against women and children.

One definition that captures the elements of this conduct as it relates to women is that given by Deborah Sinclair, in *Understanding Wife Assault* (p. 15):·

Wife assault involves the intent by the husband to intimidate, either by threat or by use of physical force on the wife's person or property. The purpose of the assault is to control her behaviour by the inducement of fear. Underlying all abuse is a power imbalance between the victim and the offender.

Examples of physical abuse abound: slapping, punching, kicking, shoving, choking and even pinching. Shelter workers report cases of women being

14

burned, beaten with belts, stabbed and even shot—sometimes with fatal consequences. Abuse can include sexual assaults, humiliation, forced and unwanted sexual acts or such things as being forced to watch pornography.

It need not involve just physical assault. Psychological abuse can often achieve the desired effect. I recall from my own practice the woman who had been hit only once but found it enough to make her feel that one false move would bring a reign of terror against not just her, but her children, her family and her friends. She dared not jeopardize anyone else because she knew that her husband could make his threats real. She suffered for years thinking that her "walking on eggshells" was actually protecting others. It justified her miserable life. She saw her clothes destroyed and her personal photos burned. She suffered humiliations and was forced to beg for money. Threats against the victim, family, children, property or pets can be quite effective.

Her abuser rivalled another husband who responded to his wife's suggestion of marriage counselling with a promise to cut her wedding-ring finger off with a pair of tin snips. She got the message—and so did her daughters. Like others I had met, she described a pattern to the terror in her home: first a period of growing tension, next an explosion of violence often triggered by some minor event, and then the "honeymoon" when the repenting man becomes the charming person she used to know. Apologies flow with gifts and lavish attention—until the next period of tension and the cycle repeats itself.

What is going on out there? Various studies in both Canada and the United States have provided us with a shocking glimpse of this problem:

- One in ten women in Canada is a victim of domestic violence.
- Less than half of the violence (44 percent) is reported to police.
- Violence will occur at least once in two-thirds of marriages.
- One U.S. study estimated that one in four wives is beaten severely during her marriage.
- In 1982, two-fifths of all homicides in Canada were spouses killing spouses; the majority (62 percent) killed were women.
- Some studies report that a woman may be beaten on average thirty-five times before she reports the violence.
- Almost one-half (49 percent) of domestic assaults result in physical injuries.
- One-quarter of all women who attempt suicide have been victims of domestic violence.
- Hundreds of thousands of Canadian households live with domestic violence every year.

Putting aside the causes of this violence, we are witnessing a modern-day plague in our own homes—with no end in sight.

What about men who are assaulted? There is undoubtedly a man reading this chapter and thinking: "Hey, this is biased. Men are assaulted by their wives, too!" Maybe I can speak to you directly for a moment. We have all heard the stories that occasionally make their way around offices about some burly guy who gets knocked around by his wiry wife and is too ashamed to admit it. Everyone laughs or nods knowingly as if, yes, it happens all the time. Maybe it did happen, but it doesn't happen much and certainly does not approach the scale of violence against women and children. This is not to say for even a moment that those men who are assaulted should not be helped. Of course they should be helped. But those occasional occurrences should not be allowed to diminish the magnitude of the bigger problem. When we talk about a big ugly secret in Canadian homes we are talking about violence against women and children by men.

What about those children?

I mentioned the woman whose daughters learned a lesson from seeing their mother assaulted. The lesson was in how to be a victim. Girls who witness violence against their mother pick up a not-too-subtle message about how women are supposed to relate to men. Similarly, young boys who see their mothers being beaten learn that this is how men treat their intimate partners, their future wives and the mothers of their children.

The emotional trauma these children experience is well known. The profile for these children of battered women describes a child filled with fear, anger and confusion. Statistics can sometimes be boring, but not these:

- 70 percent of all women seeking shelter from abusive partners have children
- 17 percent of them have more than three children
- one study in Toronto found that children were present during 68 percent of 2,910 assault cases
- one-third of the men who abuse their wives abuse their children, too.

I think you probably have the picture now. In this chapter I examine some aspects of domestic violence. My primary goal is not to propose a cure-all. That task is well beyond this book. I intend to deal with the violence on a more practical level and look at how to identify the pattern of domestic violence, the victims and the perpetrators. Most importantly, I provide some advice about how to deal with it should it happen to you or to someone you know.

THE MYTHS

Experts in this area have identified nine common myths about domestic violence. The prevalence of these popular misconceptions has allowed the secret to be kept so long. Consider the following:

1. "Men who assault their wives are mentally ill."
   Not necessarily. Many function quite well at work and among their friends. This violence is not caused by mental illness.
2. "Men who assault their partners are drunk."
   Not necessarily. Studies have found that the violence can occur

whether alcohol is consumed or not. It does sometimes contribute
to the violence but it is not a cause.

3. "Domestic violence occurs only among the poor."
   Dead wrong. Money cannot buy protection from this violence.
   The partners of lawyers, doctors and successful businessmen are
   all victims.

4. "The woman does something to provoke it."
   Yes, something like breathing. The violence has no connection to
   her conduct. Women who were sound asleep have been beaten.

5. "The woman actually enjoys it."
   This is a particularly disturbing myth because it not only minimizes
   the violence and blames the woman but it actually suggests that the
   violence is desired. The stream of women and children seeking
   refuge in shelters should be proof enough that this is simply
   not true.

6. "If she didn't like it, she would speak up or leave."
   The same way hostages on airplanes complain to terrorists that they
   don't like the way they are being treated, I guess. The syndrome
   that develops from the domestic violence is an invisible cage that
   keeps the woman from leaving.

7. "The men who do this are a danger to the rest of the community."
   Maybe in the long term, but day by day they function well and can
   appear quite charming and friendly to everyone outside the home.
   They beat only their wives and children because they know that
   they can get away with it.

8. "At least nothing will happen while she is pregnant."
   On the contrary, pregnant women are frequently the victims, with
   blows deliberately aimed at their abdomen.

9. "It happens to other people."
   Right. Sure. You should be so lucky.

WHY ARE WOMEN ASSAULTED?

It is a complex combination of things that has put women in this position.
I hope the following is not too much of an over-simplification:

- Our society conditions women to be dependent, to be victims. Many
  have seen and learned to accept violence at their parents' knees.
- The privacy of the home allows it to occur out of sight.
- There is pressure to preserve the family. Reporting violence in the
  home may break it up.
- Those who do report it have found that they are blamed—"What did
  you do to provoke him?"
- There has been, until recently, little community support when
  victims of domestic violence finally leave the home.
- Society has not thought it necessary, until recently, to punish
  the offenders.

- In many cases the woman and child have been so financially dependent on the male provider that they could not afford to leave.

These factors combine to mould a woman who is afraid and feels helpless, who blames herself, feels ambivalent about her life, has no self-esteem, and feels inferior to everyone around her. She comes to believe that she can do no more than pray for a change. These factors form themselves into a syndrome of domestic violence that keeps her from leaving.

WHY DO MEN DO IT?

Again, a complex combination of elements in our society has contributed to this problem:

- Society has tolerated it over hundreds of years. The expression "rule of thumb" has its origins in an actual rule governing the thickness of the stick with which a man could beat his wife. Men think it is acceptable to beat those with whom they are angry.
- Given the prevalence of this type of violence in the home it is likely that thousands of men have learned this behaviour from their own parents.
- Society has been quick to blame the victim rather than the offender. Why should men change when "it's not their fault"?
- Men who are violent with their wives and children generally have poor impulse control and an inflexible method of dealing with frustration.

These factors, coupled with poor self-esteem, produce a man who denies he is violent, blames everyone else, is highly dependent emotionally on his partner, is very traditional in his views of male-female relations, and handles life in one of two speeds (either everything is "OK" or he is furious). This is a man who is emotionally isolated and who lashes out at easy prey—his family.

WHAT CAN BE DONE?

As frustratingly impossible as this situation appears, there are some things that can be done on a practical level and a legal level.

On the practical side, consider the following suggestions:

- Get out. It won't be easy but it's possible. Others have done it and so can you. But rather than just walking out, make a plan. You put your life and the lives of your children at risk by staying.
- Protect yourself and your children at all costs. Do not fight back, but do practise self-defence. Be alert to the building tension if possible and stay out of the line of fire.
- Call the police. Press charges. Follow through. One study found that

when the police laid charges the probability of violence was reduced by half.

- Have a friend available for support.
- Tell your doctor about the violence. Don't make excuses; your doctor may have helpful suggestions and offer support.
- Investigate the availability of shelters in your community. Not every community in Canada has shelters for battered women, but many do. Unfortunately, even when they are available, demand far exceeds places. In Toronto, for example, shelters are reported to have only one space available for every six requests.
- Keep a record of the abuse and any resulting visits to doctors.
- Develop an escape route for emergencies. Discuss it with the children if necessary. Ask a neighbour to call the police if trouble occurs.
- Set aside some extra money for a cab in an emergency.
- Leave a supply of extra clothes for yourself and the children with neighbours. Have extra keys made for the house and car.
- When you go take all your identification—health insurance numbers, passports, personal I.D., birth certificates. You will need them if you apply for public assistance.
- Check the availability of social assistance in your community in advance.
- Consult a lawyer about your plans. Check out the availability of legal aid in your community. Some legal aid plans will expedite a request for legal aid where violence is involved.
- Don't wait for him to change. He won't and you know it.

As you can see from this list, a great many steps can be taken in advance. Little by little, step by step, you can plan an escape from an abusive home.
    On the legal side, consider the following options:

- Press charges. This assault is like any other in that it is a crime and police intervention is necessary. Many forces now have special training for officers and other personnel responding to such calls.
- Every province has a procedure for obtaining a "peace bond." This is a relatively straightforward procedure, which requires the abusive husband to post a bond subject to certain conditions. If the conditions (such as keeping the peace, staying away from the home) are breached the bond or money (often about $500) is forfeited or he may be arrested .
- All provincial family laws permit a court to make an order restraining a spouse from having any contact with his family or, in some provinces, limiting the contact to certain days and certain times. These are called "restraining orders."
- Again, check the availability of legal aid.
- All provincial family laws allow for *ex parte* motions to the court. *"Ex parte"* means that the court is asked to make the order without the other side being notified of the court appearance. This type of order is used under limited circumstances but is well suited to a situation where a woman fleeing an abusive relationship

would be at risk the moment her abusive partner received notice of going to court.

- If your children are at risk, apply for custody of the children as soon as possible. The court will grant custody but may also consider some form of access for the other parent if it will not endanger the children. Ask your lawyer to consider your own risk at the time access is exercised by him. It is possible to arrange access in such a way that the parents do not have to deal with each other.
- If you have been assaulted and injured consider the availability of compensation from two sources:

    (i) A civil law suit for damages: Essentially, you sue your partner for damages. Damage awards have been made for women injured by an assault but relatively few women sue.

    (ii) An application to a provincial Criminal Injuries Compensation Board: All provinces allow women who are victims of domestic violence to apply for compensation.

Discuss both with your lawyer.

It is not going to be easy, but with organization, planning, support, the right timing and a stiff upper lip a woman and her children can escape an abusive relationship. If you are in that position, a lawyer will be absolutely necessary, especially if the full force of the law is to be exercised in your favour. Good luck.

3

Taking a Look at Lawyers: Forewarned Is Forearmed

On the subject of lawyers, it is difficult to know where to begin. No trade or profession has been so vilified in recent times as this bedraggled group to which I belong. Lawyers have been called everything in the book and then some. Do they deserve it? Of course they do. But it does not change the fact that at some point you are going to need one. The purpose of this chapter is to provide a few insights into the legal profession with a view to helping you as a client make intelligent decisions about which lawyer you are going to use and how you are going to deal with him or her.

The blanket criticism of lawyers that I made above ignores two important things. First and foremost there are many excellent family law lawyers. I have met dozens of lawyers who genuinely care about their clients, their clients' families and their future. Secondly, you must understand that clients of lawyers can be responsible for much of their own misfortune in dealing with lawyers. I am not blaming these clients. However, I am pointing out that generally people are very poorly informed and very undemanding consumers of legal services. So, rather than debate whether all lawyers are vipers or not, let's focus on how you find a good family law lawyer and what to demand as an informed consumer once you are in his or her office.

FAMILY LAW LAWYERS

Family law is a specialized area of practice and tends to attract different types of lawyers. It is therefore difficult to generalize about them as a group, but some observations are possible. The selection of your lawyer could be the single most important decision you make about your own case, so take the time to do it properly.

It is not uncommon to hear non-family law lawyers remarking to family law lawyers: "How can you do that stuff?"; "If I wanted to be a social worker or psychiatrist I wouldn't have gone to law school"; "Family law? It's not challenging enough—every case is decided on the facts, not the law," and so on. While lawyers recognize that a family law case *is* a legal matter and can be quite lucrative, still they do not flock to this area of practice. Lawyer burnout is common. This is because family law problems are emotionally charged. Files are injected with added intensity, stress, emotion and, too frequently, violence.

Are lawyers trained to deal with this special aspect of family law—this one aspect that sets it apart? Of course not. Which means the people who choose to practise in this area do so either because they have an interest and aptitude for it or because they think of it as just another file and are unaware of the emotions it arouses. In this latter group we have the lawyer who sees motor vehicle accident victims in the morning and domestic violence cases in the afternoon without any change in attitude. By this I do not mean that a lawyer must practise family law and only family law to be good enough for your case. However, you should be aware that lots of people practise family law for different reasons; what you want is somebody who does it because he or she wants to do it and is good at it. Let's consider what it means to "be good at it."

Ontario has established a method of accrediting lawyers as specialists in fields such as family law, criminal law and so on. This represents a quantum leap for consumers who before had to rely on word of mouth, the Yellow Pages and "hit and miss." The lawyer who did granddad's will, Aunt Mary's car accident and Mom and Dad's real estate deal often inherited the family's first divorce.

Contact your provincial law society and ask if they have an accreditation system for family law lawyers and a list of those in your community. (You can find a list of law societies in Chapter 17.)

In addition, some provincial law societies have established "Lawyer Referral Services." This free service lists lawyers in the province by city and preferred area of practice. It lets you pinpoint family law lawyers in your community. These referral services can also give you information about the availability of legal aid, which we will discuss in more detail shortly. In Ontario, a lawyer who receives a client through this service will give the first half hour for free—not a bad deal if you are shopping around.

With systems such as accreditation and lawyer referral services clients have a fighting chance of finding at the very least an experienced family law lawyer. Assuming that you have found your way to a lawyer, let's consider in more detail what makes a lawyer "good."

In my opinion the ideal family law lawyer is experienced, honest, a good listener, blessed with a sense of humour and respected by his or her peers. This person does not lose sight of people, especially children, in the heat of practice. He or she is punctual, considerate and professional.

The ideal lawyer lets you participate in a discussion about your situation and is not afraid to tell you at the outset things you may not want to hear. After spending thirty minutes with this lawyer you can answer three questions: Do I feel comfortable with this person? Do I respect his or her opinion? Does this person respect mine?

Do not be influenced by designations such as Q.C. (Queen's Counsel). Ignore lawyers who bluster about past "wins" or "big cases" and have a hired-gun attitude. If somebody comes across as a stuffed shirt that person probably is. Is Arnie Becker (of "L.A. Law" fame) out there? If he is, who wants that kind of shallowness?

You do not need the "most expensive lawyer in town." He or she is not necessarily the best. You do not need the biggest law firm in the city, either. Do not pass over a lawyer who appears too young or too old. They may both have special skills. It is experience, not age, that counts.

Some clients have preferences for a lawyer of a particular sex. It has been noted recently that more women than men practise family law. There are lots of theories to explain why this is occurring but all that matters is that it is a positive development. Why some clients prefer men as their lawyers, and others women, can be quite a convoluted matter. I have met male clients who feel they need a female lawyer because (a) they can "con" her or (b) they want their ex-spouse to see how enlightened they really are. This theory I have heard taken as far as the belief that the judge will like them more if they have a woman lawyer. (Oh brother! Now we know why the marriage ran into trouble.)

On the other side of the coin we have the female client who thinks that she must have the toughest male lawyer because that will intimidate her husband and "earn his respect": "He will only listen to a man. He'd never respect a woman." So the male lawyer becomes a personal gladiator. These kinds of clients end up having fascinating conversations, like "My lawyer says your lawyer ..." or "Well, my lawyer never heard of your lawyer, and ..." They are ignoring the fact that they should be picking their own lawyer, not letting their spouse do the picking for them. (Why should their spouse's opinion suddenly have so much value, anyway?)

Family law has also become a bit of a battleground for the "rights movements"—fathers' rights, mothers' rights, grandparents' rights, women's rights, men's rights (can pets' rights be far behind?). There are lawyers out there who are fighting causes while they practise law, lawyers who describe themselves as a "fathers' rights lawyer" or as a lawyer who practises with a "feminist perspective." This is not to say that these lawyers do not fulfil a role or make some important contributions to the law through, for example, test cases. If you want to be a test case and are prepared to pay for it then that is your choice. But I believe that these people have an admitted bias and should be avoided. Their cause becomes your cause—at your expense. You have enough to worry about without somebody else having an extra agenda.

In a similar vein you do not want a lawyer who says things like: "I never send anybody to mediation ..."; "I don't approve of joint custody ..."; "I never agree to ..." Their strait-jacket probably doesn't fit you.

You do want a lawyer who is going to actually *be* the lawyer. You do not want someone who meets you at the initial interview, sniffs the file and then passes it to a junior until the discoveries or trial.

Get the names of several experienced family law lawyers and take the time to meet at least three of them. For the first interview make a list of questions about the important issues. (I have some suggestions at the end of the chapter.) In preparation for the interview you may want to prepare your own written "history of the relationship." Collect as many important documents as you can (marriage certificate, financial records, mortgages, previous orders or agreements, and so on). See the Family Law Client History form in the Appendices.

During the interview be as complete and as frank as possible. The lawyer needs to know everything to be able to provide an objective analysis. Resist the temptation to colour the facts in your favour. Just be straight.

You should also be aware of any potential conflict of interest when hiring a lawyer. Do not use a lawyer who has previously done work for your spouse or your spouse's family. The lawyer may have information from these sources that will put him or her in a difficult position. Similarly, the lawyer should never act for both of you. It is impossible to provide objective advice to two people at the same time when they have opposing interests. If the lawyer is aware of a potential conflict, he or she should alert you to it and decline to act for either of you.

FAMILY LAW AND LEGAL AID

Every province has a form of legal aid for people who cannot afford legal services. This usually entails applying for the aid, passing a "means test" (which judges your neediness) and receiving a "Certificate of Legal Aid." The lawyer to whom you present this certificate then sends his or her bill to the provincial legal aid plan. The amount that can be charged for particular steps is restricted by a tariff, so lawyers tend to receive less for their work on an hourly basis than if you hired them directly. On the other hand, payment of the account is guaranteed.

To find out about legal aid for family law in your province contact the following:

Legal Services Society
P. O. Box 3
1140 W. Pender St., Suite 300
Vancouver, B.C.
V6E 4G1
(604) 660-4600

The Legal Aid Society of Alberta
#300, 10320 - 102 Avenue
Edmonton, Alberta
T5J 4A1
(403) 427-7560

The Saskatchewan Community
    Legal Services Commission
820-410 22nd St. E.
Saskatoon, Saskatchewan
S7K 2H6
(306) 933-6767

Legal Aid Manitoba
402-294 Portage Ave.
Winnipeg, Manitoba
R3C 0B9
(204) 985-8500

The Law Society of Upper Canada
The Ontario Legal Aid Plan
Office of the Director
481 University Ave., Suite 200
Toronto, Ontario
M5G 2G1
(416) 979-1446
Toll free: 1-800-666-8258

Commission des services
     juridiques
C. P. 123, Succursale Desjardins
Montréal, Québec
H5B 1B3
(514) 873-3562

Legal Aid New Brunswick
P. O. Box 666
88 Prospect Street
Wandlyn Corporate Offices
Fredericton, N.B.
E3B 5B4
(506) 459-1911

Prince Edward Island Legal Aid
Law Courts Bldg.
P. O. Box 2200
Charlottetown, P.E.I.
C1A 7N8
(902) 368-6020

Nova Scotia Legal Aid
5212 Sackville St. - #301
Halifax, Nova Scotia
B3J 1K6
(902) 420-6565

Newfoundland Legal Aid
     Commission
Centre Bldg.
21 Church Hill
St. John's, Newfoundland
A1C 3Z8
(709) 753-7860

Judicial Administrator
Govt. of Yukon Territory
Box 2703
Whitehorse, Yukon
Y1A 4Z2
(403) 667-5210

Legal Services Board of the
     Northwest Territories
P. O. Box 1320
Yellowknife, N.W.T.
X1A 2L9
(403) 873-7450

HIRING THE LAWYER TO WORK ON YOUR PROBLEM: THE RETAINER (OR WHAT EVERYONE ELSE CALLS A CONTRACT)

The word "retainer" can mean a number of different things. It can mean the amount of money you give a lawyer up front. He or she may request the money to cover disbursements that will be incurred for couriers, court filing charges or similar relatively small expenses. The amount of such a retainer can range from a few hundred dollars up to ten thousand dollars or more.

"Retainer" can also mean the actual contract the client signs to hire the lawyer to do the work. It is this type of retainer that I would like to spend a few minutes examining.

It never ceases to amaze me that a person will go into a lawyer's office, discuss the most intimate details of his or her life (details they have often never shared with anyone else) and then turn their whole life over to this virtual stranger without so much as discussing how much the lawyer charges per hour, the estimated time for completion of the work, disbursements, billing policy, quality of work—I think you get the picture.

This same individual leaves the lawyer's office, goes home and decides to get the house painted by a couple of college students. What does he do? Well, first he asks all the neighbours about painters they have used and whether they would recommend them. Once he has found his painters he spends an hour walking around the house telling them exactly what he wants and how he wants it done. He demands written contracts, guarantees, a fixed date for completion and references. He wants to control the kind of paint that is used and to know whether these two budding entrepreneurs have public liability insurance. Once he has the estimate in hand and the students have jumped through every conceivable hoop ... he says that he wants to "think it over."

The hapless students may make a couple of hundred dollars *if* they get the job. The lawyer on the other side of town is casually opening a file with what amounts to a blank cheque, having given few, if any, commitments.

How can this contradiction be remedied?

The answer is not to stop asking the painters for a written contract. Start asking your lawyer for one! The lawyer is not going to throw up his or her arms, stamp around the office or sulk as if you have offended him or her. Lawyers know what retainers are; they use them all the time. Do you think that businessmen who hire lawyers don't pin them down on the cost? Of course they do, and they insist on answers to a lot of other questions, too. Why should decisions about your life be any different or any less important?

This need not be a painful experience. You are simply asking someone, who is supposedly a highly skilled professional, to make available to you a copy of his or her retainer form. Remember, it does not matter what lawyers call it, it is still a contract. It will describe the parties to the contract (you and the lawyer), the work that is to be done, the fee that will be charged for the work (hourly rate) and other important terms. A basic retainer which I developed from my time in private practice is included among the three in the Appendices.

You have my permission to photocopy any of these forms (but please, not other parts of the book) and present it to the lawyer you wish to retain (if the lawyer does not have his or her own retainer form). If the lawyer balks at the use of a retainer, you don't want him or her to handle your case. There is absolutely nothing in this contract or the other retainers that is unusual or offensive to an experienced lawyer.

Two further cautions concerning the fee to be charged and the service to be rendered: Do not hesitate to ask that a provision be incorporated into the retainer placing a ceiling on the fee that can be charged without further consultation and further written retainer. Matrimonial proceedings that begin quickly (perhaps in anger) have a way of consuming bundles of money in a very short time. A clause that states simply "Fees not to exceed $1,000.00 without prior further written authorization" can be a valuable inhibition for those lawyers tempted to litigate first and negotiate later.

In addition, when describing the service to be rendered, a simple "Obtain divorce" is the equivalent of a blank cheque. (Would you ask the students simply to "Paint house"?) Insist on a specific description of the work and execute a retainer authorizing perhaps only the first few steps (you will find them listed in Chapter 4). This again inhibits the litigation and gives you control of the work that is being done. If you are not satisfied with the work that has been done, don't authorize any more until you are.

Some other cautions are appropriate at this stage. They concern disbursements, inquiries about fees and relations with the lawyer you have retained.

As I mentioned earlier, lawyers by the nature of the process must spend money from time to time. It costs $60—$100 to issue a divorce petition, for example. It can cost as much as $300 to have a copy officially delivered to the other spouse (called "service of the petition"). There are dozens of small out of pocket items that can cost varying amounts. As lawyers disburse or spend money on these items they would prefer to be spending the client's own money. Consequently, most lawyers ask for an amount up front (sometimes also called a retainer). The amount varies depending on the type of case and the degree of complexity, but for out of pocket expenses it rarely exceeds $500. So be prepared to provide the lawyer with some money to be applied towards disbursements.

You will note that paragraph 4 of the first sample retainer refers to client inquiries about fees and disbursements. At no time and under no circumstances should you ever feel inhibited about inquiring about the state of your account, the lawyer's disbursements or fee policy or any other matter related to your file. Leaving a concern in doubt or unclear in any way is an invitation for disagreement at a later date. If you are not sure— ask! If it's still not clear—ask again! Why pay for something you do not understand?

The final caution concerns your relationship with the lawyer during the course of his or her work for you. Lawyers employ junior lawyers, articling students, support staff and secretaries to assist with the work on files. Without their assistance little could be done. Do not think that your lawyer is shirking his or her responsibilities by delegating to support staff. Nevertheless, you have hired a particular lawyer and you are entitled to meet with that lawyer on a regular basis to discuss your case.

I continue to be shocked by the number of family clients who complain justifiably loud and long about the fact that they met with their lawyer three or four times during the course of the entire case: at the initial interview, after the first court appearance (usually some interim matter), at the discoveries and at the trial. I'm surprised lawyers are not more sensitive to their clients' needs but even more shocked that the clients put up with it.

I suggest that you discuss this matter during the initial interview. If you want personal attention, then tell the lawyer at the first interview, not after the trial or settlement.

CONFIDENTIALITY

One of the most important features of the lawyer's relationship with the client is the promise of confidentiality. It is the basis of the client's trust and confidence in a lawyer.

To solve a client's problem, the lawyer must know everything about the client. In order to feel comfortable telling everything, the client must trust the lawyer to keep every word in confidence. Not only is indiscreet chatter about the personal details of clients' problems totally unprofessional and a breach of their trust, it is dangerous. It risks the law firm's and lawyer's reputation and may be considered professional misconduct. The Canadian Bar Association's Code of Professional Conduct provides as follows:

> *The lawyer has a duty to hold in strict confidence all information acquired in the course of the professional relationship concerning the business and affairs of his client, and he should not divulge any such information unless he is expressly or impliedly authorized by his client or required by law to do so.*

Commentary #9 under this rule clarifies this need for confidence in relation to the law firm's staff and states as follows:

> *9. Confidential information may be divulged with the express authority of the client concerned, and, in some situations, the authority to divulge may be implied. For example, some disclosure may be necessary in a pleading or other document delivered in litigation being conducted for the client. Again, the lawyer may (unless the client directs otherwise) disclose the client's affairs to partners and associates in the firm and, to the extent necessary, to non-legal staff such as secretaries and filing clerks. But this implied authority to disclose places the lawyer under a duty to impress upon associates, employees and students the importance of non-disclosure (both during their employment and thereafter), and requires the lawyer to take reasonable care to prevent their disclosing or using any information which the lawyer is bound to keep in confidence.*

Every lawyer is bound by this rule of confidentiality. The confidentiality is known as solicitor-client privilege. The lawyer cannot be forced to disclose this confidential information even if the court orders it. The lawyer can only reveal the information if it is necessary to advance your case or if you expressly authorize it.

In limited situations lawyers are able to breach this privilege, for example, to prevent a crime.

FIRING A LAWYER

A client may end the retainer or contract with the lawyer at any time. It may surprise you to learn that the lawyer cannot do likewise. The circumstances under which a lawyer can refuse to continue to act for a client are very, very limited. If a client asks a lawyer to mislead the court or do some other unethical act the lawyer can refuse to continue representing the client. Similarly, if the client does not pay the lawyer then he or she can refuse to take any further steps. However, if the client provides instructions and pays the lawyer's account the lawyer cannot refuse to act.

I think most clients are intimidated by the prospect of telling a professional that they are unhappy with the services rendered and intend to seek help from someone else. You will recall my analogy to the hiring of the college students to paint a house. Few people would have trouble putting an end to that work if they thought it was unsatisfactory. Imagine, if you can, hiring a contractor to renovate your kitchen at a cost of $15,000 or $20,000. If the work was shoddy, the contractor uncommunicative, and your instructions were not followed, I think that you would not hesitate to sit the contractor down and air your grievances. Why do we hesitate to do the same with a lawyer? The answer lies, in part, in our expectations.

When we hire the kitchen renovator we probably have a good idea of what we want, when we want it, what it should look like, when it will be finished and how much it will cost. The same is not generally true when we hire a lawyer. We have a very vague idea about what we want or need, no idea how quickly work can begin, no idea about what it should look like when it's under way—let alone finished—no idea about when it will be complete and only fear about how much the case will ultimately cost. (Perhaps more than the kitchen!)

Unlike the kitchen, we have no way of knowing whether the legal work is being done, let alone done well. That makes it very difficult to complain, doesn't it?

If the suggestions in the first half of this chapter have been followed then you will be in a much better position to evaluate the lawyer's performance from time to time. If you have a specific retainer you will know whether or not your instructions are being carried out within the cost limits established.

What happens if you are not satisfied?

Let's examine this in two parts—first, what is likely to make you unhappy, and second, what to do about your dissatisfaction.

One of the chief complaints law societies receive from clients about lawyers is that they don't return telephone calls promptly or, in some cases, at all. Why don't lawyers return telephone calls? The telephone is often the only means by which they can stay in contact with their clients, so why wouldn't they use it?

There are, I think, a variety of reasons. First, most lawyers are too busy to return every telephone call they receive in a working day. In some cases it is just physically impossible. Second, lawyers are often out of the office, in court, on discoveries, in transit and so on. Again, their work itself makes it physically impossible to return the calls.

Third, and this is a large part of the problem, many lawyers are procrastinators. If they have no good news, only bad news or no news at all, then they are less likely to pick up the telephone.

Experienced family law lawyers will use personalized answering services or will have their secretaries return calls. And yet, I have heard of lawyers who do not return telephone messages for days or even weeks. That is inexcusable. If these lawyers are to be cured of it then maybe they need to lose a client or two. I recommend a polite but firm warning after the first time this becomes a problem: "Return my calls promptly or I'll get someone who will." We will leave for the moment what to do when you have to act on your promise.

Another complaint that clients have about lawyers is the lawyers' failure to keep them abreast of developments. An experienced family law lawyer will meet with the client regularly and provide thorough periodic letters reporting on the status of the matter (called "reporting letters"). A prudent lawyer will not only report on the status of the matter but will summarize what happened, what options were open, which course was recommended, what the client's instructions were and any other considerations.

At the time of retaining the lawyer it should be made clear that you expect regular and complete reporting letters. If the letters are not forthcoming you may have to remind the lawyer about your intention to find someone who will provide regular written updates.

I place a great deal of emphasis on regular written reporting letters for good reason. The goal of this book is to make you an informed consumer of legal services *before* you enter a lawyer's office. It will have taken some effort on your part to have achieved that status. It will only be maintained if your lawyer takes over the job of informing you about your own case. Reporting letters are no more than a form of continuing education about your own case and the legal system. They provide a record of decisions which have been made and enable you to make intelligent choices about the future. Insist on them.

Another frequent area of disappointment and disagreement is the accounts that are rendered by the lawyer during or at the end of a matter. I have already set out the essential matters that need to be discussed at the time the retainer is signed—the amount of the fee per hour, the specific service to be rendered, the estimated time of completion and so on. You may also wish to discuss the *method* of billing. If an accurate estimate can be given, then some clients prefer to be billed in regular monthly instalments rather than letting a huge bill accumulate. Others cannot afford to pay until the case is finished and successful. In either case, make a point of discussing with the lawyer the method by which you would like to be billed.

Generally lawyers will insist on billing the disbursements to you as they are incurred. For example, if a $200 bill is incurred to serve the documents on your spouse then that amount will usually be invoiced to you immediately. If you have an amount on deposit with the lawyer for the purpose of paying such disbursements then you should receive a statement from the lawyer stating that the disbursement was incurred and was paid out of the amount held on deposit. This type of account is known as a "Disbursements Only" account.

Any account, whether for disbursements only or for services rendered, should also include a specific description of what was done to justify the fee. An example of a typical lawyer's account is included in the Appendices.

As set out earlier, lawyers charge hourly rates, but for obvious reasons lawyers cannot work in blocks of one hour at a time on each file. Sometimes it is a 6-minute telephone call with the opposing lawyer, or a 45-minute period of preparation for court or 18 minutes of research on a particular issue. To accommodate work of less than an hour the lawyer divides his or her work hours into tenths, or units of 6 minutes. Ten units of 6 minutes make up each hour. Regardless of how much time was actually spent, the lawyer will never record less than a tenth (.1) of an hour being spent on a matter, because that is the smallest unit of time the lawyer measures.

As the lawyer works through the day he or she will keep track, either by written docket or computer, of each tenth of each hour. For example, the telephone rings: it's the client making an appointment and the call lasts 3 minutes. The lawyer will fill out a time docket for .1, or 6 minutes. (Yes, you get billed for phone calls. Time is money.) If the call lasted 12 minutes the lawyer would fill out a docket for .2—two units of 6 minutes. As each docket is filled out the lawyer writes down what service was rendered. A typical time docket could look as follows:

Mike C.
Jan. 5, 1991
10:00 - 10:06
Client - Brown #161
Telephone call re: husband's
breach of restraining order .1

The lawyer accumulates these dockets, in the file or in the office computer. When it is time to render an account, a touch of a button yields a full chronological list of all services rendered with a breakdown of time. It will also total the time and multiply it by the lawyer's hourly rate. Once any disbursements are added on you have a full account.

This is the way it should be done, so insist on full itemized statements of account whether the account is an interim one or the final account. They will provide a detailed picture of what was done for you and how much was charged for the work.

Under no circumstances should you accept the old chestnut—one small sheet of paper as a statement of account—with "To Services Rendered - $15,000.00." You deserve a lot more. Insist on it.

Those are some of the areas in which you may have reason to be dissatisfied with your lawyer. Let's take a look now at what to do when you think it is better to part company.

Before dismissing your lawyer, take a few minutes to ask yourself what the real reasons are for your unhappiness. It might even be prudent to re-examine where you are emotionally. Re-read the checklist at the end of Chapter 1 and consider the questions posed there concerning motivation. You should also take a few minutes to put in the balance the investment you have already made in this lawyer's handling of the problem. Be aware of the fact that when a new lawyer takes the matter over many of the hours of preparation by that lawyer in familiarizing himself or herself with your case will be a duplication of time and expense.

I add these words only as a caution because all lawyers who practise family law are wary of the client who dismisses lawyer after lawyer and is always unhappy with the service. Experienced lawyers can see these clients for what they frequently are—spouses stuck in stage one of the emotional stages described earlier. Like terminal patients who deny the illness and shop for a second, third or fourth opinion, clients have been known to fire lawyers until they find one who will simply do as he or she is told. They might be happy with that lawyer until they move on to the later stages and suddenly look back on a lot of wasteful angry litigation. The lawyer, perhaps out of inexperience, perhaps out of other motivations, will have always done as the client asked but will not have served the client well.

Assuming you are comfortable with your decision to fire your lawyer, what do you do next?

Do not expect to pull this off without speaking to the lawyer face to face. (You coward!) I still recall clients who would call my secretary and ask that the file be bundled up and left in the reception area. They promised to attend with a cheque for any balance owing (not always, but most of the time) and swap it for the file. "No," they were told. They insisted. "There is no need to see Mr. Cochrane. Just tell him I'm unhappy and will take my file to another lawyer."

Try as they might they could not pull this off. Most, if not all, law firms will only end a retainer after a personal interview has taken place to discuss why the problem arose. If you are intent on ending the retainer then schedule an interview with the lawyer, tell him or her what you want to discuss, and attend to the matter with the same resolve you would use to scold the college student painter or fire the kitchen contractor.

It was never my practice to argue with clients on such occasions. If they were unhappy then I considered it their right to have a lawyer with whom they felt comfortable. Tell the lawyer what is on your mind and ask to have the file turned over with a written summary of its status (if you have not received one recently).

You should understand that you will likely receive an account for work done but not yet billed to you at the time the retainer comes to an end. If there are monies being held in trust by the lawyer they will be applied toward the account, and the balance (if any) returned to you.

Once paid, the lawyer has two obligations: first, to return your file to you promptly and second, to render whatever assistance he or she can to your new lawyer. If a new lawyer has been found in advance of ending the retainer your lawyer may be prepared to simply courier the entire file to the new lawyer.

The file that arrives at your new lawyer's office (or is turned over to you directly) may not be identical to the file you saw sitting in front of your former lawyer at the time the retainer ended. The lawyer does not simply slide the entire file into an envelope (or a box, in some cases). He or she is entitled to remove certain materials. The following things, however, should be in the file:

- legal documents (pleadings)
- letters written by you to the lawyer (originals)
- letters to the lawyer from the opposing lawyer or others (originals)
- copies of all other letters
- originals of all evidence
- any other material needed to advance the case and not available elsewhere.

The lawyer may remove from the file such things as:

- notes and memos to file
- legal research done to formulate his or her opinions.

Often a lawyer will turn over everything in the file but keep copies for his or her own records. The lawyer may do this if there is any concern that arguments may arise at a later date about the quality of work done.

All of the above is premised on the words "once the lawyer has been paid." If the lawyer is owed money for work done, then he or she is entitled to be paid before releasing the file. Until paid in full the lawyer has what is called a "solicitor's lien" on the file and its contents. Many people are familiar with a "construction lien" or "mechanic's lien" whereby a workman or contractor can register on title to a piece of property notice that he or she is owed money for work done. The property cannot be mortgaged, sold or dealt with until the lien is paid. The same is true of a client's file with a lawyer.

WHAT TO DO WHEN YOU ARE UNHAPPY ABOUT YOUR LAWYER'S BILL

This can be a painful experience. You receive the lawyer's bill for the work done on your behalf. You may even be happy with the outcome, but the cost! It seems like a lot more than you originally estimated or were told it would cost. Can the subject be dealt with in any way other than by simply paying and stewing? Yes.

An important beginning would be to discuss the matter with the lawyer face to face. Make an appointment to discuss the bill and be prepared to go through it line by line. You should have received an itemized statement of account like the one set out in the Appendices.

Mistakes may have been made, misunderstandings occur, and they can readily be remedied.

However, if you are still dissatisfied, it is possible to arrange an appointment with a court official for you and the lawyer to have an independent third person assess or "tax" the lawyer's account. To arrange such an appointment, contact the local courthouse and speak to the "Taxing Officer." You will be given an appointment and a notice that must be delivered to the lawyer.

Once at the meeting you should be prepared with notes, your account and your retainer to discuss the agreement you thought you had with the lawyer. The court official will look at the retainer, the number of hours worked, the amount charged, the normal standard for such work, out of pocket expenses and so on. He or she has the power to reduce the account—and often does. It is never increased.

It is not an embarrassing hearing for either person. Lawyers' accounts are taxed all the time. (Some lawyers say if you're not being taxed you're not charging enough.) It does not take long, and could save you several hundred dollars. There are some cases where lawyers' accounts were reduced to zero. That's right, zero. The officer thought the work was worthless and a court subsequently agreed when the decision was appealed by the lawyer.

CONCLUSION: HIRING A LAWYER/FIRING A LAWYER

It should be clear from the comments set out above that the act of hiring a lawyer is a critical point in your handling of your own marriage breakdown. It should be done from a position of power, which means from the position of an informed consumer. The checklist set out at the end of this chapter can be consulted during the initial interview to ensure that the lawyer has a clear understanding of your needs as a client. If you have read the entire book and understand your own emotional position and your legal needs in a reasonably specific way, then your lawyer will know from the outset that the necessary standard of work and communication will be a high one.

In addition, if the lawyer is an experienced family law lawyer he or she should welcome a client who is in touch with his or her own emotional and legal needs. You will be recognized and respected as a client who provides instructions from a position of informed self-interest and nothing less.

Should you determine that it is necessary to terminate your relationship with your lawyer, you can at least do so with confidence by following the guidelines set out above. Every client cannot be happy with every lawyer. The individual needs and idiosyncrasies of both are too diverse and personal for there to be perfect harmony. If you have followed the guidelines set out above then you will have significantly reduced the likelihood of a mismatch. However, if your choice has proved unfortunate or circumstances have changed (perhaps a new lawyer in the firm took over the file) do not settle for less than you need and deserve.

Examine your reasons for wishing to terminate the retainer. If you are confident in your decision, arrange the interview and set about finding someone who can move your case to a conclusion quickly, inexpensively and, with luck, happily.

LOOKING AT LAWYERS: A CHECKLIST

1. Have I called the provincial Lawyer Referral Service?
2. Does my province accredit family law specialists?
3. Have I spoken with trusted friends about recommendations?
4. Do I understand the meaning of "retainer"?
5. Does this lawyer have a sample retainer form to examine?
6. Will I need legal aid?
7. Do I qualify for a legal aid certificate?
8. Does this lawyer accept legal aid clients?
9. What is the hourly rate? Estimated cost?
10. What are the billing practices? Interim? Final?
11. Will he/she accept a ceiling on the fee in the retainer?
12. What experience does this lawyer have with this type of case?
13. Does this lawyer have any biases?
14. Will this lawyer be doing the work or passing it to someone else? At every stage? What will the role of paralegals, students and juniors be?
15. Does he/she have any potential conflict of interest?
16. How would he/she describe the services needed in the retainer?
17. How are disbursements handled? How much is needed in advance?
18. How does the lawyer handle questions about fees that arise while the case is under way?
19. How will he/she stay in touch with me? Telephone calls? Reporting letters?
20. Will the accounts have full itemized statements of services rendered?
21. Is this person honest, with a sense of humour, considerate, professional?
22. Do I feel comfortable with this person assisting me with this matter?
23. Do I respect his/her opinion?
24. Does this person respect mine?

4

Taking a Look at the Process:
Family Law
and the Legal System

Some general background knowledge about family law is valuable if you are to become an informed consumer. I do not intend to frighten or intimidate you (or bore you, for that matter) with the constitutional intricacies that account for which jurisdiction—federal or provincial—has responsibility for laws that affect your family. In fact, the easy answer is that they both have responsibility and that they both have enacted laws that complement each other.

Most people understand that the federal government has responsibility for such things as "national defence" or "criminal law." These are areas that affect the entire country and therefore one law is required for everyone, regardless of the province in which he or she resides. We have a Criminal Code that applies to everyone regardless of where he or she lives in Canada. The same is true of the law of divorce. Our Constitution provides that the federal government has responsibility for passing laws that permit people to divorce. The people of Prince Edward Island use the same *Divorce Act* that is used by people in British Columbia and Ontario. The *procedural* rules governing the way in which the divorce is moved through the courts may vary from province to province, but the substantive divorce provisions are the same in every province.

The applicability of the *Divorce Act* is triggered by one thing and one thing only—a request (or petition, as the Act calls it) for a divorce. *The* Divorce Act *only applies if a divorce is sought.*

When the Act applies it provides guidelines for making orders concerning custody, access, support (for a spouse or a child) and, of course, the divorce itself. The *Divorce Act* does not say anything about dividing property, the matrimonial home, marriage contracts and so on. We all know that those issues can be an important part of family law, so where are they? The answer lies in provincial law.

By virtue of our Constitution, the provinces have responsibility for laws concerning "property"—including the way in which property is to be divided when a marriage breaks down. What this means is that if someone seeks a divorce and wants the court, at the same time, to divide the family's property, then provincial property division laws and federal divorce laws must work together.

If a couple separates and they only want their family property divided (but not a divorce) then the *Divorce Act* will not apply. We know that provincial law will provide the law for division of their property, but what if they also need to sort out custody of their children, access and support? Again, the answer lies in provincial law.

Each province supplies a complete package of alternative law in the event a couple does not seek a divorce, but needs legal assistance with property division, spousal support, child support, custody, access and dozens of other matters.

For example, consider the Ontario provincial law. The *Family Law Act, 1986* sets out the law for property division on marriage breakdown and divorce. It also sets out the means by which spousal and child support are calculated, special rules concerning the matrimonial home, and the requirements for domestic contracts (marriage contacts, cohabitation agreements and separation agreements).

The Ontario *Children's Law Reform Act* sets out the law for determinations of custody and access and applies when a divorce is not being sought. We will look at all of these areas in more detail in upcoming chapters, but at this point we only need to see the interconnection between federal divorce law and provincial family law. They are designed to work together so that every possible circumstance is covered. The key is to remember that when a divorce is sought the *Divorce Act* does everything except divide your property. Provincial law is the only law that divides family property.

There are other federal and provincial laws that are relevant to family law. Many of the provinces now have provincial enforcement agencies to collect support owed by virtue of an order or an agreement. For example, Ontario has enacted the *Support and Custody Orders Enforcement Act* which sets out the structure and powers of an agency that will collect support payments ordered under either federal or provincial law. In other words, the agency will enforce a support order whether or not it was made as a part of a divorce. Unlike other provincial enforcement agencies the Ontario agency will also enforce custody orders and separation agreements.

Manitoba was the first province to establish a support enforcement program, in 1980. Since then, every province has established some form of support enforcement assistance program. The degree of assistance may vary from province to province. Saskatchewan's Maintenance Enforcement Office will collect on orders made after 1985 but not before. Other provinces try to collect no matter when the order was made. Chapter 13 has more to say about this.

The *Federal Orders and Agreements Enforcement Assistance Act* provides information to those trying to track down support defaulters. It facilitates the work of the provincial enforcement agencies. In general, the support enforcement area is a good example of recent attempts to enact complementary family laws in Canada.

In most cases, when a couple decides to separate and they cannot agree on how to settle their differences, a Petition for Divorce (see the examples in the Appendices) is issued, coupled with a request for a division of property under the relevant provincial property law. In Ontario, between the *Family Law Act, 1986* and the *Divorce Act* all the necessary court orders can usually be made whether for custody, access, property division or the divorce itself.

The important piece to this puzzle is understanding that there is no easy solution in the federal or provincial law. If you cannot agree with your spouse, then the law serves as a guide and the judge decides for you. These different laws make up a patchwork designed to help the court sort out the problems experienced when a family splits up.

I know you must think I am ignoring the most obvious questions of all: Why is it organized like this? Why doesn't one level of government make all the laws? Why don't all the provinces get together and agree to have the same laws? History has a lot to do with it. The original framers of the *British North America Act* divided the responsibilities this way, and changing the Constitution can be a very difficult thing to do. There has been talk of transferring jurisdictions between the federal and provincial governments but very little has come of it—or is likely to come of it in the near future. The provinces do try to co-ordinate their family laws but there are differences in attitudes and needs that result in different approaches. Some provinces could afford to spend money setting up support enforcement agencies, some could not. Some provinces think property division should not affect a spouse's business assets, others think it should. So it can be difficult to agree on one law—but we try. (You don't like it, you say? Then turn to Chapter 17, "How to Complain.")

THE LEGAL SYSTEM

There are some other general aspects of the legal system that you should understand, if only to place your particular dispute in context. Proceeding in the absence of some of this general knowledge would be like beginning a game of "Snakes and Ladders" or "Monopoly" without even knowing how the board works.

In every province there are two distinct parts of the legal system—civil justice and criminal justice. Most people are at least vaguely familiar with the criminal law because so many news stories concern the justice system's handling of crime. Less well understood, but equally important, is the civil part of the justice system, which encompasses virtually anything not related to criminal justice.

Legal disputes over wills, property, motor vehicle accidents, commercial contracts, defective products and, of course, family law, are all handled within the civil justice system. Each province is the same in this respect. What you need to know at this stage is that family law is but one of many areas handled by our civil justice system. With minor variations, disputes concerning family law enter our civil justice system in much the same way as disputes over motor vehicle accidents or breaches of contract.

The differences between the civil justice system and the criminal justice system have caused confusion for many people. Often the two systems operate in the same building, use the same judges, lawyers and court staff and for all intents and purposes look the same. But they are not.

First, we should understand that civil and criminal justice systems vary from province to province—especially civil justice systems. The criminal justice system tends to be more uniform because it has one national law to apply—the Canadian Criminal Code. Civil justice systems process cases that involve provincial law, which can vary widely from province to province.

Second, the two systems do not reach conclusions the same way. The differences concern the amount of proof required to get the court to make a decision. This is generally called the "burden of proof." In a criminal case the Crown Attorney (not District Attorney or D.A.—that's in the United States) must prove "beyond a reasonable doubt" that someone is guilty of a crime. In other words, the judge or jury must be left with no doubts about this person's guilt. There must be no other reasonable explanation for what happened. In the civil justice system (including family law) the burden is different. A person must prove that his or her version is correct "on the balance of probability." This is a lower standard than that of the criminal system. Here each person tries to tip the scales in his or her favour with the proof. It doesn't have to be "beyond a doubt"; it just needs to be "probable."

Understanding this subtle but fundamental difference between a family law case and, say, a murder trial, may change your approach to solving the problems in your own case. The family law judge is not trying to find out who is "guilty." He or she is trying to choose between two possible solutions to the problem. The one the judge picks is the one that in his or her opinion is probably correct.

FAMILY LAW AND THE COURTS

It is a constant source of amazement to me as a lawyer and, I am certain, to those people who must actually use the courts for resolving family disputes, that there is not simply one court capable of handling all family law problems. The provinces vary in this respect, but many of the provinces have more than one level of court for family law matters. Ontario—until recently—did not have one court for family law disputes, but four. That's right, four!

In Ontario, depending on the specific nature of the dispute, the geographical location, the wishes of the lawyers and the availability of court time, a person's request for help from the court could have ended up in one of four courts.

The Personnel of the Courts

Within these different courts you may encounter a variety of people performing the functions that make the justice system operate. These people include:

  (i) Judges
 (ii) Masters
(iii) Trial Co-ordinators
(iv) Registrars and Clerks
 (v) Court Reporters
(vi) "My friend ... my learned friend"

We will take a brief look at each person's role in order to become a little more comfortable in our dealings with family law.

JUDGES

This job—and make no mistake, that is what it is, a job—continues to be endowed with a great deal of mystique by the Canadian public. It is admittedly a powerful position, for it gives this handful of men and women control over our property, our children and, in some cases, our liberty.

Judges are appointed to their position by either the federal or provincial government. It is a lifetime job and can pay quite well compared with other jobs ($100,000+), and it includes a pension and other benefits. Judges are free from political interference and cannot be fired or removed from "the bench" except in the most limited circumstances.

Most judges have been lawyers for at least ten years and therefore have a certain degree of legal experience. By and large we have good judges in Canada, although women and minorities are underrepresented in their ranks. That is changing. The quality of judges continues to grow rather than decline in Canada.

Once appointed to the bench, judges are treated differently by their former colleagues and many complain that it can be an isolating experience. It can be difficult to let your hair down in public when so much decorum and respect is necessary for the work of the judge in the courtroom.

The judge's function in the courtroom goes beyond rendering a decision at the end of the case. He or she must listen to the theory of each lawyer's argument, listen to the witnesses, watch their demeanour, take notes, rule on questions of evidence and control the entire courtroom process. It means following each and every question, protecting witnesses in some cases and prodding them in others. It is a very difficult job and many times judges have sat in frustration as a lawyer did a poor job for a client in the courtroom—knowing full well they could present the client's case better if they themselves jumped down and did it for the lawyer. But they can't. They sit patiently taking notes of everything said, with observations or questions, and develop their own opinion about how the problem should be solved.

Sometimes the judge will give his or her reasons for judgment or decision at the end of a case; sometimes the judge does not, but "reserves" or promises to give the decision later, after he or she has thought about it.

Most judges are called either "Your Honour" or "My Lord." When in doubt, use "Your Honour"—and resist "Your Majesty," which some poor witness called a judge in a traffic case. (The judge was slow to point out the error.) Judges don't expect people to grovel. They only expect lawyers to be clear and concise, witnesses to be direct and easy to hear.

The judge is the focal point of the courtroom and you should be mindful of that fact should you have occasion to appear before one.

MASTERS

Some provinces have an official known as a "Master," and you should understand that in those which do, a Master performs functions very similar to a judge's. However, the emphasis tends to be more on the procedural aspects of the case rather than substantive issues. A Master also tends to deal with interim matters rather than final determinations of the parties' rights. For example, a Master might make an order for interim spousal support or interim custody of a child.

TRIAL CO-ORDINATORS

In some large cities road traffic is controlled from one computerized control centre. The flow and volume of traffic is monitored and when bottlenecks occur vehicles are diverted to an alternative route. This is essentially what a trial co-ordinator does for a living, except that what he or she manages is the litigation flowing through the courts.

A large courthouse may have ten or more courtrooms hearing motions, trials and even appeals. The trial co-ordinator makes sure that the right judge gets the right case, at the right time, in the right courtroom. This means getting lawyers, clients (and their witnesses), court clerks and a court reporter to the same place as well. Last and certainly not least the trial co-ordinator must ensure that the judge has the court file and appropriate materials in advance of the hearing. Of course, once the whole thing is ready to go the clients will decide to settle out of court, which means that another group of ready, willing and able lawyers and clients must be found. And so it goes. Sometimes a matter scheduled for thirty minutes in Courtroom #1 unexpectedly stretches into a whole day. A bottleneck forms and cases waiting for that judge and courtroom are diverted elsewhere—or simply sent home to wait.

Some courts use a "fixed date" method, which means that once the lawyers alert the court that they are ready for trial the trial co-ordinator assigns them a fixed date for the hearing. This is easier on the lawyers and clients but can result in down time for the courts unless some creative overbooking is done to accommodate the inevitable out-of-court settlement.

REGISTRARS, CLERKS AND OTHER COURT STAFF

There is a barely visible world that processes the justice system's paperwork. Tens of thousands of lawsuits are started each year and your case is just one of many files in courthouses around the country.

The Registrar is the chief administrative officer of a particular judicial district. He or she is responsible for the staff of the courthouse and for ensuring that lawsuits are processed in accordance with the rules of the court. The Registrar takes responsibility for opening files, checking documents for rule compliance, taking fees for filing and so on.

Important steps in lawsuits are recorded not only in the file kept at the courthouse but also logged in record books. In this way orders, judgments and other important matters can be tracked down relatively easily. The Registrar's staff does many of these things but he or she has ultimate responsibility for the nuts and bolts of the administration of justice locally.

The court staff also assist the judges and trial co-ordinator in making sure the right file and materials are available for hearings.

One of the least pleasant aspects of family litigation—any litigation, for that matter—is the need to line up to file material at the courthouse. In larger cities the courts are very overburdened and court staff cannot keep up. It is not unusual to see law students or paralegals, or even secretaries, lined up at the courthouse waiting to file some important material. This bustling office is a stressful environment and a mystery to first-time observers.

COURT REPORTERS

Court reporters are used at trials, appeals and discoveries. In some other significant matters, such as an important motion, they might also be used. Their sole purpose is to record everything that is said during the proceeding. This includes the opening introduction of the judge by the clerk right through oath swearing, to every question and answer.

Theirs is a unique skill that I still do not completely understand— especially when they accurately record every word said when three people are speaking at the same time!

Different methods are used by different court reporters. Some reporters use a steno mask, which is a large plastic device that fits over their mouth and nose. They simply repeat every word said by anyone who speaks, whether it is the judge, lawyer, witness or clerk. Other reporters take the proceedings down in shorthand with a pen (this is on the decline) and others use what is known as a silent typewriter. The typewriter is set up at the front of the courtroom and the reporter silently types the proceedings.

In Quebec City there is a very modern courthouse that uses tape recorders controlled by a central studio. It is very impressive, and probably represents the future for many courthouses.

The reporters can produce (overnight if necessary) a transcript of the proceedings. This transcript is used to prove what was said by whom at trial—for example, on an appeal. Often it is used to "impeach" a witness. This means to challenge his or her present statement by showing the person the transcript of what he or she said on a previous occasion under oath. This type of impeachment often used to end with the brilliant question: "Were you lying then, or are you lying now?!"

Most witnesses seem to forget about the court reporters as they go about their invisible work.

"MY FRIEND ... MY LEARNED FRIEND"

Lawyers often refer to the opposing lawyer in the courtroom as their "friend." For example, the lawyer may say "Your Honour, my friend's point is well taken; however, he neglected to mention ..." Clients are seen shaking their heads as if to say, "Hey, wait a minute, if he is such a good friend how can he do a good job for me?" They may soon realize that the last thing that these two lawyers are is friends. They may have never even met before or may dislike each other intensely. I have yet to hear one lawyer call another "my learned friend" without at least a hint of sarcasm or a smile—or both.

It is simply a courtesy developed to maintain some decorum or civility. Lawyers are reminded that they are merely advocates for clients who come and go while they are there in the courts as adversaries day after day throughout their careers.

Many courts still require lawyers to wear gowns to court. These include the black cape, black waistcoat, wing-tip collar shirts and tabs. Some lawyers wear formal striped trousers while many just wear dark dress pants and black shoes.

No one wears a wig to court and no one ever has in Canada—except perhaps a witness or two.

Oh—as a final note to this section on the personnel of the courts, if during your own case you see a jury in the courtroom, slowly stand up and, as quietly as possible, leave—you're in the wrong courtroom. Family law disputes are never heard by juries.

The Rules of Court

You may recall the first time you played "Monopoly" and everyone sat patiently (well, nearly everyone) and listened while someone who had played before read out the rules. Coloured markers were selected, a little money counted out, the dice were cast and away you went. Well, in its handling of family law matters, our court system is not unlike that, except that you are the coloured marker and the money is real.

If you will bear with me for a minute I shall "read the rules," so to speak. Remember, too, that this a general overview.

The court system, lawyers, all of the other people discussed earlier, and your own case respond to or initiate action in the system through the use of sets of rules. These rules, which are very specific, actually have the force of law because they are regulations made pursuant to provincial law. Without these detailed rules no one would know what to do next on a particular case. Everyone would be going off in different directions without any guidance or control or, worse yet, everyone would simply sit and do nothing. Each province has its own set of rules governing procedure in its courts.

The rules of the game are known as "The Rules of Practice" or "The Rules of Court." They provide for virtually everything that can happen between the institution of proceedings (starting the case into the court system—for example, by getting the Registrar to authorize commencement of an action) and the obtaining of a judgment at the end of the case. One published version of the Rules and the summaries of cases that interpret them is 1090 pages in length. The Rules also provide for appeals, enforcement of court orders and hundreds of other matters.

The various levels of court within each province have their own sets of rules. So a provincial court has its own set of rules and the Unified Family Court has, of course, another set of rules all its own. Every level of court for family law has its own set of rules (and you thought this was going to be easy).

The only good news in all of this is that, by and large, the rules are helpful and provide very much the same procedures for the different courts, with variations. If used properly they can provide a great deal of control over the progress of a case.

The Rules prescribe all of the steps that must be taken to move your case from beginning to end as well as all of the forms that must be used to make the documents acceptable for filing at the court. A system as overburdened as ours would not last fifteen minutes if everyone filed documents in whatever form they wished. So the Rules prescribe everything from the colour and size of the paper to their form and content. You may want to take a minute now to look at some of the forms reproduced in the Appendices at the end of the book.

The basic steps in any legal proceeding are essentially the same:

1. exchange of letters between lawyers
2. exchange of legal documents (called pleadings)
3. discovery of each other's case
4. motions (mini-trials on matters that come up from time to time)
5. pre-trial (settlement discussion before a trial)
6. trial and, if necessary,
7. appeal

The following is a brief summary of what happens at each of these steps.

1. EXCHANGE OF LETTERS
Assuming you have settled upon a lawyer and completed a retainer authorizing the lawyer to act on your behalf, the matter will inevitably begin with your lawyer writing to either your spouse or his or her lawyer, if he or she has already hired one. On the other hand, it may be you who receive a letter and consult a lawyer about what you should do in response. These letters often say the following:

"Without Prejudice"
Client/Spouse's name and address

Dear _____

Re: Family Matters

We have been consulted by [client's name] with respect to your present family difficulties. [Client's name] has instructed me to explore the possibility of resolving these difficulties through negotiations which would lead to the signing of a separation agreement containing terms acceptable to both of you.

Please have your solicitor contact me within the next few days so that we can amicably resolve the outstanding problems as quickly as possible.

I look forward to hearing from your lawyer.

Yours very truly,

Lawyer's name

Sometimes this type of letter contains a deadline, such as "If I have not heard from you within ten days of the date of the letter I will commence court proceedings." These letters often mention the need to complete financial statements.

These initial letters are important. They can set the tone for the negotiations. They often list a person's demands and therefore shape the issue. If appropriate, they can open the door to alternatives to the courtroom such as mediation (see Chapter 12). Given the letter's importance I suggest that you ask to see the letter your lawyer plans to send. You should also ask about the circumstances under which it will be delivered. For example, it is rarely necessary to have such letters delivered to a person at work, but some lawyers will arrange such a delivery out of thoughtlessness or stupidity. A person embarrassed at work will not be interested in negotiating anything. Discuss this with your lawyer and make your wishes known. Do not accept standardized letters run off a word processor. Insist on a personal touch.

I have seen entire separation agreements (see Chapter 10, "Settling Your Differences") negotiated by letters over a period of several months. In other cases it becomes clear early on that a settlement will not be possible without some other methods being used. *Do not* go from this letter-writing stage to the next stage, legal proceedings, without a written opinion from your lawyer about what happened and what is likely to happen if legal proceedings are started. This opinion should also contain an estimate about fees and out of pocket expenses that might be incurred.

2. EXCHANGE OF LEGAL DOCUMENTS

If the letters have not led to a settlement (which would likely be incorporated into a separation agreement) then your lawyer may recommend starting legal proceedings. All unresolved issues are submitted to the court, saying, in essence, "These people cannot decide, so you decide for them."

The proceedings can be started in a number of ways by using documents contained in the Rules of Practice. These are court forms printed by legal stationery companies. Law offices keep hundreds of them on hand and simply fill in the blanks when necessary. Family law proceedings can be started by Divorce Petition, Statement of Claim, Application, and in some cases by Notice of Motion. The names of the forms may vary slightly from province to province but they all have the same effect and seek to achieve the same goal. That goal is to give the court an orderly and uniform summary of what the dispute is all about. The form will describe the people involved, children (if any), where they live, what they want, when they are scheduled to appear to present their case and so on. Often, evidence is included in an Affidavit or Financial Statement.

Once the appropriate forms have been completed, the lawyer's staff will take the material to the court office to be "issued." This means that the clerks at the courthouse examine the documents to see if they have been completed properly, charge a fee and then sign them to make it all official.

Many provinces require the financial statements to be filed before they will issue the proceedings. Given the amount of detail needed, completion of these statements can delay the start for several days. The financial statements should give the court (and the other side) a picture of your current financial circumstances and your plans for the future.

Once issued, the material must be delivered to the other side; lawyers call this "serving the papers." If the other side has a lawyer it may be possible to facilitate service by the lawyer's accepting it on the client's behalf. If this cannot be arranged then a professional document server (bailiff or process server) may need to be hired. Except in the most unusual cases the service of documents should be done with sensitivity and not be done to embarrass the other side. (Remember—what goes around, comes around. And it's all at your expense.)

Once the other side has received your pile of material (it can swell to a couple of inches of paper very quickly) they must file material in response. If it is a divorce, then they must file an Answer to the Petition or even a Counter Petition, Affidavits, and of course the financial statements that, more often than not, tell a very different financial story from those issued by your side.

But we are not done yet. You may need to respond to the material you have just received. This can include a Reply, more Affidavits and Amended Financial Statements.

For historical reasons, these have all come to be known as "the pleadings." When lawyers used to plead for relief on behalf of their clients the documents themselves were called "pleadings." The point of the exercise where one person's documents respond to the other person's documents has not changed—it is designed to narrow the controversy until the key issues are identified.

At the end of this barrage of material everyone should have a good idea about where the argument lies. "Everyone" includes you as the client, so *do not* go to the next step (discovery) unless you have received a written opinion from your lawyer telling you what has happened and what is likely to happen. This again should include a bill for the work done and an estimate of the cost of the next step.

3. DISCOVERY

In the next four sections we will examine the most time-consuming and therefore expensive aspects of family law litigation—discovery, motions, trials and appeals. At this stage I will provide a general overview, because in a later chapter (Chapter 11, "Not Settling Your Differences") I will examine this part of the process in greater detail. What you need to know for the time being is that discovery includes oral examination of the parties under oath and examination of documentary evidence needed to prove one's case in court. Once the pleadings have been exchanged each lawyer is permitted to sit down with the other lawyer's client and ask that person questions about the pleadings—under oath, remember. The lawyer probes the written version set out in the documents.

This all takes place in a small room with a court reporter present. Both lawyers are present while the other lawyer asks you questions. The court reporter takes down all the questions and answers and marks all the exhibits for ease of reference and to be able to make some sense of the transcript later. (For example, the lawyer may ask you to identify a copy of your mortgage and will ask the reporter to mark it as Exhibit #1.) If there are many exhibits,the lawyers may bind photocopies of them into a book for ease of reference. This question and answer session may take an entire day, or it may only take a few hours. It depends on the complexity of the case.

It is unusual for your spouse to be present during your discovery, and vice versa. However, sometimes the lawyers may ask for the clients to be present if it is necessary to be able to consult with them as the questions and answers evolve. Personally, I think the clients should *not* be present so that no intimidation occurs, and to ease the anxiety for everyone.

In advance of this oral discovery the lawyers should have completed their documentary discovery. This means that if the client intends to rely on a particular document at trial then the client must produce a copy of it in advance of the oral discovery. "Document" has a wide meaning, and can include tapes, letters, photographs, drawings, computer discs and so on.

Discovery—oral and documentary—is designed to further narrow the issues and prevent surprises at trial. Nobody wants to go all the way to the court to suddenly see a document that proves the other side was right all along. In fact, the court can penalize with legal fees a person who does so.

After the discovery the lawyers will ask the court reporter to prepare a transcript of the questions and answers. The first page usually lists all the exhibits. Once the transcript arrives—two or three weeks later—the lawyers and their staff review it to evaluate the likelihood of success. They also look to see if there were any questions that the client was unable to answer. In such cases the lawyer and client sometimes "undertake" or promise to get the information and send it along later.

These promises are called "undertakings," and must be kept, or you risk being penalized.

The lawyer should now prepare a written opinion setting out what has happened and what is likely to happen at the next step. This opinion should include the lawyer's opinion on the likelihood of success. It should speak in terms of "If this matter went to court I think the court would do as follows ..."

You are paying the lawyer for his or her opinion on what will happen: make sure you get it in writing. Do not do anything until you have this opinion in hand. Be prepared to sit down and discuss it with the lawyer— *not* the student, the paralegal, the secretary or anybody else. You will also want to discuss the expected cost of going to the next step—trial.

4. MOTIONS

A motion is an application to the court for an order on a particular issue. Motions can occur any time after the proceeding has been issued at the courthouse, right up until the time of trial. Lawyers will use motions to sort out interim problems and procedural matters. This amounts to asking the court to settle an issue until the final trial. It could involve asking the court to decide a matter such as custody, or who should reside in the house, until the trial.

The motion is held in front of a judge or Master, and often does not include the clients. Two documents are needed for a motion—the motion itself, and an affidavit. The motion itself is a two- or three-page document that identifies the people involved, describes what they want from the court and sets out a time and date for the presentation to the judge. Motions can be difficult to schedule since the date and time must be co-ordinated with the court office and available "judge time."

The motion is then supported by an affidavit sworn by the client. This affidavit is evidence that takes the place of the client's appearing and giving testimony orally. There is nothing to prevent you as the client from attending a motion if you are able to schedule the time off work. Your attendance might help to keep your lawyer on his or her toes. I have always found it fascinating to watch other lawyers at work when their clients are not present as compared to when they are present. It is a real insight into who cares and who does not. (Be forewarned though—there can be a lot of waiting.)

The motion may be adjourned, indefinitely or to a specific day, to allow the lawyers to cross-examine the clients on the contents of any affidavit filed. In such a case the discovery process is repeated, but only with respect to the affidavit. A transcript of the question and answer session may be requested by the lawyer and filed on the motion. Once the motion is again before the judge the matter is discussed and the judge makes an order. The motion may be dismissed (rejected), the order sought may be granted or some other order may be made somewhere in between what the lawyers were asking the court to do. For example, a wife may ask for an order that she have exclusive possession of the home until trial (approximately one year away). The husband, on the other hand, may ask the court to order that the house be sold immediately and the proceeds of the sale be divided equally. The judge could order that the wife have exclusive possession until the house is sold and fix the terms of sale to include a stipulation that the deal not close for at least six months.

If an order is made the judge will usually just scribble his or her endorsement on the back of the papers in the file. The lawyer's staff will get a photocopy of the judge's order and have it typed up into a formal order, which is then approved by both sides as accurate and filed with the court clerks. The order is issued by the court staff and becomes an official order of the court.

Motions may cost approximately a thousand dollars each, not including the cost of disbursements such as the court reporter's transcript of a cross-examination (three hundred dollars plus). Lawyers should not be instructed (or permitted) to bring motions without your express consent, and then only if there is no other way of solving the problem.

5. PRE-TRIALS

Every province has some method of screening family law cases before they go to trial. In many cases this is known as a pre-trial or a settlement conference. It takes place once the people involved have indicated that they are unable to resolve the matter and are ready for trial.

An experienced person—often a family court judge—examines the pleadings and meets with the lawyers and their clients. In all but the most unusual cases the clients should be available for—and should participate in—the pre-trial conference. Once again, the goal of this exercise is to help the people settle part, if not all, of the case. The issues may become narrowed even further or part of the case may settle simply by having a four-way discussion.

The pre-trial also allows the lawyers and clients to get a second opinion about their positions. The judge who conducts the pre-trial will not hear the trial, so he or she is free to state frankly that "if I heard this case I would decide as follows ..." This can have a powerful effect on a difficult lawyer or client. In most systems this type of conference is a precondition to being given a trial date.

Again, *do not* go to the next step (trial) unless you have the written opinion about what happened and what is likely to happen next.

6. THE TRIAL

Settlement discussions have produced nothing, pleadings and discoveries are finished, motions have been exhausted and a pre-trial has not resolved the matter. It may have taken years but you now stand near the end of the trail—the trial.

Assuming you have actually got a judge, a courtroom, all the witnesses, an opponent and are ready to go, most trials take more than one day. The approximate cost is $1,500 per day and it is therefore not unusual to see a three-day trial run $5,000—each.

We shall discuss this in upcoming chapters, but you should understand at this stage that everything you have written in affidavits, explained at discovery, or achieved on motions must now be recounted orally for the court. From the most obvious questions (What is your name?) through the most complex (Can you explain the differences between your financial statements for 1989, 1990 and 1991?) all will be traced in public in the courtroom with the goal of persuading the judge that you, after all, are correct and have been since the proceedings were commenced a year and a half ago.

After the evidence has been reviewed by the judge, he or she will render a judgment on the issues placed before the court—custody of your children, access rights, property division, and, if necessary, the divorce itself.

The judge will also order who must pay the costs of the lawyers and how much, depending on how the case was conducted.

7. APPEALS

Almost any order or judgment can be appealed to a higher court. Although some orders are considered to be of such a minor nature that they cannot be appealed, most orders of any significance can be appealed.

Judgments are always appealable but must contain some serious error in fact or law to be successfully appealed. If an appeal is undertaken a further six months to one year may be required. A transcript of the entire trial must be ordered at a cost of thousands of dollars just to be able to determine whether an appeal is feasible.

I have set out the foregoing for one primary reason: you must appreciate that when a case is not resolved and it goes to court, it must then wind its way through the procedures I have set out above. And remember—I have set out a *brief* version of events.

Lawyers who promise quick results in court are either misleading you or haven't been there enough to know better. In either case, think twice about anyone who promises fast results in court.

You now know as much or more about the legal system and family law than most law students. It should be clearer why starting proceedings in court is like playing "Monopoly": everyone gets a turn, the game rarely ends quickly, and then only when one person has all the money.

Remember also that you will be paying for this with your own money at rates in excess of one hundred dollars an hour. It can be an expensive proposition, to say the least.

This is not to say that you should never go to court; sometimes it is simply unavoidable. But if you must use the wheels of justice, remember, they turn slowly—using up time, energy and money.

5

Divorce

As hard as you may find this to believe, I thought we should start with something easy—the divorce itself. It is not difficult to forget during the intensity of a dispute that one goal is to actually end the marriage, to dissolve it. One of the reasons that it is easy to forget is that the granting of the divorce itself can in many cases be the least contentious issue. This wasn't always the case. Before 1985, when significant changes were made to the *Divorce Act*, the list of reasons for divorce included such things as adultery, homosexual activity, bestiality, prison sentences, rape and so on. Little wonder that people felt they had to defend themselves in a divorce proceeding when such horrible allegations could be made.

In 1985 and 1986 the *Divorce Act* amendments ended many of those disputes by going to an almost completely no fault system of divorce in Canada. The amendments themselves came into force on June 1, 1986, and apply to all divorces subsequent to that date. We shall examine these "grounds for divorce" in a moment but first let's consider some background information to put this chapter in perspective.

You will recall that the *Divorce Act* is federal legislation and applies only to people who are legally married. If a divorce is sought then the Act provides the court with the authority to make orders for custody, access, spousal and child support as well as other miscellaneous orders. In this chapter, however, we shall consider only the divorce itself, the order that dissolves the marriage.

THE NATIONAL PICTURE

When thinking of your own predicament it may be comforting to know that tens of thousands of other people are going through similar circumstances. Consider the following facts about divorce in Canada:

- The Canadian divorce rate has increased steadily from 124 per 100,000 population in 1969 to 339.9 per 100,000 population in 1987.
- In 1987 there were 80,000 divorces in Canada. Estimates for 1990 and 1991 are for approximately 100,000 divorces per year.

- Statistics Canada estimates that between 28 and 30 percent of all marriages will end in divorce. This actually turns out to be good news, because a few years ago they estimated that approximately 40 percent would end in divorce. The new, lower estimate is considered to be more accurate.
- Most divorces occur after about eleven years of marriage, although there is a group of about 11 percent of couples who leave their marriages after twenty-five years.
- About half of all divorces involve children. This meant that in 1987 approximately 74,000 children were affected by divorce.
- Despite all that we read and hear, lawyers, judges and other commentators seem to feel that divorce is becoming less adversarial.
- Couples who divorce seem to have fewer children than couples who remain together.
- 84 percent of men and 61 percent of women have full-time employment at the time they separate.
- 71 percent of men and 86 percent of women have legal representation for their divorce proceeding.
- Lawyers and judges estimate that about 5 percent of divorces actually require a trial to resolve them while other estimates place it a little lower, at about 3.8 percent.
- Most divorce cases (70 to 95 percent) settle through negotiations and do not require a trial.

With these facts in mind let's consider what the *Divorce Act* actually says about ending marriages.

GROUNDS FOR DIVORCE

There is only one ground for divorce in Canada—"marriage breakdown." The *Divorce Act* sets out three circumstances in which the marriage will be considered to have broken down:

- the husband and wife intentionally live separate and apart for one year or longer
- either the husband or wife commits adultery, or
- either the husband or wife subjects the other to intolerable physical or mental cruelty.

When you consider that the previous *Divorce Act* required people to be separated for three years, you can appreciate how these amendments have made access to the divorce procedure itself easier.

For a one-year separation to be used as a reason for the divorce, the separation must have occurred because there were difficulties in the marriage. A man could not file for divorce because his wife went to study at a university in another city for a year or because he or his wife went to work for Bell Canada in Saudi Arabia on a short-term contract. At least one of the spouses must intend to live separate and apart because the marriage was having problems.

If this circumstance of marriage breakdown has occurred, there is no need to describe the problems or lay the blame with anyone for the marriage's difficulties. The separation itself is the proof of the marriage breakdown.

Separation need not mean separate houses, although that is certainly the case in most situations. The courts have considered cases in which the husband and wife lived separate and apart but under the same roof. For example, if a husband and wife had marital problems but could not afford separate accommodations, then they could agree to share their home but live separate from each other in it. This would mean no sexual contact with each other, separate sleeping arrangements, separate meals, separate lives and minimal communication, with both left to fend for themselves with respect to cleaning and other domestic work.

In most cases, however, the couple separates into their own new lives and it is not difficult to see that they are intentionally living separate and apart from each other.

We have all heard the old melodramatic line in the movies: "She won't give him a divorce!" You will be relieved to know that it has no application in Canada now, because once the separation has occurred either the husband or the wife can file for divorce. When I say that the separation has occurred I do not mean that the full year of separation must be complete, but rather that the day after the separation has occurred either of them may file for divorce. The court, however, will not make the divorce order until the year of separation has expired. If the ground of marriage breakdown is met the court will grant it no matter what the other spouse says or wishes. There can therefore be no withholding of consent to the granting of a divorce.

A recent survey of Canadian lawyers found that 83 percent of people filing for divorce seek the divorce on the basis of the one-year separation.

Adultery has always been one of the more lurid allegations hurled by one spouse at the other. It is, if proved, considered proof of marriage breakdown and will result in an immediate divorce order. This method of establishing marriage breakdown is being used less and less because of the availability of the one-year separation method.

The spouse who has committed adultery cannot start the divorce; only the other spouse may do so. This prevents spouses from going out and committing adultery simply to entitle themselves to an immediate divorce. The only restriction on the making of a divorce based on adultery is that the court is careful to ensure that the spouse who is seeking the divorce did not "forgive" the adultery. Forgiveness will excuse the conduct and prevent the divorce from being granted.

Strangely, homosexual conduct will not entitle a spouse to a divorce on the grounds of adultery. The adultery can only be committed with a member of the opposite sex. If a spouse is engaging in homosexual activity that the other spouse finds objectionable it may constitute mental cruelty and be evidence of a marriage breakdown.

One spouse's physical or mental cruelty towards the other spouse is the third method of proving that the marriage has broken down. The result of the abuse must be that it makes the possibility of living together intolerable. Again, the spouse responsible for the abuse cannot seek the divorce. It must the abused spouse. He or she may seek a divorce any time the abuse becomes intolerable.

The law books are filled with cases in which the court has been asked to decide whether or not the physical or mental cruelty is sufficient to render the continued cohabitation of the partners intolerable. These cases have developed a set of guidelines that are used in such divorces. They are as follows:

1. Each case must be determined on its own merits. The key question is whether this conduct by one partner towards the other constitutes cruelty.
2. The cruelty, either physical or mental, must render intolerable the continued cohabitation of the spouses.
3. The parties must be living separate and apart, since life together that is intolerable would prevent them from sharing the same accommodations.
4. The acts of cruelty that are complained of must be "grave and weighty." One judge has described them as "more than flesh and blood can stand."
5. The acts that the spouse complains of must be more than mere incompatibility within the marriage.
6. Cruelty should not be used as a way of securing a quick divorce where evidence of separation or adultery is not available.
7. The cruelty must be exercised by one spouse directly against the other and should not arise from the nature of their living circumstances or the acts of third parties.
8. Evidence of cruelty must be clear and corroborated and should not be based simply on the hurt feelings of an injured spouse.
9. While it is not essential in every case, there usually should be an element of fear that renders the cohabitation intolerable.
10. The spouse's conduct that is complained of need not be intentional. It can result from illness, alcohol abuse or even total insensitivity.
11. What is considered intolerable conduct may vary from era to era. What one generation tolerated, another generation may not.

With those general guidelines in mind, consider the following situations which were considered examples of mental cruelty:

- The husband had a habit of leaving home after the evening meal and not returning until the early hours of the morning, a course of conduct to which the wife consistently objected.
- The husband concentrated most of his time on his work and refused to make time for his wife and family, was not involved with the children and did not communicate with his wife in any meaningful way.
- The husband totally disregarded the family and spent time with other women.

- The husband was hostile, rigid and had a domineering attitude towards his wife.
- The husband was a perfectionist who was subject to bouts of depression and was occasionally violent.
- The husband drank heavily, refused to work and refused to have sexual relations with his wife, although he was prepared to harass her at work and refused to participate in marriage counselling.
- The husband's personality was loud, obnoxious and authoritarian.
- The husband had thirty jobs in twenty years and subjected the family to intense pressure from creditors.
- A wife concealed from the husband a physical abnormality that made conception impossible.
- The wife was a severe alcoholic.
- The wife was constantly suspicious of her husband's supposed infidelity and publicly accused him of having affairs with other women and on several occasions physically assaulted him.
- The husband forced his wife to quit working with an all-male landscaping crew. This was coupled with verbal and physical abuse.
- The husband began to lead an active gay sexual life.
- The couple engaged in mutual sarcasm and public belittlement.
- The wife constantly referred to the husband as "the bastard" and considered him to be a less worthy person because he had been born out of wedlock.
- The couple had arguments about finances and the husband's keeping of a loaded shotgun.

Mental cruelty was not established in the following situations:

- The wife obtained an abortion without her husband's consent.
- The wife's children from a previous marriage were undisciplined and unsupervised.
- The husband complained of eighteen years of constant nagging by his wife.
- The wife complained that her husband did not have sufficient empathy for her future. He considered her idea of communication unreasonable.
- The spouse failed to obtain employment and provide support.
- The wife in a second marriage could not cope with the children's behaviour and was dissatisfied with the carpeting in the home and the husband's failure to repaint the house.
- The wife was not happy with the husband's friends and called him a fool in his business activities.
- The husband was attacked by the wife's son from a previous marriage.

Cases involving physical cruelty are a little easier to comprehend. The courts have not required particularly vicious conduct in order to justify the granting of a divorce on that ground. Canadian cases describe physical cruelty as including punching, threatening with a knife, dragging the wife by the hair, locking the other spouse in bathrooms, inflicting abrasions and bruises and, in one case, the husband subjecting the wife to a brutal exorcism ritual.

Spouses who conspire to create evidence for any of the above situations of marriage breakdown or who forgive the conduct of which they complain will lose the right to obtain a divorce.

In a nutshell, then, you may be entitled to a divorce if you separate for at least a year, if your spouse has committed adultery, or if your spouse has been physically or mentally cruel to the extent that you cannot tolerate living together. These rules apply to any marriage, regardless of where it took place in the world. Whether you were married in the United States, Europe, India or elsewhere, as long as you have lived in Canada for at least a year prior to the application for divorce, you may use the *Divorce Act*.

Note, however, that some of the more unusual forms of marriage may require a second look by a lawyer. There are a few types of marriage (such as polygamous marriage) that we do not recognize for "reasons of public policy." If in doubt, have a lawyer check out the circumstances of your marriage to determine whether it is recognized as a marriage for the purpose of divorce in Canada.

Reconciliation (getting back together) is always a possibility. I remember cases of couples reconciling shortly before the court was going to deal with their divorce. They were less than twenty-four hours from what they thought would be freedom and they decided to give the marriage at least one more try. Some couples try reconciling more than once, and this is fine, since no one wishes to discourage people from attempting to work things out. However, we need to keep in mind the effect this may have on the one-year period of separation. The couple cannot have it both ways— either they are separated or not. The *Divorce Act* sets a limit—a ninety-day total of living together. If you go over the ninety-day limit, the one-year period of separation is interrupted and you must start over again. The ninety-day total can be made up of more than one attempt. So, for example, a husband and wife could try living together for a week in the summer, then a month in the fall and even another month at Christmas and still be entitled to a divorce on the basis that they have been separated for a full year.

Incidentally, reconciliation attempts are not considered forgiveness of cruelty or adultery, so couples are given some flexibility in working things out.

A survey of lawyers found that the ninety-day recohabitation provision was not, in fact, used that much. About one-third of divorcing couples report that they separated and attempted reconciliation before they actually went ahead with their divorce.

THE PROCEDURE FOR A DIVORCE

Most lawyers will tell you that there are only two kinds of divorce— contested and uncontested. It can actually be a little more involved than that, but the dynamic of the divorce does depend very much on whether the couple agrees or not. The consequences of settling or not settling are examined in upcoming chapters. At this stage, however, we want to focus on what it means in terms of procedure to seek a divorce from the court. (Here again, remember that we are thinking now only about the divorce itself, not the custody, access or property division orders.) You will recall from Chapter 4 that there are different levels of court in each of the provinces. Since the *Divorce Act* is federal, only federally appointed judges may make orders for divorce. These judges sit on what are called "superior courts," which have different names depending on the province in question. In Manitoba, Alberta, Saskatchewan and New Brunswick they are called the "Court of Queen's Bench." In other provinces they are called simply the "Supreme Court." In Ontario this court is now known as the "Ontario Court of Justice." Regardless of their names in the different provinces, it is these courts that grant divorces.

Whether you use the court in one province or another is dictated by whether one or both of you have been ordinarily resident within the province for at least the previous year. "Ordinarily resident" does not mean the province where your cottage is located or where you took a summer university course. It means the place where you normally have your home. In one case, a young woman moved from Ontario to British Columbia following her husband to attempt a reconciliation. After two months, they realized the marriage would not work and she tried to file for divorce in British Columbia. She was not considered to have been ordinarily resident in British Columbia (nor was he) and they could not file the Petition for Divorce. You may wish to take a moment to examine the example of a Divorce Petition in the Appendices. In order to complete that Petition, at least one of the spouses must have been ordinarily resident for at least a year in the jurisdiction in which the divorce is sought.

The one-year residency requirement prevents people from shopping around for the least expensive or least difficult divorce procedure, and also prevents a spouse from trying to file for divorce where it would achieve maximum inconvenience for the other spouse.

A Central Divorce Registry in Ottawa collects statistics on divorces filed across Canada. It ensures that when two spouses residing in different parts of the country file for divorce without either one knowing of the other's filing, the one who filed first is permitted to continue with the divorce action and the other, subsequent, action is discontinued.

It is not only the residence of the spouse that will determine the location of the divorce. If a child is affected by the divorce, the court reserves the right to transfer the entire matter to the province that is most convenient for the child. So, for example, where a child is resident in Ontario with his mother and attending school, but the father seeks the divorce in Newfoundland, along with a particular custody or access order affecting that child, the Newfoundland Supreme Court could transfer the matter to Ontario. Those best able to comment on the child's life would then be available for the court's consideration.

Uncontested Divorces

In many cases there are no outstanding issues to be resolved, since any problems concerning custody, access or property division may have been solved by a separation agreement (see Chapter 10, "Settling Your Differences"). The parties are then able to ask the court to simply dissolve the marriage and in some cases incorporate the terms of the separation agreement into the court's order at the same time.

Years ago, even when the divorce was uncontested, it was necessary to attend court for a hearing. This was considered by many to be a waste of time and money for the court and people involved. So when the *Divorce Act* changes came into force on June 1, 1986, the provinces were given the power to create a procedure for granting divorces without requiring the people to attend a court hearing. Every province except Newfoundland has created such a procedure; in some provinces as many as 98 percent of divorces are granted in this way. In Quebec, the availability of the procedure is limited to cases that do not involve children. Nationally, about 68 percent of divorcing couples use the "no hearing" method.

Following this procedure, the couple simply fills out the appropriate divorce forms and supporting documents and files them with the court. It was expected that this system would lower legal fees for the couple involved. Unfortunately, this has not been the case everywhere. The simplified procedure has not reduced cost significantly.

One positive development with this procedure is the increase in speed with which the uncontested divorce can be processed. On average, it now takes about seventeen weeks when no hearing is needed—much less time, as we shall see, than most contested divorces. In addition, clients rarely like attending court, so it makes it all less of a strain for the people involved. It also tends to steer them away from the courtroom generally in resolving family law disputes.

Joint Petition for Divorce

An interesting innovation introduced in the recent *Divorce Act* reforms was the Joint Petition. If the couple can agree on the ground for the divorce and no other matter is in dispute, then they are able to issue a Petition for Divorce jointly. Only about 4.7 percent of divorcing couples in Canada have made use of this procedure, although its popularity is increasing.

The research available on the use of Joint Petitions suggests that those who use this method tend to pay considerably less in legal fees, have their divorce finalized more quickly, are more likely to favour joint custody and are slightly more generous with the amount of support paid. Researchers also speculated that couples who are able to divorce on a more friendly basis use the Joint Petition to symbolize their co-operation in divorce. An example of a Joint Petition is included in the Appendices.

Contested Divorces

A contested divorce is one in which the parties cannot agree on some issue and this forces them to exchange the "special" pleadings for a divorce action. A Petition must always be issued to begin the divorce claim. It is the equivalent of a Statement of Claim; an example is included in the Appendices at the end of the book. However, what makes the case contested is the need for the Respondent to deliver an Answer or a Counter Petition. In the Answer the Respondent replies to all the allegations made by the Petitioner. A Counter Petition is needed if the Respondent needs some kind of order from the court. For example, the Answer might deny an allegation of adultery made by the Petitioner and the Respondent may also counter petition for a divorce on the basis of a one-year separation.

Once a case is contested it is difficult to predict how long it will take to resolve or what the ultimate cost will be. Many contested divorces go on for years—particularly, research indicates, if the dispute concerns property. Where custody is an issue and assessments are needed or trials occur, it takes on average twice as long to finalize as an uncontested divorce does. (Therefore it can be expected to take more than two years.)

Regardless of the contested or uncontested nature of the divorce, once the court actually deals with the dissolution of the marriage it becomes effective thirty days after the judge has made the divorce order. The marriage is therefore over and dissolved on the thirty-first day. This thirty-day period is designed to give either of the people involved an opportunity to appeal. If one of them appeals, the divorce cannot be effective until the appeal is resolved once and for all. Once launched, the appeal can wait several months before it is heard.

In some cases the husband or wife needs the divorce order to be effective before the thirty-first day. For example, he or she may be remarrying. A remarriage cannot take place until the divorce order is final and effective. All jurisdictions therefore allow the couple to have the order made effective sooner if they both undertake in writing not to appeal and if special circumstances require the earlier effective date. Most family law lawyers have witnessed the look of panic on those who wish to remarry within that thirty-day period because the bride-to-be is expecting and the couple wants the child to be born in wedlock. In such a circumstance the court would abridge the thirty-day period and grant the divorce immediately. In some cases it can be effective with no waiting period.

What do you get for all this work? A Certificate of Divorce! It is available at the court office and provides an official record of the marriage's dissolution and the effective date of dissolution. The Certificate may come in handy if you plan to remarry at a later date. With it, you can prove that your previous marriage is in fact over.

Legal Fees for Divorce

Most men and women are represented by lawyers for their divorce proceedings. Recent studies determine that women are four times more likely than men to have legal aid lawyers acting on their behalf. Little is known about the actual expense of divorce proceedings and the one study that has been done developed some very conservative estimates for the average cost of legal representation in a divorce action. That study found that the estimated cost of legal representation was $2,322 for men and $2,338 for women. The maximum legal bill reported by a woman was $23,000 and by a man was $20,000. If a trial occurred, men reported on average a legal bill of $7,571 and women reported bills of $3,133.

Most lawyers find these figures a little difficult to understand. High as they may seem to you, to the lawyers they seem too low! One explanation is that the thousands of routine, uncontested divorces are artificially lowering the average cost of family law litigation. It is no secret that one motion alone in a family law case can cost $3,000. Some cases involve several motions. So while these average figures are interesting, they should not be considered benchmarks in any way for the expense of contested family litigation. Most family law lawyers will not undertake a contested custody dispute unless they receive $10,000 or $15,000 in advance. So much for national averages.

In conclusion, you may wish to consider the following checklist of questions before you file for divorce:

1. What is the basis of the claim for marriage breakdown? One year's separation? Adultery? Mental cruelty? Physical cruelty?
2. Will my divorce be contested or uncontested?
3. If it is uncontested, is a Joint Petition possible?
4. If the marriage breakdown is to be evidenced by adultery or cruelty, is it likely that a one-year separation may apply by the time such a hearing could be arranged?
5. Where were we married? Does the *Divorce Act* apply to our marriage?
6. Is there any chance of reconciliation?
7. Do I understand the ninety-day-total rule governing an attempt at reconciliation?
8. If cruelty or adultery is the evidence of marriage breakdown, has there been any forgiveness of this conduct?
9. Will a child be affected by the divorce? Will that affect the jurisdiction most suited to hearing the divorce?
10. If a divorce is granted, will I require it to be effective within the thirty-day period after the order is made?
11. Is remarriage or the birth of a child a factor?

I hope the above information gives you a feel for the particular issue of marriage dissolution. It may in retrospect turn out to be the easiest part of the entire process.

6

Dividing the
Family's Property

A recent headline in the *Toronto Star* proclaimed: "Did no work, husband loses share of house." The story underneath it described a woman who had "lived like a pauper" to buy her house while her husband contributed almost nothing to its purchase or care. The judge in a divorce hearing felt that the husband's contribution was so completely absent that he should receive none of its value. It is an interesting case from a number of perspectives.

It underscores the importance of the family home as what is usually the largest and most significant asset owned by a family. In this particular case the home was valued at $185,000 and was located in a suburb of Toronto.

The trial involved neighbours of the couple being called to court to testify that the husband had spent most of his day, during the summer, sitting in his lawn chair drinking out of a coffee cup. One witness testified (in what must have been a dramatic moment) that the husband had occasionally mowed the grass.

The wife in question testified that her husband had lost his job at a dairy just before they married and that he had done just a little cooking and cleaning while she did most of the household chores as well as working at a full-time job. At the end of the trial the judge found that the wife should keep the entire value of the home and that the husband should receive none of it.

The case is an excellent example of the expense such family law litigation can generate. The wife reported that, while she was happy with the "victory," she faced a legal bill of $40,000. She had already paid $20,000, but owed an additional $27,000 in lawyer's fees. She received her costs because she was successful in the case. This amounted to approximately $8,000. The husband, on the other hand, having lost his interest in the house, was faced with a bill of $25,000 in legal fees. The most recent newspaper account of this decision reports that the husband has launched an appeal.

Property division in a marriage breakdown situation is governed entirely by provincial law and therefore varies from province to province. Because virtually each province has its own property division scheme, this chapter was one of the most difficult to assemble. Likewise, the number of generalizations that we can make about property division law in Canada is limited. So in this chapter I shall attempt to provide a sense of the common goals of property division and examine some of the more practical aspects of this area. In some areas of this discussion I shall pay particular attention to the property division scheme recently enacted in Ontario in 1986. I do so not out of preference for that particular scheme but rather because it is so comprehensive that it provides some valuable insights.

It is safe to say that the goal of property division schemes in all of the provinces and territories is to attempt to divide equitably, if not equally, the value of all of the assets acquired by the couple between the date of the marriage and the date of their separation or divorce. Marriage has become, for all intents and purposes, an economic partnership between a man and a woman. The partnership, like any business, sees each partner bring a contribution to it; assets and liabilities are acquired over the life of the partnership and at its conclusion the assets and liabilities are divided equally between the partners.

This partnership is created upon becoming legally married in Canada. In another chapter, dealing with common-law spouses, we examine the very serious limitations on their entitlement to share property at the end of a relationship. The rules and guidelines we are discussing in this chapter concern only legally married spouses.

While it is difficult to say whether or not married couples are any better off materially now than, say, twenty or thirty years ago, it is safe to say that married persons are subject to a much more complex scheme of provincial property division and that they are acquiring assets that are much more complex in nature and value. The typical Canadian family may own (or rent) a home, own a car, own furniture, have an interest in a pension plan, and have miscellaneous other personal items. If they are lucky they may own more than one vehicle, a cottage, recreational vehicles, stocks and bonds, RRSPs, Guaranteed Investment Certificates and so on. The case law that is reported in the family law property division area has considered hundreds of different types of property that spouses have acquired in marriages whose appropriate method of division they have been unable to agree upon. Assets argued over have included oil paintings, coin collections, books, heirlooms and just about every conceivable personal effect, and yes, even pets.

The complexity of the property division schemes and the types of property that couples own demand the involvement of lawyers and in many cases chartered accountants and valuators. So we begin this chapter with a caution that you will need to rely heavily on legal advice if you set out to divide your property and that you will be bearing a great deal of the responsibility yourself for locating, describing and valuing your own marriage's assets.

The importance of this issue vis-à-vis all others can be seen from the fact that property division is the issue the court prefers to settle first. Once the family's property has been divided the court then turns its attention to questions of custody of the children, access to them, child support and, depending on the amount of property received, spousal support.

I have reproduced in the Appendices to the book a copy of Ontario's Financial Statement, which is by far the most comprehensive effort to describe property and liabilities that a couple may acquire during the course of their marriage. You may wish to take a moment now to examine that form. While it does not apply in any province except Ontario, it is a useful way of determining precisely what a couple has and what a couple owes.

As with any claim that can be made in a court, you will face certain time limitations. Each province provides its own cutoff date for claiming such things as property division and spousal support. If you have separated, one of the best reasons to consult with a lawyer as soon as possible is to ensure that you have an accurate view of the precise time frame within which you must make a claim for property or support.

The definition of "property" varies from province to province. Some provinces make the distinction between "family assets" and "non-family assets." Family assets are generally those items most frequently acquired and used by the family. They include such things as the home, the family car, furniture, joint bank accounts, cottages, recreational equipment, and other similar assets. Non-family assets, on the other hand, include such things as business interests of the spouses, inheritances, special assets that were never used by the family, and so on. Provinces that make a distinction between these two categories do so to distinguish between assets that are divided equally upon marriage breakdown and assets that are not divided upon marriage breakdown at all. So, if a family held family assets of the nature I just described upon the date of their marriage breakdown, the net value of those assets would be divided equally between the husband and the wife.

I use the term "net value" in describing the value that would be divided because the value must include a deduction for any debts that are owed in connection with a particular asset. So, for example, if a couple owned a cottage that was worth $200,000 but was subject to a $100,000 mortgage, its net value would be $100,000 and it is that net value that is divided between the couple when their marriage breaks down. The same is true for a car that is subject to a bank loan, a home that is subject to a mortgage and even stocks that are purchased on a line of credit provided by a bank. The debts must be repaid first and any remaining value is divided.

Ontario has not made any distinction between family and non-family assets since 1986. Under Ontario's scheme, all property owned by either spouse, subject to some very limited exceptions, is divided between the spouses at marriage breakdown. A sometimes complex formula is used to divide that property. Essentially the formula has each spouse calculate his or her net worth in assets acquired between the date of marriage and the date of separation. The lower net value is deducted from the higher and the difference divided in half. In the final result the spouse with the higher net value pays half the "differential" in order to equalize the values they take out of the marriage.

Each province provides a list of exceptions for assets that need not be divided upon marriage breakdown. For example, every province allows a couple to exempt property from division by use of a marriage contract. If, at the time they were married, a couple agreed that a particular piece of property, such as the matrimonial home, would not be shared if the marriage broke down, and that agreement was contained in a marriage contract, then the home would be exempt. No two provinces exempt property in exactly the same way, but the following types of property are typical of the types of exemption:

- any asset owned in advance of the marriage
- a gift or inheritance received during the course of the marriage
- a court award or a settlement giving a spouse damages for personal injuries suffered, for example, in a car accident
- items of exclusively personal value
- business assets
- family heirlooms
- proceeds from a life insurance policy (for example, if a husband's mother died and left an insurance policy payable to him, the amount of money received could be exempt)
- gifts from one spouse to the other
- traceable property (this means property that started out in one exempt category but may have ended up in some other form; so, for example, if a wife took her damage award for injuries suffered in an automobile accident and purchased Guaranteed Investment Certificates, the Certificates are still exempt because they can be traced back to the original exempt category)
- assets exempted by virtue of a marriage contract; and finally
- assets that are acquired after the date of separation and before the trial.

One of the first issues that you will want to explore with your lawyer when discussing the property division in your own case is which categories of exempt property are applicable in your province or territory.

A difficult question that can arise in the area of property division is the value that should be attached to a particular asset. The following example is a good illustration of how diametrically opposed valuations can be: A man and woman had been married for approximately twenty years and have operated a dairy farm that had been passed down through five generations in the husband's family. Over those generations, the dairy operation was gradually surrounded by suburbs from a major metropolitan centre. The dairy operation was successful and the husband and wife intended, throughout most of the marriage, to pass it on to their children. The marriage experienced difficulty, the couple separated, and the value of the dairy operation came into question. The husband pointed out that the dairy operation had a particular book value of approximately $700,000 and that he was prepared to divide that value with his wife. The wife, on the other hand, had a valuation of the property performed and reported that the farm should be valued at $3,500,000. Why the discrepancy? The wife's valuation was dependent upon ending the dairy operation and selling the land to developers for a new housing subdivision. Which valuation is correct?   Both.   If the dairy operation continues, the business is worth $700,000; however, if the dairy operation is terminated and the property is sold for its value as a housing development, it is worth $3,500,000. Which is the best solution in this particular case?   Neither of the alternatives satisfied any of the people involved, particularly the children, who had expected to inherit the property.

The point of the above example is to illustrate that valuations can be quite different. You will want to explore with your lawyer the various alternatives that are available in your province. Some provinces such as Manitoba and Saskatchewan specify that the value to be used is the "fair market value." Other provinces do not specify the basis of valuation and allow each case to be decided on its own facts. This means that in cases involving difficult or unusual assets, various approaches will be used, including "current market value,", "fair market value," "cost," "book value," and "liquidation value."

Another twist that can be applied to the valuation issue is whether or not tax obligations and other costs should be taken into consideration when arriving at a value for an asset. For example, if an asset's owner would incur tax consequences for a particular disposition, such as the sale of the asset, should those tax consequences be factored in to reduce the value of the asset as divided? Similarly, if a piece of property when sold would involve costs of disposition, a question arises as to whether or not those costs of disposition should be deducted from the value as divided. So, for example, where a couple own a home and its value is to be divided, but one party does not wish to have the property sold and will therefore buy out the other person's interest, a question arises: Should the value be the fair market value of the home after the deduction of an amount for real estate commission?   If the property were sold on the open market a commission would be paid. Should the commission be taken into account in reducing the amount that must be shared with the other spouse? These are all questions that must be answered in the effort to arrive at an equitable division of the family's property. Valuation methods will vary from asset to asset and province to province.

Each province, as indicated earlier, has its own method for division of property. Generally that method is to add up the total value of all assets, add up the total value of all liabilities against those assets, and divide equally the net value that remains. Every province, however, provides a method for the court to divide the net value in a way that is *not* equal. Every provincial legislature has recognized that there may be circumstances in which it would not be fair to divide the family assets equally between the two spouses. But they have taken different approaches in describing the circumstances in which the court can exercise that discretion.

Some provinces, such as Ontario, Manitoba, Newfoundland and Nova Scotia, have said to their courts that assets should be divided unequally only where to divide them equally would be unconscionable or grossly unfair. This is a very high standard. It means that the court would need to find that it was almost shocked by the effect of an equal division for it to depart from that general rule. Other provinces, on the other hand, give the court the discretion to depart from an equal division of the value of the asset where to divide equally would be merely unfair.

You will recall the Ontario case I described at the opening of this chapter, involving the division of a house. Ontario only allows the court to divide unequally where to divide equally would be unconscionable. The judge in that case found it offensive to the conscience of a reasonable person to give the husband any interest in the home because of his lack of contribution. It is one of the rare decisions interpreting unequal division in unconscionable circumstances in Canada.

Because of the existence of this provision in the laws of some provinces, you will wish to discuss with your lawyer the circumstances under which your provincial legislation will allow the court to depart from an equal division of the property. You should be aware, of course, that unequal division of assets can be a two-edged sword.

A special asset that requires separate consideration is the matrimonial home. All provinces provide for a restriction on one spouse's ability to dispose of or encumber the matrimonial home without the other spouse's consent. Therefore, one spouse cannot sell the matrimonial home or place a mortgage on the property without the other spouse's consent. This protects the value of the property for sharing at marriage breakdown.

Another consideration is possession of the matrimonial home at the time the marriage breaks down. Possession does not necessarily relate to ownership of the matrimonial home. Manitoba, New Brunswick, Newfoundland, Nova Scotia, Ontario, Prince Edward Island and Saskatchewan all provide an automatic equal right to possession of the matrimonial home at the time of marriage breakdown regardless of ownership of the home. This means that if the couple separates it is open to either or both spouses to apply to the court for an order giving one of them exclusive possession of the matrimonial home. Alberta, British Columbia and Quebec do not provide this automatic right to possession of the home. In cases of family violence or where there is a need to keep children in a particular neighbourhood where they attend school or have their friends, for example, an order for exclusive possession can be a valuable tool. For further discussion of exclusive possession and its enforcement see Chapter 13, concerning enforcement of family law orders.

You should therefore discuss with your lawyer the availability of orders for exclusive possession in your particular jurisdiction.

A question that is related to the enforcement of family law orders is the availability of a restraining order with respect to property. Again, this is discussed in Chapter 13 but you should be aware at this stage of the possibility of obtaining an order from the court prohibiting your spouse from dealing with any of his or her property until further order of the court. This allows the court to preserve the assets until the end of trial, if necessary, so that there will be property available to divide and to pay for satisfaction of the judgment.

Payment of the judgment can be an interesting exercise. The goal of the formulas provided by provincial family law is to calculate a sum of money that is owed by one spouse to the other. The judgment can therefore be paid simply by a cash payment from one spouse to another or by the transfer of particular pieces of property. If, for example, the court finds that the wife is entitled to $100,000 for her interest in the family property and finds that the matrimonial home has an equity of $100,000, it could simply order that the matrimonial home be placed in the wife's name alone in satisfaction of her interest in the family property.

Another special asset is a pension. It is quite common for one or both spouses to have separate, private pension plans. If the particular province considers the pension to be a family asset, then it must be valued and divided like any other asset owned by the family. Valuing pensions is an intriguing experience, with values varying from pension to pension and pensionholder to pensionholder. Since the amount of the pension to be divided may only be the amount of pension accumulated during the marriage it may not be the entire value of the pension that needs to be calculated. Different methods used by valuators and accountants include the "termination method" and the "retirement method." In examining the value, the person doing the valuation will also consider mortality tables, the role of interest, early retirement provisions, death benefits that may be available after retirement and the tax consequences of the benefits upon receipt. Indexed pensions are a separate matter again.

You should be aware that those who do pension valuations—or valuations of any assets, for that matter—do not work for free. Their bills for valuations can represent a significant disbursement on your lawyer's account, a disbursement that is eventually passed on to you. It is important that you receive an estimate from your lawyer in advance before authorizing the valuation of an asset as significant as a pension.

One area of special interest in the area of pensions is the Canada Pension Plan credit sharing scheme. The Canada Pension Plan was amended in 1978 to provide for the sharing of the pension credits accumulated by one or both spouses during the years of their cohabitation. This sharing of credits takes effect upon the dissolution of the marriage. It was designed to ensure that low- or non-income earning homemakers whose marriage has ended are provided with some pension coverage.

The class of persons who can claim a division of pension credits includes married spouses who have been separated for at least one year as well as common-law spouses whose relationship has ended with the death of the other spouse or a separation lasting at least one year. The general rule applied to this class of persons is that upon the dissolution of the marriage or the ending of the common-law relationship, all unadjusted, pensionable earnings of either spouse during the eligible years of cohabitation are added together with one-half the total being credited to the Canada Pension Plan or provincial pension plan account of each of the spouses. Spouses whose divorce became absolute or effective prior to January 1, 1987, are treated differently than spouses whose divorce became effective after January 1, 1987.

The method by which the credits are divided is related to the contributions made by the respective spouses to the Canada Pension Plan.

A wife who never worked and was therefore never eligible to contribute to the Canada Pension Plan but whose husband always made the maximum allowable contribution would benefit to a large degree from the division scheme. If, however, the spouses had incomes throughout the marriage that were relatively equal, their pension credits would remain relatively unchanged.

Your precise entitlement to a sharing of Canada Pension Plan credits can vary. Therefore, you should consult your lawyer during the discussion of property division to determine whether or not you are entitled and, if so, to what form of credit.

Returning to some of the more practical considerations of property division, we should consider the all-important financial statements for a moment. Each province prescribes its own particular form of financial statement. Whenever some form of financial relief or property division is sought from the court, these forms must be filed. Consequently, if spousal support, child support or property division is claimed by either party then financial statements must be filed. Only in the very limited circumstances of an uncontested divorce where all financial matters have been resolved can financial statements be dispensed with.

It is very likely that the first document a lawyer will present you with, after a Family Law Client History form, is your province's financial statement. You will be sent home with a direction to complete the form to the best of your ability and return it to the office for typewritten preparation. So much depends upon the accuracy of this statement that it must, of course, be a full statement. It must be complete, it must be up-to-date and it must be meaningful. There is no point in trying to avoid a description of an asset, of artificially undervaluing an asset or of describing it in such vague terms that it cannot be understood. The content of the financial statement will be scrutinized by the lawyer for your spouse and ultimately, by the court.

While it is your job to locate the information and supporting documentation for these financial statements, the document should be prepared under close supervision by your lawyer. Remember, the form is designed to save time and money by ensuring complete financial disclosure as early as possible in the legal proceedings.

Your all-important credibility in a legal proceeding is at risk if the financial statement is not prepared accurately. The courts look with disfavour upon a party who has neglected to give full and complete disclosure. You should remember that these financial statements are sworn affidavits, and so they must be completed honestly and kept up-to-date throughout the proceedings. It may be necessary, from time to time, to file amended financial statements showing updates and corrections. I have seen a client's case improved immeasurably at trial when the client has withstood a probing cross-examination of the financial statement and demonstrated to the judge and the opposing counsel complete honesty and accuracy in completing the financial statement.

In some cases, clients worry about the disclosure of confidential financial information in a public proceeding. Many provinces have now incorporated provisions into their rules of procedure that allow the financial statement to be shielded. If this is a concern you should immediately consult with your lawyer so that you receive the benefit of that type of provision.

CONCLUSION

Property division is the area of family law that varies most from province to province. Its goals, as you have seen from the above, are relatively consistent in seeking to divide on an equitable basis the value of assets acquired by the marriage partnership between the date of marriage and the date of separation or divorce.

Both you and your lawyer have a special role in the preparation of the information that will guide the court in its effort to divide your family property. Your primary goal is to ensure that your lawyer prepares, on your behalf, the most complete, honest and accurate financial statement possible. It is your job to ensure that the statement retains that status from the beginning of the proceeding until the trial.

7

The Children

It is safe to say that custody of children is *the* issue in a family dispute. No other issue can dredge up such strong emotions or such total commitment by a parent to achieve his or her purpose. It is not uncommon to hear one parent threaten the other with a "scorched earth" policy in the approach to custody of children. I am familiar with one case in which a husband told his wife in venom-filled language that he intended to sell off all the family assets to finance his fight for custody of their children. She knew that he meant it, and refused to contest his request for custody of their children.

In this chapter we examine the meaning of "custody" and "access," the considerations used by the court in ordering them and some of the more important features of custody and access orders. We'll also examine the method of dispute resolution in custody as well as its cost and some of the tactical considerations.

Both federal and provincial family laws contain provisions with respect to custody of and access to children. The *Divorce Act* provides the court with the power to make an order respecting custody of or access to a child at the time of the granting of the divorce judgment and on an interim basis ("interim" meaning until a final order can be made). Virtually all provincial and territorial family laws contain similar provisions and, as described earlier, the choice of a provincial, territorial or federal law is dictated entirely by whether there is a request for a divorce. Under the *Divorce Act*, an order for custody or access is another type of "corollary relief." It is an extra, related order made at the time the court grants the divorce.

The *Divorce Act* states that an order for custody of a child or access to a child can be made in favour of one or more persons. It is this language that enables the court to make a sole custody award in favour of one parent or to divide custody between two parents by means of a joint custody order. Both the federal *Divorce Act* and provincial and territorial family laws contemplate custody being with more than one parent or, in some circumstances, with a non-parent (see Chapter 14, "Grandparents and 'Other Interested Persons' "). We'll examine these terms in more detail in a moment but it is important to understand that the court has wide discretion in deciding who shall have custody of and access to children.

The necessity for custody and access orders calls into question the status of the child. Who is considered a child for the purposes of the *Divorce Act* or the purposes of provincial law? As a general rule, a child under the age of sixteen can be the subject of a custody or access order under the *Divorce Act*. A child under the age of majority (which varies from province to province but usually is eighteen or nineteen) can be the subject of a custody or access order under provincial or territorial law. However, in some circumstances, an illness, disability or some other cause may require a child to remain in the charge of a parent. This can extend the time period for which a custody order can be made.

In order for the court to have jurisdiction to make a custody order it is a requirement that the child be in the jurisdiction of that particular court. So in order for a Saskatchewan judge to order custody of a child to one party that child must reside in Saskatchewan. The importance of this safeguard is expressed in the *Divorce Act* provision under which a judge has the power to transfer a divorce from one province to another if to do so would better enable the court to assess the child's best interests with respect to custody, access and support.

This last expression—"the child's best interests"—is an important one in custody and access matters. The determination of what is best for a particular child is the overriding consideration in all applications to the court concerning children. Provincial family laws have made an effort to set out considerations that the court should follow when attempting to determine the best interests of a particular child. Ontario's *Children's Law Reform Act*, for example, provides a list of examples of the needs and circumstances of a child that should be considered. These include:

(a) the love, affection and emotional ties between the child and (i) each person entitled to or claiming custody of or access to the child, (ii) other members of the child's family who reside with the child, and (iii) persons involved in the care and upbringing of the child;

(b) the views and preferences of the child, where such views and preferences can reasonably be ascertained;

(c) the length of time the child has lived in a stable home environment;

(d) the ability and willingness of each person applying for custody of the child to provide the child with guidance and education, the necessaries of life and any special needs of the child;

(e) any plans proposed for the care and upbringing of the child;

(f) the permanence and stability of the family unit with which it is proposed that the child will live; and

(g) the relationship by blood or through an adoption order between the child and each person who is a party to the application.

The above list is not intended to be exhaustive but does provide a very broad guide for assessing a child's best interests.

Nationally, the following general considerations have emerged as guides for the court in making custody and access determinations:

- the physical well-being of the child

- the emotional well-being and security of the child
- the plans for the education and maintenance of the child as described by those requesting custody or access
- the financial position of the parents (so that the court is able to apportion responsibility for support)
- the religious or ethical needs of the child
- the moral and ethical standards of the person seeking custody or access vis-à-vis local community standards
- the sensitivity of the person seeking custody or access as a parent and in particular that person's understanding of this particular child's needs.

One method that the court uses to address these questions is called an "assessment." It can be ordered by the court against the wishes of the parties or it can be arranged on a voluntary basis. During the assessment a skilled professional, often a social worker or psychologist, will meet with the family and the children to assess each particular child's needs and the ability of the parents to meet those needs. The assessment will often produce a recommendation for the court. It can take several visits with those involved.

Whether through the court process itself or through an assessment, some of the issues that the court and the assessor look for concern whether the child's needs are being met in a positive environment, whom the child has bonded most closely with, the sexual orientation of the parents, the child's relationship with brothers and sisters and other family members, the child's religious and moral upbringing, and his or her biological ties with each parent.

Some experts describe the assessment process as a search for the "psychological parent." It is not uncommon, particularly for younger children, to have a greater bond with one parent than the other. This may be related in some ways to the child's stage of development and the sex of the parent. Nonetheless, the person doing the assessment and the court are searching for that person, who will be the one best able to meet the child's needs. If the psychological parent has certain shortcomings, such as inadequate resources, the court can address that by ordering financial support from the other parent. This search for the psychological parent can present quite a dilemma when that parent is in fact not the biological parent of the child. In some cases the psychological parent is a grandparent or other family member and could even be a daycare worker or babysitter.

Another consideration is the behaviour of the parents. The *Divorce Act* is explicit in its direction to the courts and divorcing couples to consider which parent is most likely to facilitate the maximum contact for the child with both parents. In other words, maintaining the child's ongoing relationship with both parents is considered a factor in determining what is best for the child. If a parent seems obstructive or appears to be reluctant to facilitate the other parent's contact with the child, that person runs the risk of not being named the custodial parent.

This type of provision has come to be known as the "friendly parent" rule. That is to say, it has the effect of leading each parent to try to present himself or herself to the court as "friendly" to the other so as not to jeopardize a claim for custody. It is also called "the maximum contact" rule.

The court is not supposed to consider a person's past conduct when making custody or access orders unless the conduct is relevant to the ability of that person to act as a parent. That means the court will concern itself with conduct by a parent that may adversely affect the emotional, psychological or spiritual welfare of a child. These concerns can extend to a parent's relationship with a third party, a parent's sexual preference, the presence of physical or mental addictions and, in one recent case, whether the parent smoked to such an extent that it aggravated a child's asthma.

Homosexuality of a parent is not considered to be a bar to custody of or access to a child. However, it is a factor that is considered in the context of the particular community's standards and its effect on the child in question.

It is not uncommon to hear a parent's invitation to "speak with the child" in a custody case, as if here must be conclusive evidence of who should have custody of the child. Each parent may well have received assurances from the child that the child wished to be in the custody of that particular parent. In fact, upon subsequent investigation it is found that the child is really attempting to communicate that he or she wishes to be in the custody of *both* parents and does not wish to see the separation take place. Similarly, some children do not wish to be seen to be preferring one parent over another and often express a preference that they feel the parent wants to hear.

This raises the question of the value of the child's views and preferences. The answer lies in the particular child's age and level of maturity. There are two ways of looking at this question of age and maturity. First, as the child grows older he or she is better able to articulate in a positive way what he or she wants. At the same time, it is more difficult to impose on an older child a situation that the child does not wish to live in. The court recognizes this and makes an effort to ascertain the child's wishes and preferences and to give effect to them if it believes that the child was able to form the opinion objectively. The court is very conscious of the ability of a parent to "assist" the child in forming an opinion. This is sometimes called "poisoning the child's mind" against the other parent.

Where the court considers it necessary, the child's preferences can be ascertained in a number of ways:

1. by calling the child as a witness in court
2. by having a private interview with the judge in chambers
3. by having an assessment done by a child-care professional who would later report back to the court, and
4. by providing the child with his or her own lawyer to assist in determining and describing what are the child's wishes.

However, some jurisdictions use the child as a witness or arrange private interviews with the judge only as a last resort.

The presence of brothers and sisters is also a consideration in custody and access matters. The general rule, whether under the *Divorce Act* or provincial law, is that brothers and sisters should not be separated. A strong effort is made to preserve the family despite the absence of one parent. Children often see the presence of brothers and sisters as a very important support during difficult times. It is difficult to imagine the court concluding in anything but the most unusual circumstances that the separation of children could be in the best interests of any of the children involved.

An interesting concept that is described in custody and access cases is something known as "the tender years doctrine." This doctrine considered it to be a general rule that the mother was entitled to custody and care of a child during its nurturing years. This came to mean that any child, regardless of who was actually the child's psychological parent, would be given to the mother until at least the age of seven years, its "tender years." Obviously, the "tender years doctrine" has undergone some revision over the last decade. The emphasis is now put almost exclusively on what is best for the child regardless of the child's age. Some courts have commented that the "tender years doctrine" is now irrelevant given the best interest test.

CUSTODY

Before examining the circumstances in which custody is ordered and the methods by which it is ordered, it is important to understand the full meaning of the term. One judge defined custody as follows: "To award one parent the exclusive custody of a child is to clothe that parent, for whatever period he or she is awarded the custody, with full parental control over, and ultimate parental responsibility for the care, upbringing and education of the child, generally to the exclusion of the right of the other parent to interfere in decisions that are made in exercising that control or in carrying out that responsibility."

The distinction between custody and access is basically the difference between having the right to make all decisions regarding a child and simply being entitled to information about the child's health, education and welfare, and to occasional time with the child.

The changes that have occurred in the area of custody and access over the last few years have been directed towards a sharing of this decision-making power that was formerly exclusive to one parent. Non-custodial parents have sought to enhance their entitlement to information, their participation in decisions affecting the child, and their right to have equal or sole responsibility for important decisions affecting the child.

The traditional expressions "custody" and "access" have been challenged of late: separating couples have begun to use terms such as "co-parenting," "shared parenting" and "co-operative parenting." Each of these new terms is an attempt to describe the new division of responsibility for the child.

There are two types of orders with respect to custody of a child—sole custody and joint custody. Sole custody vests all of the decision-making power in one parent and usually leaves the other parent with an entitlement to time with the child. As we shall see in a moment, these sole custody orders are becoming increasingly laden with conditions and stipulations that detract from the full traditional custodial power.

Where the other type of custody order, a joint custody order, is made, the parents (or other person if that is the case) share the custodial decision-making responsibility. Some parents have made a distinction between "joint physical custody" and "joint decision-making responsibility" over a child. In the case of joint physical custody, the child resides in two homes for fixed periods of time. These arrangements can include splitting a week, where the child resides with one parent for half the week and the other parent for the other half of the week, alternating weeks, alternating months and, in some cases, alternating six-month periods or years. While the child is in the physical custody of one of the parents, that one parent has all necessary custodial decision-making power. The other parent gains the same power when the child changes homes. In such an arrangement there is a requirement for a high level of co-operation between the parents if it is expected to work in a way that meets the child's needs.

The case law on joint custody continues to evolve, but the current state of affairs sees the court ordering joint custody in circumstances where the parents consent to such an order. In other words, the courts are unwilling to impose a joint custody arrangement on the parents or the child if it would be against the wishes of one of the parents.

In cases where the physical custody of the child is not shared, the child resides with one parent exclusively but important decisions are made jointly. So while the child resides with the mother, for example, she would not make any major decisions without involving the father.

Joint custody awards, particularly those for joint physical custody, may result in a corresponding reduction in the need to pay child support. So, for example, where the parents are of a relatively equal earning power and there is joint physical custody, it is unlikely that child support would be required from one parent to the other. This has caused some people to oppose joint custody on the grounds that it is simply a means by which non-custodial parents can avoid obligations for child support. No doubt some parents have been motivated by this mercenary approach, but there is no doubt that the values of joint custody may exceed such disadvantages and there are ways of sorting out those who do not genuinely seek joint custody.

A word of advice for those who would attempt joint custody arrangements: They do not work unless there is a high degree of co-operation and flexibility between the parents. Where a child alternates between two homes, it can be particularly difficult to manage the child's affairs, whether it be with respect to clothing, sporting activities, hobbies, visits with friends, visits with relatives, or other pursuits, unless there is maximum co-operation. The goal of joint custody is not the convenience of the parents, but the maintenance of maximum contact with the parents in pursuit of the child's best interests.

Even where sole custody awards are made it is not unusual for the courts to impose conditions upon the arrangement. For example, it is not unusual now to see a restriction placed on the mobility of a custodial parent. Non-custodial parents who wish to protect their access visits have been seeking, in separation agreements and in court orders, specific geographic restrictions on the custodial parent's mobility. These terms can take the form of specific references to living within a certain distance from a city, for example, residing within a 300-kilometre radius of the City of Toronto.

The *Divorce Act* provides the court with the power to require a custodial parent intending to change his or her place of residence to notify the other parent at least thirty days before the change and advise that parent of the planned date and location of the move. The court can, if it sees fit, impose an even longer period of notice.

Another restriction that the courts are prepared to place on the custodial parent concerns the effect of moving on the non-custodial parent's ability to visit with the child and the cost of such visits. Where a custodial parent expresses a wish to move further away from the non-custodial parent and has good reason (such as new and better employment), the court may order a reduction in the amount of child support that corresponds to the increased expense of travelling to visit with the child. In one case, where a mother moved from Toronto to Calgary, the father's child support payments were reduced by a hundred dollars per month to compensate for travel expenses he would now incur.

As we know, not all separations and custody cases are conducted reasonably and amicably. After acrimonious custody disputes the custodial parent often lives in fear of child abduction; the courts will make orders of custody or access subject to a condition that one parent surrender his or her passport to ensure that he or she does not leave the country with the child.

In a vein similar to the surrendering of a passport, the courts have also ordered that a parent post some form of financial security such as a bond or recognizance to ensure compliance with the court order. In one case where the mother wanted to take the children from British Columbia to Iowa, she was permitted to do so only on condition that she forfeit a $10,000 recognizance if she failed to return.

Supervised custody and access is another concept that is becoming increasingly popular. In such a circumstance, the court orders that a third party supervise the custody or access periods. This supervision is often focused on the exchange of the child from one parent to the other in cases where there has been ongoing hostility or suspicion. We'll examine this in more detail in the section dealing with access.

ACCESS

Access has been characterized as anything left over after custody. It has been defined in court cases as being an entitlement to spend time with a child and during that time to exercise some of the powers of a custodial parent. Other jurisdictions, particularly in the United States, call access "visitation rights," although some have noted that it is improper to characterize the time a parent spends with a child as being merely a visit. In Canada, the term "access" enjoys more popularity.

Aside from the right to spend time with the child, the right to access can include, at least under the *Divorce Act*, the requirement described earlier that a custodial parent give thirty days' notice of his or her intention to move the child. This new provision is in keeping with the emphasis on giving a non-custodial parent information about the child whether it be with respect to the child's health, welfare or education. If a parent received such notice of the custodial parent's intention to change locations, he or she would then have the opportunity to move for a variation of the custody order.

Other entitlements to information include the right to be kept abreast of the child's performance in school, the child's medical needs and care, and the child's general welfare. It is not unusual for courts to provide the non-custodial parent with an opportunity to make a contribution to the child's religious upbringing. There are cases reported in which the non-custodial parent has been given an opportunity to expose the child to his or her religion.

The form of an access order can be extremely important. For years it was common for the courts and for lawyers, in drafting separation agreements, to stipulate simply that one parent would have custody and the other parent would have "reasonable access," or "liberal access," or "generous access," at times to be agreed upon by the parents. Such a provision can be satisfactory where the parents are co-operative and where they can in fact agree on times to be spent with the child. However, the moment such co-operation breaks down, the non-custodial parent is left in a very difficult position, since it is next to impossible to obtain court enforcement of these vague expressions. In fact, the non-custodial parent is left in a position of returning to court for a variation of the access provision to provide for specific dates and times.

Parents who anticipate difficulties or require some predictability often stipulate the precise days and times for the access to take place. An example could be as follows: every second weekend from Friday at 7:00 P.M. to Sunday at 7:00 P.M.; alternating Wednesdays from 5:00 P.M. to 7:00 P.M.; alternating birthdays, Easter vacations, Christmases, New Years, or other important family events to be agreed upon. In the event the access is then denied, the non-custodial parent can point to the specific entitlement when seeking enforcement. (For a description of access enforcement difficulties see Chapter 13, "Enforcing Family Law Orders.")

The concept of supervised access was mentioned earlier in the section dealing with custody as a means of watching the exchange of the child between the parents. In some provinces, volunteer or government facilities will supervise the exchange as a service to the court. Supervision can be ordered or arranged voluntarily and is useful where one of the parents is under a cloud from allegations of sexual or physical abuse. Sometimes the supervision is needed because the custodial parent suffers abuse at the time of the exchange.

Even where facilities are not available it may be possible to have an objective, trusted third party supervise the visits. This could be a family member, priest, rabbi, community worker or other reliable person.

This is as good a time as any to introduce the "neutron bomb" of custody and access—allegations of sexual abuse. Sexual and physical abuse of children by parents is a sorry fact of life that is only beginning to be understood, and even believed. Every effort must be made to encourage parents, neighbours, friends and whoever else has contact with a child to come forward with their suspicions. We need to err on the side of caution with children in such a position.

We know it's out there. But what about the false allegation of abuse? It happens. Rarely, but it happens. Sometimes one parent will try to use the allegation as a means of blocking access or of trying to ensure that they get custody. When it does the entire family must suffer, but no one more than the children.

Fortunately, fewer and fewer parents are putting their children through the trauma of a full custody trial. The success of mediation in solving custody and access disputes is well known. For a more detailed description of mediation, see Chapter 12, on mediation and arbitration. For a description of the type of process your child will experience should you decide to go to trial, see Chapter 11, "Not Settling Your Differences."

Of course, with any trial or custody dispute, the cost is an important consideration. When I mention cost here I mean the financial, not the emotional cost. It is not unusual for lawyers taking on a custody dispute to ask for an advance on fees of between $10,000 and $15,000. Custody trials can consume a great deal of court time with absolutely no promise of a monetary recovery at the end. Consequently, lawyers are anxious to ensure that their fees are secure in advance since the loser of a custody trial is a notoriously unhappy client.

One final consideration in this chapter is the tactical aspect of custody and access. In order to appreciate the tactical considerations, we need to understand the difference between an interim order and a final order. Interim orders are orders that are made pending the final decision of the court. Naturally, it is necessary to make temporary orders with respect to custody of children until the court has an opportunity for a full consideration of the dispute. This means that the court must consider on an interim basis where the child should reside and who should have full decision-making power with respect to the child's needs.

The courts have in the past been very reluctant to move the child from the home of whichever parent has what is known as "*de facto* care and control of the child." This means that whoever has the child at the time the interim application is made is very likely to have custody of the child until the trial. The court will only depart from this general rule if it is clearly not in the child's best interest to remain with that parent. At the trial, the judge will often ask: "Where has the child resided pending this hearing?" "How has he or she been cared for?" "Are the child's needs being met?" "Is the child comfortable?" "Does the child go to neighbourhood schools? have friends nearby? day care?"

You can see that the court will be very reluctant to disturb the child's world if it has been meeting his or her needs. Interim custody often means final custody.

As I said at the outset, custody is *the* issue in marriage breakdown and therefore may be the most emotionally charged of all. People under the stress of a collapsing relationship may be hard pressed to put their children's best interests first. At a time when they may need to look out for themselves they must look out for someone even more vulnerable. It is a time not for showing how awful someone else may be as spouse or parent but rather how good you are as a parent and how you can offer the softest landing to the children displaced by divorce.

8

Support

As I came out of my office in downtown Toronto one Sunday morning a couple of years ago, I encountered a group of "fathers' rights activists" who were picketing our office. Several of them wore black T-shirts that declared in large white letters "Support is the screwing you get for the screwing you got." I could only shake my head in disbelief at their misdirected anger at former spouses and the family law system. Support, in fact, is one of the key issues at marriage breakdown. Discussions about dividing RRSPs, cottages and homes are fine for those who enjoy such material wealth, but for most people the financial burden of separation can only be met through a division of one spouse's income for the benefit of both spouses and the children. That essentially is what support is all about—how to divide one spouse's salary to maintain two homes, one possibly with children.

How can it be done in cases where new marriages occur after the separation and new families are started? How should support be calculated after a twenty-year marriage? After a two-year marriage? What if one of the spouses has never worked? What if ill health of a spouse is a factor? You can see fairly quickly that support can open a complex series of questions that can only be answered in dollars and cents. Add to this that the question will be quite different depending on whether you are talking about support for a spouse or for a child.

As noted in previous chapters, the provincial, territorial and federal governments have all provided for support upon marriage breakdown in their various laws. It is known under the *Divorce Act* as a type of "corollary relief," that is, an additional related order the court can make at the time it grants the divorce. In this chapter we will examine the areas of spousal support and child support in order to understand the goals of such orders and how they are calculated. But before doing so I would like to provide some context to what you are about to learn. Recent studies of our *Divorce Act* and spousal and child support provisions tell a sorry tale about how we provide for needy spouses and children upon marriage breakdown.

With so many divorces each year, more and more support orders are being made under federal law—the *Divorce Act*. An analysis of these orders, therefore, provides a valuable insight into the effect of support in society generally. Consider the following facts:

- Two-thirds of divorced women with custody of their children had total incomes which put them below the poverty line in 1988— including their support payments.
- The likelihood of a divorced woman with custody of the children living below the poverty line has increased, not decreased, in recent years.
- A major consequence of separation and divorce is the impoverishment of women and children.
- The average amount of child support per family declined in real terms over the last five years.
- Men paid 18 percent of their income in child support in 1986 but in 1988 were paying only 16 percent.
- The more a man earned, the smaller the proportion of his income was spent on child support.
- Spousal support is now rarely requested (only 16 percent of applications sought spousal support) and even more rarely granted (6 percent of all cases).
- Most spousal support orders are made for a fixed term; in other words, they end at a specific time or at the occurrence of a specific event.
- Lawyers are negotiating separation agreements containing spousal support provisions that are *less favourable* than what the courts are ordering.

The picture that emerges is a dark one. Support is not acting as a cushion for families undergoing marriage breakdown, it is barely meeting the needs of women and children. Let's look at the system in more detail, beginning first with child support and then turning to spousal support. After the section dealing with spousal support we will briefly consider a new phenomenon—parental support.

As I mentioned at the outset, provincial and territorial family laws provide an entitlement to claim support and guidelines for the calculation of support upon marriage breakdown. (In this chapter I refer to marriage breakdown as a triggering event for the claiming of spousal support. However, as you will see from a reading of Chapter 9, dealing with common-law spouses, this is one of the entitlements that a common-law spouse has after a relationship breaks down. Consequently, any references to spouses in this chapter apply to both common-law spouses and legally married spouses.) The federal *Divorce Act* also provides an entitlement to claim support and guidelines for calculating it for couples who are divorcing. While we will attempt to identify some of the different approaches taken by the provincial, territorial and federal legislation, the goal of the chapter is to identify general guidelines that have emerged in this area.

You will recall the financial statements that figure so prominently in the division of family property. Here again they play a key role in revealing to the court potential sources of support. Take a moment to review the sample of the financial statement reproduced in the Appendices.

Women are awarded sole custody of children in approximately 72 percent of the cases, while men receive sole custody in about 16 percent of the cases. Child support is ordered in approximately 70 percent of the cases where there are dependent children, one study found as of 1988. The same study found that 90 percent of women with custody requested child support and 93 percent of those who requested support were granted it.

So we have a snapshot of those who seek child support in our court system. The snapshot is of women receiving custody of children in the vast majority of cases, and asking for and receiving child support. Yet the poverty persists. Why? The answer lies in the method of calculating support and in the child's actual needs.

The minimum cost for raising a pre-school child in a single-parent family in Canada has been estimated to be approximately $350 per month per child if no child care is needed. If child care is needed, the minimum cost rises to $790 per month per child. Compare that with the average amount of child support ordered per child according to one study of the *Divorce Act*—$250 per month. What we see, therefore, is a shortfall of $540 per month per child in situations where parents require child care. It is that shortfall that produces, in part, child poverty in Canada.

Let's consider the laws that produce these results.

CHILD SUPPORT: THE *DIVORCE ACT*

Upon marriage breakdown and after a determination of custody, the court turns its attention to the question of child support. In doing so, in the context of a divorce action, it considers the two objectives of child support as described in the *Divorce Act*:

1. to recognize that spouses have a joint financial obligation to maintain the child; and
2. to apportion that obligation between the spouses according to their relative abilities to contribute to the performance of the obligation.

In making a child support order the court considers a list of factors which include the condition, means, needs and other circumstances of the child, and any order, agreement or arrangement relating to the support of the child. The *Divorce Act* also requires the court, before granting a divorce, to satisfy itself that reasonable arrangements have been made for the support of any children of the marriage and, if such arrangements have not been made, to stay (or delay) the divorce until arrangements have been made.

In applying the *Divorce Act*, the courts have reached a general consensus that child support should be set at a level which would maintain the child at a standard of living as close to that which the child would have enjoyed had the family breakup not occurred. The courts have also agreed that the cost of achieving that standard should be apportioned between the parents in proportion to their incomes. This potential standard of living should be sought for the child even if it is at the expense of the non-custodial parent's standard of living.

Provincial family laws also deal with the question of child support and in many cases set out in more detail than the *Divorce Act* the types of things that the court should consider in assessing support. They include

- the parents' current assets and means
- the child's assets, and any that he or she is likely to have in the future
- the child's capacity to contribute to his or her own support
- the child's age, and physical and mental health
- the child's aptitude for and reasonable prospects for an education
- the child's need for a stable environment.

Both provincial law and the *Divorce Act* impose on each parent this joint obligation to provide for a child's support.

The courts have developed a variety of approaches to assessing child support in Canada. One judge described the ideal solution as the calculation of a sum that would be adequate to care for, support and educate the children, then dividing the sum in proportion to the respective incomes and resources of the parents and directing the payment of the appropriate portion by the parent not having physical custody.

Other approaches talk of "resource sharing" or "cost sharing," the "crumbs off the table approach," the "equal living standards model" and the "fair share of responsibility" approach. For some comparison of these approaches, consider the following: The "crumbs off the table approach" takes the non-custodial parent's income, subtracts reasonable living expenses and then uses the balance to meet the need for child support. The "fair share of responsibility" approach calculates a reasonable cost for the support of the children and then allocates it between the parents in proportion to their gross income. In one such case the "crumbs" approach yielded $360 per month per child while the "fair share of responsibility" approach, on the same facts, yielded $300 per month per child.

The court's approach is never entirely clear; despite the various theories, courts have rejected a rigid formula approach. Nevertheless, some guidelines and rules of thumb have emerged across Canada:

- The court tries to meet the child's reasonable needs.
- The court tries to maintain the same standard of living as if the breakup had not occurred.
- The child's standard of living should be appropriate to the parental incomes.
- The child's basic necessities come ahead of a parent's perks such as recreation and vacation.
- Child support should not be used as an indirect means of spousal support, but a parent's indirect benefit from child support is no reason to reduce the amount of child support.
- The custodial parent's needs are irrelevant to the calculation of child support.
- A custodial parent's wish for a higher standard of living with a new partner is irrelevant to the calculation of child support.

- The amount of child support should recognize the custodial parent's exclusive possession of a matrimonial home.
- Child support is a joint obligation. Just because one parent could pay it all doesn't mean that the other parent is relieved of his or her obligation.
- Where a parent has wilfully refused to work, the court will attribute income to him or her in order to calculate the appropriate amount of child support.
- A parent cannot adopt a semi-retired lifestyle at a child's expense.
- All sources of income, including investment and employment income, are considered in calculating the amount of support.
- The income tax consequences of a child support order should be taken into account when calculating the order in the first place.
- Support can include coverage of prenatal expenses.

Courts have also tried to develop rules of thumb for calculating the amount of child support, such as:

- it costs a minimum of $400 per month to support the first child of a marriage
- the cost of maintaining one child is greater than maintaining each of two or more children
- each child requires $250 to $300 per month (although some provincial ranges have been as low as $175 to $250 per month).

Frequently, the support is a monthly fixed amount designed to cover all child-care expenses such as food, lodging and so on. However, the court often considers specific expenses incurred with respect to the children such as those related to special hobbies, pursuits or activities. Special extra-curricular activities expenses can relate to high school activities, special dance schools, sporting expenses, tuition at camp, private schools, synagogue and Hebrew school expenses, remedial reading tutors and even bar mitzvah expenses.

Child-care expenses, which may range from babysitting to a full-time nanny, are considered in fixing support. In one case, a father who had moved to Kentucky was ordered, as a part of support, to pay the travel costs of the child and the nanny as well as the nanny's salary while in Kentucky. (OK, it's rare but it happened.)

Medical expenses for children also play a role in assessing the amount of child support. The courts have considered cases involving special care for a child with cerebral palsy, the costs of orthodontic work, and the expenses of learning disabilities and epilepsy among other medical needs.

Housing costs naturally figure prominently in assessing child support, as can the child's travel expenses to visit the parent if the parents reside in different locations. In contrast, there have been cases where child support has been reduced by the amount of travel expenses a parent incurs in travelling to see the child.

As you can see, a variety of considerations figure in the calculation of child support. Despite the theories and mental gymnastics that leap and spin around the calculation, the only thing that is truly predictable is that it will in all likelihood not be enough.

Let's turn for a moment to the another aspect of child support—the making of support orders that are not periodic payments but lump sums.

As mentioned earlier, the court prefers to make orders that the payment of support be on a periodic basis—monthly, for example. However, in certain circumstances the court is prepared to consider the payment of a lump sum where to do so would meet the special needs of the individuals in question.

Lump sum payment is available both under the *Divorce Act* and provincial legislation, and is made in the following general situations:

1. where there is a likelihood that the spouse who is to pay support will disobey an order for periodic payment
2. where the circumstances of the spouse who is to pay support would likely prohibit him or her from making periodic payments
3. where the parent is unable to make periodic payments because his or her income from employment does not generate enough cash to be able to make a support payment for a child
4. where the order for periodic support would only draw the spouses into ongoing conflict
5. where there is some suggestion that the parent who is to pay support will leave or has left the jurisdiction
6. where to do so would compensate for arrears that are owing due to non-payment or where an order is made for periodic payments but it is retroactive
7. where the non-custodial parent has not had a relationship with the child and is not likely to do so in the future, and a clean break can be established through a lump sum payment
8. where a substantial change in circumstances has resulted in a greatly increased ability to pay child support (such as one case in which the father won $1 million in a lottery and his periodic child maintenance payments were increased to $1,000 per month from $100 per month and a lump sum order was made in favour of the child)
9. where the parties consent such an order will be made
10. where the parent is asked to meet a specific expense that has arisen that can be met only through a lump sum payment (as in one case where a child needed $6,000 worth of orthodontic work and a lump sum payment of $2,000 was ordered from the father).

These types of orders are unusual; the vast majority of payments are periodic. However, in the circumstances described, a lump sum payment can most certainly avoid many of the difficulties described in Chapter 13, dealing with support enforcement.

Another issue that arises with respect to child support payments concerns the need from time to time to increase or decrease the amount of child support. This is known as a "variation proceeding" and is quite common. The circumstances of both parents can change, as a result of illness, unemployment, a change of job and even in some cases some good fortune. Both the *Divorce Act* and provincial family law permit either parent to apply to the court for the amount of support to be increased or decreased to reflect these new circumstances. The catch phrase that is applied is "a material change in circumstances." What this really means is that there must be some significant change in the parent's situation that necessitates an increase or a decrease in the amount of child support.

On a variation application, the court considers all of the criteria described above with respect to the making of the order, but places particular emphasis on the alleged change in the parents' circumstances.

When Is a Child Eligible for Support?

The *Divorce Act* contains an extended definition of the expression "child of the marriage," which includes any child for whom the person has stood in the place of a parent and any child of whom one is the parent and for whom the other partner stands in the place of a parent. Essentially this means that biological parents and adoptive parents can be obligated to pay child support. In addition, even if a person has not actually adopted a child but has treated the child as if he or she were that person's own, a support obligation may arise.

In attempting to determine whether a person has acted as if he or she were a child's parent even though that person is not the biological or adoptive parent, the courts have asked questions such as the following:

- Did this person provide a large part of the financial support necessary for the child's support?
- Did the person intend to step into the shoes of a parent?
- Was the relationship between the person and the child a continuing one with some permanency?
- Can any inferences be drawn from the treatment the child would receive were he or she living with the true parent?
- Has the person at the time pertinent to the claim for support ceased to act as a parent of that child?

The court will also consider such things as the affection between the person and the child, the length of time of the association and whether the child has taken the surname of that person and lives in the same dwelling.

An interesting question with respect to child support concerns not the making of the order or its amount but rather when it ends. There can be quite a debate over the circumstances under which the child support order should terminate, a debate that is only made worse by differences in provincial and federal law. Child support under a provincial order can end at a different time than a child support order made under the *Divorce Act*, even when the children are in quite similar economic circumstances.

The *Divorce Act* extends its definition of "child of the marriage" to mean a child who at the time in question is under the age of sixteen, or is sixteen years of age and over and under the parents' control but unable by reason of illness, disability or other cause to withdraw from the control of the parents or to obtain the necessaries of life. It is not uncommon for separation agreements or court orders to provide simply that child support shall be paid so long as the child is a "child of the marriage," a provision that is also found in the *Divorce Act*. The winding up of the child support order can be fairly straightforward if it is simply a case of the child turning seventeen years of age. However, if the child is sixteen or over but for the reasons described above is unable to care for himself or herself, an argument can develop. For example, is a child attending university unable to withdraw from the control of his or her parents and obtain the necessaries of life?

The questions of illness and disability can be dealt with without much difficulty. Once a child passes the age of sixteen but for reasons of illness or disability must continue to be cared for and supported by the custodial parent, there will be a corresponding financial obligation for the non-custodial parent to support.

A far more difficult question concerns the other causes for inability to withdraw from a custodial parent's control. There is no doubt on the basis of cases that have been decided across Canada that the expression "other cause" includes attendance at secondary school and university. The courts have placed a broad and liberal interpretation on this provision, so that children have received financial support through undergraduate degrees at university. This support is provided even though the children are eighteen or nineteen years of age and older.

Some cases have decided, however, that a child who is attending school is not a "child of the marriage" once he or she gains a regular part-time job or other employment. In such cases of employment during education, the court examines the child's intentions and needs to determine whether or not the child is truly unable to withdraw from the custodial parent's charge or to provide necessaries of life for himself or herself. Other cases have considered interruptions in the child's education for medical and other reasons and decided that even though the child was over the age of eighteen and was not in attendance at an educational institution, he or she was still a child of the marriage and dependent upon the custodial parent.

It should come as no surprise that there has actually been judicial consideration of the status of a child who was expelled from school. In that case, which originated in British Columbia, a court decided that a child expelled from school was no longer a child of the marriage for the purposes of support.

Aside from the above guidelines, there are no hard and fast rules about the extension of child support past the age of sixteen under the *Divorce Act*. The court has complete discretion to determine whether or not support should be extended to a child and in exercising its discretion considers such things as the child's age, his or her academic achievements, the value of further education, the state of the job market and the ability of the parents to bear the costs of a college education. It is not unusual for the court to consider also whether the child should have reasonably expected the parents to continue to furnish support. In doing so the court may even examine the parents' treatment of their other children. If support was extended to one child through university, then perhaps support should be extended for all children who are willing to attend.

It should not be assumed from the above that attendance at university guarantees support from a parent. In several cases where the child elected to attend university after the separation the court was clear in stating that a university education is not a necessity of life and that each case will be decided on its own merits. Such courts have stated that children who are mature enough to attend university should be mature enough to recognize the necessity for self-reliance when their parents' marriage breaks down and the financial capability of one or both parents changes dramatically.

Some of you may be relieved to hear that there is little if any backing for continuation of support once the child reaches the graduate level. In Nova Scotia, one twenty-one-year-old sought financial support through his law degree but was turned down by the court. A law degree, in the court's eyes, is helpful, but not necessary. One rule of thumb that has developed is that parents who support children past the age of sixteen will only need to do so to the extent of one degree or diploma course.

To continue to receive support, a child need not reside with the custodial parent. In many cases children have been required to leave home to attend university but still receive financial support from the custodial and the non-custodial parent because of their continuing dependency. There is no firm requirement that a child live with the custodial parent in order to continue to receive support.

Provincial family law also describes support obligations as relatively open-ended, and it is safe to say that many of the cases interpreting the *Divorce Act* also apply to provincial law—that is, that there is no automatic cutoff at a particular age. One aspect of provincial law, however, is the termination of support when a child has withdrawn from parental control. In Ontario, for example, the *Family Law Act, 1986* provides that every parent has an obligation to provide support for his or her unmarried child who is a minor or is enrolled in a full-time program of education to the extent that the parent is capable of doing so. In assessing this obligation to provide support the court considers the needs of the child. The Act goes on, however, to state that the obligation to provide support does not extend to a child who is sixteen years of age or older and has withdrawn from parental control.

Withdrawing from parental control means a voluntary withdrawal, the exercise of a free choice to cut the family bonds and strike out on a life of one's own. If a child is driven from parental control by emotional or physical abuse then the court will not consider the child to have exercised a voluntary withdrawal. A parent cannot expel a child from the home and expect to terminate a support obligation. For this reason, the onus of proving that a child has withdrawn from parental control is on the parents. The case reports provide examples of children who have been driven from their home by parents or stepparents to live with friends or relatives and who have then applied for financial support and received it on the basis that, while they do not live with their parents, they did not voluntarily withdraw from parental control.

In one Nova Scotia case the applicant was a fourteen-year-old girl who had experienced difficulties with her mother. The child would not abide by the "house rules" and persisted in staying out very late at night contrary to her mother's wishes. She then moved out to live with her aunt and uncle for almost a year, but the aunt and uncle soon found the same difficulties. After a brief attempt to live with the mother again the child left on her own initiative to live with her girlfriend's family. When the child applied for support, the court having considered her two failures to abide by the rules found her to have voluntarily withdrawn from living with the parents and the parents had a lawful excuse for not providing support.

If you are faced with the issue of child support, an important aspect to focus on with your lawyer is the precise point at which support will end. Open-ended expressions such as "until the child is no longer a child of the marriage" or "so long as the child is a child within the meaning of the *Divorce Act*" are of little assistance if parents require some predictability in the end of support obligations.

Child support is considered income in the hands of the recipient and therefore taxable. Conversely, support payments that are made pursuant to a separation agreement or a court order are considered deductible by the person who pays such support. As mentioned earlier, the income tax consequences for support orders should be considered at the time the amount of support is fixed.

One final note should be made with respect to the indexing of support orders for inflation. It is now routine for courts to index child support orders so that there is no need to return to the court from time to time to have the order varied upwards to keep pace with the cost of living. Increases may be made on an annual basis.

SPOUSAL SUPPORT

The *Divorce Act, 1986* lists four objectives for orders of spousal support made under the Act. It provides that an order for the support of the spouse should

(a) recognize any economic advantages or disadvantages to the spouses arising from the marriage or its breakdown;

(b) apportion between the spouses the financial consequences arising from the care of any child of the marriage;

(c) relieve any economic hardship of the spouses arising from the breakdown of the marriage; and

(d) insofar as practicable, promote the economic self sufficiency of each spouse within a reasonable period of time.

In making support orders the court considers certain factors which are provided for in the Act including the condition, means, needs and other circumstances of the spouses. These may include the length of time the spouses cohabited, the functions performed by the spouse during cohabitation and any order, agreement or arrangement relating to support of the spouse. The courts have used three approaches to fixing spousal support at the end of a marriage: the "income security model," the "compensatory model," and the "clean break model."

A recent study of the *Divorce Act* found it difficult to draw any firm conclusions about the approaches used by the courts. They vary from jurisdiction to jurisdiction and from court to court. In an "income security model," the support obligation is considered to be derived simply from the existence of a spousal relationship. Under a "compensatory model," the spousal support is considered to be a form of compensation for the economic consequences of the marriage, such as loss of career opportunity through having cared for the children. The "clean break model" sees the objective of the support order as the severing of economic ties between the spouses so that each may go his or her own way. Support is transitional: it is paid for a fixed period of time, and then it is terminated. One author has noted that the court seemed perplexed by the list of objectives in the *Divorce Act*. The result has been a relatively uneven approach to spousal support.

Before considering the question of calculating the amount of support we should make it clear that the *Divorce Act* only applies to legally married spouses. A common-law spouse's entitlement to support arises under provincial law only. This is discussed in Chapter 9. The principles described in this chapter, however, are applicable to both legally married spouses and common-law spouses. When the court is faced with the need to fix spousal support it looks at essentially the same criteria regardless of the nature of the obligation.

As in the case of child support, spousal support is often made on a periodic basis with a monthly payment of a fixed sum payable directly from the husband, for example, to the wife.

The making of support orders, whether under the provincial family law or the *Divorce Act*, boils down to the consideration of two key factors—the spouse's need for support and the other spouse's ability to pay. Into this mix is introduced an increasingly important consideration, which is the dependent spouse's ability to provide for his or her own support.

One important change that has occurred over the last few years is the deletion of the court's power to consider misconduct of a spouse in relation to the marriage in making an order for support under the *Divorce Act*. The deletion of this criterion has taken some of the acrimony out of a support proceeding and allowed the court to zero in on the above-noted factors, need and ability to pay.

In determining the spouse's needs, the circumstances of each case must be examined. Much can depend on the nature of the marriage relationship, that is, whether it was a "traditional" or a more "modern" marriage. In a "traditional" marriage, the wife is usually the dependent spouse, and over time she can expect to find herself without job skills or income. A dependent spouse is entitled to a standard of living that is equal to what she could have expected had the marriage continued, where the parties have had a long-term "traditional" marriage.

In the following section I will attempt to set out some considerations in the area of spousal support both with respect to assessment of need and calculation of the quantum (or amount). It should be noted that these are general rules that apply nationally but there may be some variation on a province-by-province basis. They are, if you will, rules of thumb for spousal support.

- In deciding what a reasonable standard of living is the court must consider the husband's ability to pay. In one case the court decided that it was unconscionable to reduce the husband's standard of living below the poverty level in order to provide the wife with a reasonable standard of living. This was so even though the parties were married for thirty years and the wife was unable to work on a full-time basis.
- A wife asking for support is not expected to take just any job in an effort to meet her own needs.
- The objective of a spousal support order is not to equalize the incomes of the two spouses.
- The need for spousal support should be assessed after the determination of the division of the family assets. If the division of assets leaves the dependent spouse with sufficient means to meet his or her reasonable needs then the court will not order support.
- The court will consider whether the prudent investment of the assets obtained at marriage breakdown and the spouse's qualifications for work will reduce the need for support from the other spouse.
- Spousal support has been denied in cases where there was a lengthy marriage but both spouses were employed throughout, and after the marriage breakdown the funds from the sale of the matrimonial home generated additional income.

An interesting question has arisen around whether the need must arise from the marriage itself. The law is still unsettled on the point, particularly since the Supreme Court of Canada decided in 1987 that support should only be ordered if the person claiming it is able to show a connection between his or her present need and the marriage itself. The theory is that the marriage must have *caused* the need for support. This is known as a causal connection. Application of the Supreme Court principles has varied from province to province, with some provinces placing less emphasis on a causal connection and others following the causal connection test closely. A clear example of this type of causal connection occurred in a Manitoba case where it was decided that the husband had created a marital environment that was so burdensome during twenty-two years of marriage that the wife suffered an incapacitating mental collapse. Her poor health and lack of marketable skills were directly traceable to the marriage. This is a good example of a causal connection between the need for support and the marriage itself.

Similarly, where the need for spousal support is related to that spouse's role as custodial parent there will be a causal connection. Other examples of causal connections involve the marriage causing a lengthy absence from the work force, the dependent spouse putting the other spouse's career first, the roles adopted by the spouses during the course of the marriage, and so on.

The courts have refused to find a causal connection in situations where the dependent spouse was receiving social assistance both before and after the marriage, where the spouse was financially independent throughout the marriage, where the spouse seeking support did not make any career sacrifices for the other spouse, where the marriage was not a contributing factor to the dependent spouse's health problems, and where the events that caused the need for support occurred after the separation. In one Ontario case the wife was involved in an accident which caused an injury to her hand that rendered her unable to use her right hand in any normal sense. She was unable to obtain employment but because this was not causally connected to the marriage support was not ordered.

Another interesting case involved a woman who left her husband to establish a common-law relationship with another man. This relationship continued for approximately five years and then ended. The woman then sought support from her first husband but her claim was dismissed since the need for support arose not out of the ending of the first relationship, but the ending of the common-law relationship.

A causal connection for the support need will also not be found where the spouse is leaving the marriage in a better economic position than that which existed at the time of the marriage.

As indicated earlier, this approach of needing a causal connection for support is not universal. In discussing the issue of support with your lawyer it should be a priority to determine whether or not the courts of the province in question are subscribing to the Supreme Court principle of causal connection.

Methods of Payment

While periodic support orders are common, the courts also make limited term orders and lump sum orders. Let's consider these types of orders now.

The *Divorce Act* provides that the court may make an order for support for a definite or indefinite period, or until a specified event takes place. Approximately 45 percent of support orders made under the *Divorce Act* are for a fixed term and another 30 percent are tied to some other event such as the beginning of employment or the completion of education or retraining. Interestingly, one survey shows that lawyers estimated that 50 to 75 percent of their cases involved time-limited support orders.

Both provincial family laws and the *Divorce Act* contemplate these types of time-limited orders. Given their prevalence, it is worth considering how they are used. Generally, the courts have considered time-limited support orders to be appropriate where the dependent spouse is healthy and generally able to care for himself or herself but needs some financial assistance to make the jump from marriage to self-sufficiency.

The spouse may need a period of retraining, an upgrading of skills or other education in order to become independent.

Looking at it from the opposite angle, the courts have considered time limits on orders to be inappropriate in cases where the marriage was lengthy and where it could be described as a "traditional" one. This is especially so where the dependent spouse had assumed the role of homemaker, had limited education and training and had been out of the work force for a great deal of time. Also, if the spouse was in poor health a time-limited support order would not be appropriate.

An example of this type of case occurred in British Columbia in 1985 where the spouses had been married for twenty-seven years. The husband was fifty-one and the wife was fifty-five years old. The marriage had been a "traditional" one with the wife assuming the traditional functions of homemaking and childrearing. She had little education or job experience but did manage to obtain employment from time to time as a sales clerk, a babysitter and a housekeeper. The wages were, of course, always quite low, and since she had only a grade 8 education and very little job training, it was unlikely that she would ever obtain higher levels of employment. To make matters worse, she suffered from a bad back and arthritis which restricted her employment opportunities. In such a case, the court decided that a time-limited order was totally inappropriate.

On the other hand, there are a wide variety of cases in which time-limited spousal support orders have been made. The circumstances in which they have been made have, to a degree, determined the intent of the specific orders. Time-limited spousal orders have been made:

- to permit the spouse to complete a program of education or retraining
- to enable a fully qualified person to find suitable employment
- to enable physically or mentally ill persons to rehabilitate themselves
- where the person seeking support is not making a sufficient effort to be self-supporting, but could, with a renewed effort
- where the parties agreed in a separation agreement that spousal support payments would terminate at a specific time, but the court felt it was necessary to override their agreement because it had become unfair subsequently
- to provide a spouse with support pending the receipt of a property settlement or other sum of money
- where the person seeking support has established a new relationship but is not yet capable of relying upon that relationship for full support
- where there are children of the marriage who are still in daycare or of school age
- where the marriage has been of a short duration, and support is needed to offer a brief cushion after separation
- where the ability of the person paying support will be substantially reduced on a specific date in the near future, for example, because he or she is retiring
- where principles of fairness dictate that some form of support is needed on a short-term basis.

It is, of course, always open to the people involved to come back to the court and ask that the time-limited support order be turned into an indefinite one or that it be abridged (shortened) in some way. The court always retains the complete discretion to alter such an order.

The issue of time-limited support orders raises another interesting aspect of spousal support, the duty to be self-supporting. A very clear message has come from the courts in Canada over the last five or six years that each spouse is expected, upon marriage breakdown, to go out and make an effort to contribute to his or her own support. This can mean a contribution to economic well-being through part-time employment, retraining, and the active search for completely self-sustaining employment.

Another issue that affects the awarding of support and its amount is the health of the spouses. With a rapidly aging population, health concerns can often be paramount in fixing the amount of support. The court is always vigilant in ensuring that spouses do not use health concerns as an inappropriate way of reducing their obligation for support, and that where a spouse has a health concern, particularly one that arises from the marriage, related needs are met through spousal support.

As in the case of child support orders, the court retains the full discretion to vary any spousal support order at any time upon an application by either spouse. The court will vary the order where there has been a "material change in circumstances" that affects either one spouse's ability to pay or the other spouse's need.

The courts now regularly order that the amount of spousal support be indexed to keep pace with the increases in the cost of living. These are sometimes called "COLA" clauses—the acronym stands for "cost of living allowance." Some of the indexing formulas can be quite complex. You may wish to examine the cost of living clause that forms a part of the separation agreement reproduced in the Appendices. The goal of the clause is to ensure that the support increases automatically at regular intervals as the cost of living increases. This reduces the likelihood that the parties will need to return to court for support increases at a later date.

A special consideration in the area of spousal support is the presence in some provincial family laws of a cutoff date for the request for support. While the cutoff dates (called "limitation periods") vary, some jurisdictions have required that the request for spousal support be made within two years of the end of the relationship. If the support is requested after the two-year period, the spouse must have a special reason for coming forward late. If the court considers it fair at that time it may extend the time for the request for support, but the onus is on persons seeking support to convince the court that they should be given special treatment.

The court has the discretion to ignore support provisions agreed to in a domestic contract where the provision of support is totally inadequate in the circumstances and would be unfair to the spouse in need of support. You may wish to keep this in mind as you review Chapter 10, which deals with domestic contracts ("Settling Your Differences").

PARENTAL SUPPORT

The *Divorce Act* does not contain any provisions concerning parental support, but provincial family laws now provide in some jurisdictions that a parent in need of support can obtain it from a child of the marriage. The courts have had little experience with this type of provision, but some general rules of thumb have emerged.

Ontario's provision, for example, states that every child who is not a minor has an obligation to provide support, in accordance with need, for his or her parents who have cared for or provided support for the child, to the extent that the child is capable of doing so. As you can see, such an order could only be made against a child who has reached the age of majority; and again, the court looks at the parents' needs as well as the child's ability to pay. An interesting additional requirement is the fact that support will only be ordered for parents who have cared for or provided support for the child from whom they are now seeking support.

Again, as we see our population aging, it may not be uncommon in the very near future to see parents seeking support from their children where pension plans and other forms of public assistance do not meet the parents' needs.

Support continues to be one of the most important aspects of a family breakdown. Orders for spousal support, child support and parental support can be the key to sustaining a family after the marriage breakdown. Chapter 13 examines how very difficult it is to enforce these orders. You'll see from reading that chapter that it is one thing to obtain the order, but quite another thing to enforce it.

9

Common-Law Spouses
Have Rights, Too

Two very different cases come to mind when the term "common-law spouse" is used. Both involve older women. One had left a very unsatisfactory relationship with a man she had lived with for many years but never married; the other was the "widow" of a highly publicized and very colourful Canadian. These women are Rosa Becker and Yolanda Ballard, and both were considered "common-law spouses" by Canadian courts.

Rosa Becker's case is well known to family law lawyers as a textbook book example of the type of joint effort made by two people, unmarried but living as man and wife, trying to build some economic security but ultimately suffering tragic consequences. After years of toil, Rosa Becker's relationship with Mr. Pettkus broke down and she was thrown out of their home with a few thousand dollars to show for a lifetime of contribution to a successful beekeeping operation and farm just outside of Ottawa. She was not satisfied with his suggested "settlement" and hired a lawyer to get what she considered was her fair share of the operation. After litigation that dragged on for years she won and obtained a judgment for an estimated $150,000 from the Supreme Court of Canada. This was not the end of her trouble, though. She then spent another several years attempting to collect that judgment, without much success. The years of waiting, the lawyer's fees, the legal stonewalling and the fact that she never saw a cent of her judgment led her to conclude that our legal system did not have much justice to offer a woman in her predicament. So, on November 5, 1987, she put a rifle to her head and killed herself, putting her legal struggle to an end.

Canadian family law, however, has not changed one bit as a result of her death and the protest it implied.

Yolanda Ballard's case is quite different. She and Harold Ballard, the owner of the Toronto Maple Leafs and Maple Leaf Gardens, began living together in about 1984. They never married, but she spent most of her time with him and eventually changed her last name to Ballard.

In April 1990 Ballard died, leaving Yolanda $50,000 a year for the rest of her life. This she considered inadequate given the fact that she was his "common-law spouse" and had become accustomed to a higher standard of living than could be attained on $50,000 a year. She applied to the court for an interim support order of $16,050—per month. Her projected expenses included such things as $75,000 a year for clothes, $15,000 for pet care, $60,000 for vacations and so on. Two questions arose that are typical of such cases: Was she a common-law spouse? And if she was, what did that entitle her to?

On October 2, 1990, the court awarded Yolanda Ballard interim support of $7,000 per month retroactive to April 11, 1990 to run for six months. She will receive, therefore, approximately $91,000 in support pending the final outcome of her case. Incidentally, she seeks a final order of support in the amount of $381,000 per year—seven times what Harold Ballard had in mind.

Yolanda Ballard's case is a far cry from Rosa Becker's, yet both women are common-law spouses.

In this chapter we shall examine the meaning of this term, the misconceptions which surround it and identify the rights and obligations of a common-law spouse when the relationship comes to an end. These rights and obligations may include support, property sharing, pension sharing, custody of and access to children and financial support of children.

What does it mean to live "common law"? Most people would say it means "living together as if you were husband and wife but not actually getting married." The expression appears in few if any statutes passed by either the federal or provincial governments. It seems to have its origins in the English term "common-law marriage," which was a marriage not solemnized in the usual way but created instead by an *agreement to marry in the future* which was in turn followed by cohabitation (living together).

Rather than use the expression "common-law spouse" in their statutes, several provinces have instead expanded the meaning of the term "spouse" in some limited circumstances to acknowledge that there are consequences that follow from men and women living together but not marrying. Who fits the definition varies from province to province, of course. As you might expect, the federal *Divorce Act* has no interest in common-law spouses. It only applies to those who actually took the step of getting married.

Ontario's *Family Law Act, 1986*, which provides for property division and support on marriage breakdown, deals with the common-law spouse in an interesting way. Part I of the Act deals with property division and for that part "spouse" is defined essentially as one who is legally married. Part III deals with support obligations, and defines "spouse" as including three categories of couples:

- people who get legally married
- people who live together for three or more years as husband and wife, or
- people who live together in a relationship of some permanence and have a child (adopted or natural).

In Ontario this means two things. First, when property is being divided after a common-law couple separates, Part I (dealing with property division) *does not* apply to them because they don't fit that part's definition of spouse. Second, they will be entitled to claim support from each other under Part III if they fit the definition of that part. But before we look at rights and obligations let's examine the area a little more closely.

Common-law relationships do not always start in the most orderly or legalistic way. For some, living together arises out of necessity and may grow into a more intimate relationship. For others it is a conscious choice to avoid the legal obligations imposed by marriage. Still others live together unmarried because they have no choice—one partner cannot divorce for some reason and is therefore unable to remarry.

Studies have suggested that common-law living arrangements seem to be a form of premarital behaviour—a modern courtship. These same studies suggest that those who live this way do not view it as a lifetime commitment but rather as a test of marital compatibility in preparation for marriage. In most cases, either the relationship ends quickly or the people involved get married. For whatever reason, more and more Canadians are living together without taking the traditional step of marrying. Consider the following facts taken from Statistics Canada and Census figures as of 1986:

- Common-law relationships (or "unions," as the studies sometimes call them) have been rare in the past.
- 8.3 percent of all couples live in common-law unions—about 487,000 couples (Sweden has 16 percent, Denmark 13 percent).
- Quebec, the Yukon and N.W.T. have the highest number of common-law unions; Ontario has less than half the percentage of Quebec.
- Education has little to do with the choice. People of all educational levels choose it at about the same rate, although it is less common in rural areas.
- It is rare among the Chinese and Italian communities but popular with the French.
- Common-law unions tend to be young adult lifestyles, with 30 percent of females and 38 percent of males aged twenty to twenty-four in common-law relationships. Many of these are first-time unions.
- It is popular following divorce or separation, with 4.3 percent of women and 5.3 percent of men aged forty to forty-four choosing it.
- Among women aged forty to forty-four the number cohabiting rose by 81 percent between 1981 and 1986.
- Common-law unions have lower fertility rates, probably because of the stigma of out-of-wedlock childbirth and the expressed lack of commitment to the relationship.
- Interestingly, marriages preceded by common-law unions were more likely to end in divorce than those that were not.

Having considered the meaning of "common-law spouse" and looked at their number in Canada, let us now turn to their respective rights and obligations upon the end of the relationship in terms of support, property, pensions and children.

SUPPORT

Eight Canadian jurisdictions have defined "spouse" in such a way as to extend an entitlement to or duty to pay support at the end of a common-law union. Alberta, Quebec, P.E.I. and the Northwest Territories do not extend support rights and obligations to common-law spouses (although a recent court case in the NWT interpreted the NWT *Maintenance Act* to include both legally married and common-law spouses). All other Canadian jurisdictions do, in one form or another. Briefly, the variations are as follows:

JURISDICTION	CRITERIA FOR COMMON-LAW SPOUSE
• British Columbia	• 2 years of cohabitation
• Saskatchewan	• 3 years of cohabitation, or a child and a relationship of some permanence
• Manitoba	• 5 years of cohabitation and substantial dependence between people involved, or • 1 year of cohabitation and a child
• Ontario	• 3 years of cohabitation, or a child and a relationship of some permanence
• New Brunswick	• 3 years of cohabitation and substantial dependence
• Nova Scotia	• 1 year of cohabitation
• Newfoundland	• 1 year of cohabitation and a child
• Yukon	• a relationship of some permanence
• Alberta, Quebec, P.E.I., N.W.T.	• no common-law spouse entitlement to support

While the period of cohabitation may vary, the cases that have gone to court across Canada have produced a general set of criteria for what judges consider when examining a common-law relationship. The court considers the following:

- Did the partners share accommodations?
- Did one render domestic services to the other?
- Was there a sharing of household expenses? (This does not necessarily mean equal sharing.)
- Was there sexual intimacy between them?
- Are they of the opposite sex?
- What was the nature of their relationship?
- Were they husband and wife for all intents and purposes?

The courts have found that where there has been a relationship of such significance that it has led to the actual dependency of one party on another or the expectation that one will support the other in the event of financial crisis, then an entitlement to support arises where there is a case of need.

Assuming the individual qualifies, the amount of the support and its duration are calculated in the same way that they are calculated for legally married spouses who have separated (see Chapter 8, "Support"). Where there are differences, they may arise from the length of the relationship and the court's willingness to make support orders for common-law spouses time-limited, that is, not open-ended or indefinite.

In many jurisdictions this obligation for support of a common-law spouse may also apply with respect to an estate. That is, if a person dies leaving a common-law spouse as his or her survivor, the surviving spouse may be able to obtain an order of support from the estate. This was the case with Yolanda Ballard, who wanted to be considered a spouse within the meaning of Ontario's *Succession Law Reform Act*.

PROPERTY

Now, for the dispelling of some myths and misconceptions: *Common-law spouses have no statutory property rights in Canada.* Period. I have spoken to dozens of people—including lawyers—who think that once a person meets the provincial definition of common-law spouse that person is automatically entitled to every right (or subject to every obligation) that is available to a legally married spouse. In fact, it was the prevalence of this view that in part prompted me to write this book.

One woman's inquiry practically knocked me out of my seat. She called to find out how long she had to cohabit to be considered common-law. Simple enough—the Ontario *Family Law Act* says three years, I said. Oh great, she replied, only eight more months to go until she could separate from the man with whom she was living and share his property under the *Family Law Act*. Wait, I said, you don't acquire property rights, only support. Long pause. How long, I asked, have you been hanging in there? A year and a bit, she said. Bye. Yeah, bye. She never called back, so I don't know what happened.

It doesn't matter if a man and woman live together for fifty years—if they do not marry the only property they are entitled to when they leave is their own property. This, of course, raises a problem: What if they acquired property together?

A couple can acquire some significant assets over a few short years—a home, cars, furniture, RRSPs, Canada Savings Bonds, a joint savings account—all without so much as a discussion about what would happen if one of them died or if they separated. That is why lawyers hear the familiar "Well, I just assumed ..." or "I thought we would just share it equally ..." or worse yet, "I never intended to share *that* ..." and so on.

The courts have developed some general guidelines over the years to help couples sort such property division matters out:

- In the absence of an intention to the contrary, each person may leave the relationship with any assets they brought in and any acquired in his or her name alone during the relationship.
- The court will not allow one person to be "unjustly enriched" at the other person's expense.
- Where one of the persons confers a benefit on the other person and suffers a corresponding deprivation as a result and there is no other

legal reason or justification for the enrichment, the court will "correct" the situation through the use of a device called the "constructive trust." A constructive trust is simply a fancy legal way of saying to the spouse who has the property in his or her own name (called "having title"): You are actually holding that property or part of its value in trust for your partner. The court then orders the part considered to be held in trust to be paid over to the other person. This is what happened in Rosa Becker's case. Mr. Pettkus was found to be holding part of his beekeeping operation's value in trust for her. The value of the part held was the amount of the judgment.

An example might be helpful. Let's assume a man and a woman met and decided to live together. Over a couple of years they saved $10,000 each to put down on a home. They bought the house in the man's name and moved into it with a vague intention to marry someday. Over the next several years they both paid the mortgage and expenses as best they could, although not equally. A child was born and the woman agreed to stay home to care for it and the home. She then inherited $50,000, and rather than start a small business she agreed to renovate the kitchen and build a play room. For whatever reason they separated, with the house still in the man's name. Would he be unjustly enriched at her expense if he kept the whole house? Did she confer a benefit on him and suffer a corresponding deprivation by renovating instead of starting a business? Would the court correct this by imposing a trust upon him to hold a share of the house's value for her? The answer is yes to all three questions.

The same approach is true of all property acquired by common-law spouses, whether it is the home or the furniture in it. The court will look at their intentions and their contributions, and try to achieve a fair split that does not leave one enriched at the other's expense.

Other general rules include the following:

- Each case is different. The size of an interest in a piece of property will depend on the facts of the particular case.
- A contribution does not automatically entitle a person to a half interest. The court will determine what is a fair return on the actual contribution.
- The court prefers a direct connection between the contribution and the property in question. It does not necessarily have to be a contribution directly to the acquisition of the property—it could be some act that preserved the property, maintained it or improved it.
- Merely being a supportive, good partner or paying some household expenses will not necessarily entitle one to a share of a property. Remember, there must be present the aspect of one's being unjustly enriched at the other's expense. The case law is evolving on this point.
- There have been cases that found home-management, child-care and housekeeping services to have been a "contribution," but in those cases the spouse who cared for the child or did the house duties freed the other spouse to earn and acquire property.

- The court will consider the intention of each person, but does not insist that both have the same intention. It will consider what each person reasonably expected to happen or what interest in the property each one reasonably expected.
- If the property is in one spouse's name because it was a gift from the other spouse, then the court will not "correct" the situation. One cannot be "unjustly enriched" by a gift.

You should also note in the context of this discussion of property rights that since there is no matrimony there can be no matrimonial home. Those provinces that accord special status to the matrimonial home for such things as "exclusive possession" have only conferred that benefit on legally married spouses.

No formula is used to calculate the respective interests in the property in such cases. Evidence of intention and contribution over the years must be gathered up and bundled first into the lawyer's office and eventually into the courtroom. This can be a long, drawn out and expensive process, a fact to which Rosa Becker's death stands as a stark reminder.

PENSIONS

Before leaving the area of property altogether, we should look at one special area of protection for common-law spouses concerning pensions.

Everyone acquires Canada Pension Plan benefits over his or her working life. The *Canada Pension Act* provides that persons of the opposite sex who had been living together for *at least one year* and who have been separated for more than a year may apply to the Minister for a division of pension credits. So where a working spouse acquires credits the other spouse may apply to share them. An application must be accompanied by the "necessary papers," of course! Birth certificate, Social Insurance Number, addresses (current and at cohabitation), relevant dates of cohabitation and separation and—for some reason—the reason for the separation.

CHILDREN OF COMMON-LAW RELATIONSHIPS

All things considered, this is one of the less complicated aspects of common-law relationships. The *Divorce Act*, of course, has no application so all issues concerning the children are decided pursuant to provincial family law. Custody issues will be decided in accordance with the child's best interests, as will any access entitlement. (You can find a discussion of these matters in Chapter 7, "The Children.") Provincial law applies to the children of common-law spouses, and there may be support obligations when the relationship ends if a need has arisen (see Chapter 8).

LEGAL ADVICE

It is particularly necessary to consult a lawyer about division of property when lengthy common-law relationships collapse or where significant assets are involved. You should also discuss Canada Pension credits with your lawyer.

What should a couple do, who want to make joint purchases or investments? The best route, of course, is to think in advance about what you would want to happen if one of you died or you separated. This can be a difficult subject to raise, because it means confronting the possibility of two very unpleasant possibilities. Who wants to think about *that* when things are going so well? *You* do.

The best way, in my opinion, is to address the issue head on—"Honey, what would we do if something went wrong?" If the investments are significant or complicated (for example, if they involve money from either family) you should seriously consider a cohabitation agreement. This type of domestic contract is the equivalent of a marriage contract and is designed for people who will not be legally married but will live together. It is not difficult to prepare (written, signed, witnessed) but like any contract that affects your property it should be prepared with independent legal advice. You will find a more detailed description of this type of contract in Chapter 15, "Marriage Contracts and Cohabitation Agreements."

Don't be reluctant to raise the subject. If your relationship is so great it will survive this type of planning. Look on the bright side: You can have the lawyer prepare your will at the same time and save yourself a second trip to the lawyer's office!

The value of this particular chapter is to open the eyes of people who are in a common-law relationship or thinking about being in one. The rights and obligations are very limited. Essentially, they amount to the right to ask for support and the duty to pay it if the relationship has created a dependency. Sorting out property purchased jointly can be extremely difficult and confusing, and if left to the courts, property division can be very rough justice. In contrast, custody and access issues are determined in exactly the same way as with the children of legally married spouses. The same is true of the parents' obligation to support their children.

QUESTIONS TO CONSIDER IF YOU ARE LIVING COMMON-LAW:

- Do you meet your province's definition of a common-law spouse?
- Do you own property with your common-law partner?
- Have you discussed or considered how your property would be divided if one of you died or you split up?
- Have you considered a cohabitation agreement?

10

Settling
Your Differences

One of the goals of this book is to equip you to make some intelligent choices about your family law difficulties. Reasonable choices will lead, in the vast majority of cases, to settlement. I therefore want to spend a few minutes looking at how and why settlements are reached.

We have already examined the potential emotional obstacles to settlement in Chapter 1. Assuming that none of those problems is influencing your decision, at some point you and your lawyer will realize that a settlement is close, that your needs are capable of being met without going to court for an imposed court order.

When a settlement is reached, it should be because that is what the parties themselves want. This sounds so obvious, there should be no need to even state it—of course that is why a case should be settled! Unfortunately, it is not obvious to many lawyers and their clients. Cases settle for other less satisfactory reasons. Consider for the moment the client who settles because she is emotionally tired or weakened, or frightened of an abusive husband. She settles to avoid further conflict.

There are too many clients to name who have settled because the cost of proceeding outweighs the disadvantages of an immediate settlement. This can mean either that the client cannot afford to pay his or her lawyer to continue a valid cause or that the net amount recovered now will exceed that which would remain after a trial.

Sometimes a case is settled because it has not been prepared properly. Necessary evidence was not gathered, the case is called for hearing and the lawyer is not prepared to go to court or has been tactically outmanoeuvred—these are all "less than satisfactory" reasons for a client to settle a dispute.

A case that is settled on such uneasy ground is not settled for long. I have met too many family law clients who feel they were pressured into a settlement with which they were unhappy. In one case the client was summoned to her lawyer's office to discuss a settlement offer which had just been received by fax on the eve of the court appearance. The offer, as it turned out, was not very different from a previous settlement proposal. The lawyer reviewed the offer with the client after which the following exchange took place.

Lawyer: Well, basically that's it. I think you should accept it and avoid a
trial ...

Client: But it's not what I had in mind. I thought—

Lawyer: Well, if you don't accept the offer I will need a $10,000 retainer
before we go to court.

Client: What?! I can't write a cheque for $10,000. Could you wait until
we win the trial? I'll pay you out of what we recover ...

Lawyer: Oh, I can't do that. There's no guarantee we would be
successful.... In fact if we lose you may have to pay your
husband's legal costs... Your case does have some weaknesses.
There are no guarantees, especially in family law cases...

Client: But I thought we had a good case ... you said—

Lawyer: Do you want to go to court?

Client: What should I do?

Lawyer: It's your decision.

Suddenly the case wasn't as good as the lawyer made it seem six
months earlier, and the client had the unmistakable feeling that a rug was
being pulled out from under her. It leaves the clients unhappy with the
process, thinking that the settlement had very little to do with what they
want. Before long the tainted "agreement" is being twisted this way and
that way by someone looking for an advantage. Of course, once the
agreement is breached the whole struggle begins again.

In this chapter, therefore, I want to talk about the documents related to
the possible settlement of your case: Offers to Settle, Minutes of
Settlement, Orders on Consent, and Separation Agreements.

It may not always seem obvious, but the lawyers handling the matter
actually have a professional obligation to encourage you and your spouse
to settle or to compromise. For example, Rule 3 of The Law Society of
Upper Canada, *Rules of Professional Conduct*, provides as follows:

> *The lawyer should advise and encourage the client to compromise*
> *or settle a dispute whenever it is possible to do so on a reasonable*
> *basis, and should discourage the client from commencing useless*
> *legal proceedings.*

Keep that in mind as the case progresses, and hope that your lawyer
does, too.

OFFERS TO SETTLE

Offers to settle come in two forms—informal ones, contained in letters
exchanged by lawyers, and formal ones, contained in a document
prescribed by the Rules of Court. As negotiations go on between your
respective lawyers, bits and pieces of the case start to get resolved. One
letter may confirm an agreement on the sale of the home, another may fix
the amount of child support, and so on. In some cases, settlement of one
issue is conditional upon settlement of another For example, a father may

agree to pay child support fixed at $350 a month provided he has the child for two months each summer. If one part of such an offer is accepted, then the other part can be resolved. After the exchange of several letters a basic agreement may take shape.

Oftentimes an experienced lawyer will see fairly quickly an appropriate middle ground upon which the parties could settle. He or she may have the client in to discuss the possible settlement and seek permission to propose it to the other side. One letter may contain proposals on several matters. With skill and correct timing it may resolve the dispute. But in many cases it does not, and more letters are exchanged or proceedings are commenced or moved to the next step. It can call for a great deal of patience for everyone. (Keep in mind Chapter 1's advice about the emotional stresses you may be going through at just this time.)

One caution I wish to offer is in regard to the famous "Without Prejudice" letters. Lawyers often have those words at the top of each letter sent to the opposing lawyer. Many clients have little understanding of why those words appear on some letters but not others. The short answer is that we have a system that we hope tries to encourage people to settle their differences out of court. To do so, people—including lawyers—need to be able to speak to each other frankly, without fear that some remark or admission will be used against them later in court if the matter doesn't settle.

Lawyers have developed a system of shielding discussions designed to settle the case from disclosure in court at a later date. They began by saying such things as "My client did not do what your client says he did. However, without prejudice to my client's case, at a later date in court, I am willing to recommend that my client pay $15,000 to your client to settle this matter." By using the words "without prejudice," he prevents the other lawyer from even mentioning the offer to settle at a later date. Consequently, whenever you see a letter marked "without prejudice" it is usually indicative of an attempt to resolve the case without admitting the client did anything wrong.

A more formal type of offer is provided by the Rules of Court. There is even a prescribed form for it. This form is a relatively new innovation and was designed to end arguments that often developed between lawyers over who offered what in the informal letters discussed above. Usually at the end of a trial lawyers would stand up with their letters that offered to settle and said that the other person should have to pay all the costs of the trial because they had been offered the same thing (or better) long ago.

For example, a wife may have offered to accept $600 a month for support. If her husband rejected that offer, went to court and ended up paying $600, then it makes sense that he should pay for the cost of everyone's going to court. The trouble was that letters marked "without prejudice" could not be used to tell the court what the offer had been, and even if they could, lawyers frequently argued about what the letters actually meant. Judges found it confusing and often ordered everyone just to pay his or her own lawyer and go home.

To solve these problems, the formal "Offer to Settle" was developed. It operates the same way as the letter but has some important differences.

First of all, because of the Rules, all formal Offers to Settle look the same and follow the same format. This means there is less to argue about.

Second, the Offer to Settle is made with the specific understanding that it will be drawn to the attention of the judge at the end of the trial. The Offer to Settle means, in so many words, "I think the judge will decide the case as follows ... so let's settle the case on that basis ... but if you don't accept my offer to settle and the judge orders the same thing or better for my client, then I intend to show the judge this Offer to Settle."

The Rules of Court provide that if an Offer to Settle is made but not accepted and the judge orders the same terms, then the person who rejected the Offer must pay all the costs incurred between the date the Offer to Settle was made and the end of the trial. This can be particularly onerous if an experienced family law lawyer makes a shrewd, but fair, Offer to Settle early in the proceedings. One Ontario judge described family law cases as "extremely lengthy and ruinously expensive because of one or the other party's unreasonable and unrealistic demands upon the other." He went on to say that "extended family litigation has become unbearably expensive" and to state that he would insist on Offers to Settle being made.

As you can see, the Offer to Settle creates a lot of pressure. It cannot be rejected out of hand, and so it forces the lawyer and the client to think about their own case and how they think it might turn out. Whether the Offer to Settle is formal or informal, a lawyer who receives one must tell his or her client about it and provide a recommendation about possible acceptance or rejection. Even if the offer is unreasonable, the client must be told about it. It is not up to the lawyer to judge what the client might or might not accept.

Assuming an Offer to Settle is accepted, the lawyers may recommend incorporating the agreement into Minutes of Settlement, an Order on Consent, or a Separation Agreement.

MINUTES OF SETTLEMENT

Anyone who has ever been to a business or political meeting or a meeting of a volunteer organization knows that someone is usually asked to "take the minutes." This involves making as detailed a record of the discussion as possible. Minutes of Settlement are no more than the details of a settlement discussion that has taken place, usually after legal proceedings have been commenced. One of the lawyers will usually volunteer to draft up a summary of a settlement reached through the exchange of letters, Offers to Settle or even a face-to-face meeting between all the lawyers and the clients. In some cases the clients have just finished a court hearing or a "pre-trial" (see Chapter 4) and a consensus emerges while everyone is still at the courthouse.

Minutes of Settlement are always signed by the clients themselves and usually witnessed by the lawyers. In many cases they are completely handwritten, or partially typed and partially handwritten. I have often seen lawyers sitting in hallways using their briefcases as makeshift desks, furiously scribbling out a settlement just reached in another room. Their haste is often out of fear that one client or the other might change his or her mind.

Once signed, the Minutes of Settlement are binding and enforceable. To avoid any argument, many lawyers often incorporate the agreement reached into an order of the court made on consent.

ORDERS ON CONSENT

You will recall that the court makes orders in response to requests made by the lawyers and their clients. The request is often in the form of a Notice of Motion and is supported by an Affidavit (see the Appendices). In many cases the lawyers have scheduled competing motions to be heard at the same time so that several matters can be resolved at once. As the lawyers and clients wait for their turn to be heard, discussion may yield some common ground. By the time the lawyers are ready to stand up and argue in front of the judge, a settlement on one of several issues may have emerged. One lawyer may simply advise the court, "Your Honour, the parties have reached an agreement on this matter and we ask that you make the following order on consent." The lawyers are using the time booked at court to record the settlement in an actual court order. This saves time and protects the parties' settlement.

The meeting of minds doesn't always occur while the parties are waiting to be heard by a judge. Sometimes the exchange of settlement letters or Offers to Settle produces an agreement and it is then incorporated into an Order on Consent—an order that everyone agrees should be made.

SEPARATION AGREEMENTS

The separation agreement is by far the most popular method of settling family law disputes. Essentially, the parties, through their lawyers, sign a contract that sets out the terms of their settlement. We sometimes hear people refer to this as a "legal separation." The alternative, living separate from each other without a written agreement, is not an "illegal separation"—there is no requirement for people to have a written separation agreement. However, there are several advantages to a written agreement, as we shall see in a moment.

Separation agreements are used whether the couple separating are legally married or not. In other words, if you have been living common law (described in Chapter 9) and want to separate, then you could settle your differences with a separation agreement.

There is no need to commence legal proceedings in order to use a separation agreement; in fact, many people consult lawyers and negotiate and sign separation agreements without ever seeing the inside of a courtroom. They are the lucky ones. Others feel obliged to experience the courtroom and its related expense, and only turn to the separation agreement as a way out of the court system. Mediation (which is discussed in Chapter 12, "Alternatives to Court") frequently yields an amicable settlement which can then be incorporated in a separation agreement.

So, while the use of separation agreements can arise in a number of ways, their purpose remains basically the same—to settle the dispute by contract.

The technical requirements for a separation agreement are not extensive. The contract must be written, signed by the parties and witnessed. Virtually all law firms have word processing/computer systems that contain thousands of model agreements and clauses. As the lawyer identifies the appropriate settlement, he or she simply picks and chooses from a precedent book the necessary clauses and paragraphs. A law clerk or secretary plugs in the family details and related information. Then a hard copy (paper version) is produced and reviewed with the client. We will look at the agreement itself in a moment, but you can see at this point that there is no magic in the "legal separation." It is a contract like any other. If you wish to change or amend it later or even cancel (revoke) it, it must be done by the same method.

Let's consider the reasons for having such a contract. There are several advantages:

- The negotiations themselves have a way of making the couple consider things they might not otherwise have thought relevant. Not only must they resolve the disputes about the past but they must also think of the future: Where will I live? Can I move with the children to another province? What will happen to my estate if I die? and so on.
- A written agreement that the people can refer to from time to time offers predictability in the future. There is less room for debate when it is there in black and white. A related advantage is the fact that those among us (you know who you are) who have trouble honouring their verbal promises (they say things like "I never said that!") are less likely to walk away from a written promise.
- In every province separation agreements can be enforced like any other contract. They are legally binding. An added advantage in provinces such as Ontario, Manitoba or British Columbia and even the Yukon, is that support provisions in separation agreements can be filed with the court or "Support Enforcement Agency" (see Chapter 13) and enforced as if they were court orders. This can be a great advantage to a person wishing to enforce a promise to pay support.
- Also related to the question of support is the fact that tax advantages will arise if the obligation to pay support is in a separation agreement. Revenue Canada permits a person paying support to deduct the amount paid. This applies to court orders also, but no agreement means no tax deduction.
- A written separation agreement can speed up considerably any subsequent divorce proceeding. The agreement can be filed and its provisions incorporated into the divorce judgment if necessary.

As you can see, the advantages outweigh the disadvantages of having a written separation agreement. I think that people sometimes avoid negotiating one because

(a) they don't want to rock a boat that may be steady for the first time in a long time,

(b) they are concerned about the expense of the lawyers,

(c) they keep saying they will do it themselves—but never get around to actually doing it, or

(d) they worry that the lawyers will find something to argue about and get them into a battle they don't want and can't afford.

These are all valid concerns ... but the first one may happen anyway, perhaps because you don't have an agreement. The next one, (b), is controllable if you follow my advice or use mediation. Think of it as buying insurance. As for (c), let's face it, if you haven't done it by now you never will. And (d) is also controllable—if you follow my advice.

Which brings us back to the advantages.... So consider a written separation agreement.

In terms of the content of a separation agreement, there are very few limitations on what a couple can deal with in the contract. In general terms the agreement can deal with:

- ownership in and division of property
- support obligations—child and spousal
- the right to custody of and access to children
- the right to direct the education and moral training of children
- any other matter in the settlement of their affairs.

In the Appendices I have reproduced a full separation agreement, and you may want to take a moment to examine it now. You will note that like any standard contract it begins by identifying the people who are entering into the agreement. Their names appear in full along with a statement of where they reside. The date of the agreement appears at the top of the first page.

After this introduction several standard clauses appear. One sets out the particulars of the marriage (where is that marriage certificate anyway?) or the period of cohabitation if it was common law. Another paragraph sets out the date and circumstances of the separation. The couple will acknowledge that they intend to continue to live separate and will not interfere with one another's life.

Each agreement is tailored to the individual needs of the couple and can include paragraphs on the following subjects. (Check off any that apply to you and refer back later if necessary.)

- custody
- access
- division of household contents
- division of the matrimonial home (sale)
- possession of the matrimonial home and its maintenance

- future use of property (e.g., cottage sharing)
- child support
- spousal support (amount and duration)
- indexation of support
- restrictions on the mobility of parents (e.g., can't move more than 300 miles)
- restrictions on changing a child's name without consent
- methods of solving future disputes (mediation or arbitration)
- release of interest in other's estate
- general releases
- releases of interest in specific property
- division of pensions
- interpretation provisions (e.g., definitions)
- health and medical expenses
- dental coverage
- automobile division (sale) or use
- Canada Pension Plan
- life insurance
- responsibility for debts
- tax consequences
- effect of recohabitation
- effect of default
- financial disclosure
- independent legal advice
- responsibility for legal fees

There is no limit to the terms that can be incorporated into such an agreement.

Signing (or "executing," as lawyers like to say) the separation agreement can be quite an experience, although many people have commented that it seems anticlimactic after all the tensions of negotiating it. The law office staff (law clerks and paralegals) will prepare four identical versions of the agreement, one for each client and each of the lawyers. At the end of the signing "exercise" there will be four duplicate originals. I call it an exercise because it is a bit of a marathon of signatures and initials. It goes like this:

- You will sign your name on the last page on the right hand side above a line set over a typewritten version of your name as it appears on the first page. In other words, the last page will have a line with, for example, "Michael George Cochrane" typed under it. Place your usual signature on the line. You do not have to write your name out in full—your usual signature is fine. A witness will sign beside your name. This may be a paralegal or other office member. It is often the lawyer who witnesses the client's signature.
- You will then place your initials on each page of the agreement and beside any handwritten changes that have been made at the last minute. (Sometimes a name is misspelled or a birth date is incorrect.) The same witness will place his or her initials beside yours wherever they appear.

- The pages are marked with initials for two reasons: to acknowledge that you saw that page (so read it carefully line by line) and to prevent anyone from trying to substitute a new—and perhaps different—page later.
- Both people must sign the agreement as I've described it above. This is often done on different days at different times. The last page, where the signatures appear, will often show the dates upon which the couple signed the agreement.
- It is the lawyers' task to ensure that the agreement has been signed properly by both sides.
- Once it has been signed by both sides the agreement is a legally binding contract.

Wait—there's more.

There are some additional documents that are signed at this stage—a *Certificate of Independent Legal Advice* and an *Acknowledgment by Wife/Husband.* The Certificate is a sworn statement by your lawyer that he or she is the witness to your signature, believes you are the person whose signature he or she witnessed and believes you understand what you were signing and did it voluntarily. In other words, by signing the Certificate a lawyer acknowledges that he or she explained the nature and consequences of the agreement to the client, who signed knowing what they were and accepting them.

The client will then be asked to sign an Acknowledgment that he or she hired the lawyer to advise him or her about the agreement, that the lawyer did so and that the client is fully aware of the consequences of the agreement. It will also state that the person is signing voluntarily. (See the Separation Agreement in the Appendices.) At the end of it you will find these additional documents. Lots of paper, lots of signing.

You should also note that in some provinces, where separation agreements are enforced by the court, you may also need to sign an affidavit at the time of the final signing of the agreement that will facilitate filing with the court or with the police.

The signing exercise takes place only after the agreement has been reviewed with you line by line by the lawyer you hired. (Not the secretary, not the paralegal, not the articling student, not the junior lawyer, but the lawyer who negotiated it.) Do not be shy about asking questions. Look at each paragraph carefully. Do you know what it means? What does it accomplish? Don't accept statements like "Oh that's just 'boiler plate,'" "That's standard—it's in every agreement," and so on. If it is in the agreement, it is for a reason. Remember, you are going to be asked to sign the Acknowledgment I mentioned earlier. You are paying a lot of money for this contract, so understand what it does for you. If you don't, you may keep on "paying" for years.

Don't be rushed. Ask the lawyer if you can take the draft agreement home to read. Sometimes law firms have little interview rooms or a library that can be used. Review each draft from beginning to end. Review each new change. Does it do what you thought it would do? Does it accomplish what your lawyer said it would accomplish? If not, he or she should have a good explanation.

This brings us to another area—setting aside an agreement at a later date. Following the technical rules for assembling the agreement will not make it immune to a charge that it was entered into "improperly" or that a special circumstance has changed. An agreement entered into "improperly" could include an agreement signed under duress. In other words, one party forced (through threats) the other person to sign an agreement that the person would not otherwise have signed. This is why there is so much emphasis on both people having independent legal advice and acknowledging it in the document itself. It is difficult to challenge an agreement as being involuntary when a lawyer was consulted and gave advice. But it happens.

Another "improper" agreement would be one that was brought about by fraud. For example, if a person has hidden or lied about the presence or value of assets, then any calculations for the division of property would be inaccurate. If this was done to mislead the spouse then the court may set the agreement aside.

The courts will also set aside agreements entered into because of undue influence, material misrepresentation, unconscionable bargain and something lawyers call "non est factum."

Briefly, "undue influence" occurs where one person uses his or her power over another in such a way that the stronger person acquires a benefit. This has occurred in cases involving a domineering husband and an emotionally or psychologically weak wife.

A "material misrepresentation" occurs where one person hides a fact or lies about a state of affairs with the effect of inducing the other person to sign the agreement. In one case a husband told his wife the agreement was for "tax purposes." In another case a husband was told it was only "temporary." Both were misrepresentations.

An "unconscionable bargain" may be set aside by a court if it finds that the parties were in unequal bargaining positions and as a result of it the deal was improvident for one of them. This would be likely in cases where no legal advice had been obtained. In one case a husband told his wife that she was entitled to one-seventh of the property because there were two adults and five children. She signed the agreement without legal advice.

"Non est factum" is a special legal term for something that can be quite straightforward: a person signs a document thinking it is one thing but finds out it is something else. It used to be reserved for the blind and illiterate but can now apply to cases where documents are switched.

To avoid these types of situation, lawyers now insist that the clients exchange sworn statements about their assets and their value. This discourages fraud and allows the lawyers to negotiate a fair agreement. As much as this exchange of information makes sense, there are couples who will ask lawyers to prepare agreements without exchanging full financial information. If this type of client subsequently discovers that the other spouse was not completely honest in his or her disclosure it is very unlikely that the court will set aside the agreement. The moral of the story is: Don't sign a separation agreement without seeing a full, sworn financial statement from your spouse.

You should also understand that the court does not consider itself bound by any agreement that affects children. The amount or duration of child support, for example, can be changed by the court at any time regardless of what the agreement says. The same is true of custody and access. The court will always try to do what is best for the child.

In the case of spousal support, separation agreements often provide that in the event of a "material change of circumstances" (essentially, a significant change related to the marriage in some way) the amount and duration of the support can be changed. So, if a wife was receiving $300 per month and working part-time but was laid off, then her support could be increased by the court until she finds a new position.

One special situation deserves mention: What if the people get back together after the separation agreement has been signed? The answer is like many in law: It depends. Of course there are reconciliations that don't last. The couple may have second thoughts about their decision to separate and begin to cohabit again, but after a few months the same old problems surface and they are left wondering what happens now. The court will look to the agreement itself and see if reconciliation was contemplated. It often is, and the agreement may provide that certain terms become invalid if reconciliation occurs. For example, the agreement may provide that any provision dealing with spousal support will be invalid if the couple gets back together. On the other hand, the agreement will also be likely to provide that any transactions that have already occurred (such as the husband's transfer of his interest in the cottage to the wife) are *not* invalid because of a reconciliation. As a general rule, the reconciliation will terminate the separation agreement with respect to future dealings such as support, their estates, or custody and access. Transactions that were intended to be complete, however, are not undone by the cohabitation. Property that was transferred stays transferred.

The intention to resume cohabitation must be bilateral. That is, both partners must wish to reconcile. Evidence of such intention in one case was the occurrence of several acts of intercourse—but the court disagreed, finding that evidence from one of them testified to the contrary.

Separation agreements are valuable tools for settling family law cases, both large and small. Their real value, though, is found in recording the agreement the couple wants and needs. This result can only be achieved by understanding the process and giving informed instructions to your lawyer.

In conclusion, there are a number of ways to document the settlement of a family law case: Offers to Settle, Minutes of Settlement, Orders on Consent and Separation Agreements. Each method has its own value, depending on the circumstances of your case, but all are based on arriving at a settlement that meets your needs and the needs of your children. That is the only valid criterion for settlement—that your needs have been met. Fatigue, cost or other factors will enter the picture—but they should not obscure your needs.

11

Not Settling
Your Differences

In the previous chapter we saw how cases can be settled when the people involved find a way to resolve their differences. *Not* settling means only one thing: going to court for a full trial. This aspect of family law is becoming less common due in part to the expense of full trials and because clients and lawyers are using more creative methods of solving problems, such as mediation. But there are still many, many full courtroom trials every year in every province and territory at an appalling cost to the people involved.

A trial, at its most basic level, means that the people involved have not been able to agree on a solution to their problem and are left asking the court to solve it for them. All the issues discussed in the previous chapters can be and have been decided by a judge in a courtroom. When people stand back from the process and consider, for example, the meaning of a custody trial, I believe they are in part ashamed of their inability to resolve the problem. They are admitting that they, the child's parents, cannot agree on what is best for this child, so they will ask a complete stranger, the judge, who has minimal familiarity with their lives, to decide this most important aspect of their lives for them. Yet this is precisely what happens with children, property, spousal support and even the entitlement to a divorce itself.

The best beginning we can make in this area is to separate reality from the misconceptions created by television. Family law trials in Canada bear very little resemblance to the trials we see on television, particularly on shows such as "L.A. Law" and "Street Legal." I'm always amused by how the "TV clients" who consult the "TV lawyer" for the first time at the beginning of the show are having a trial by the end of the program, about an hour later. We should all be so lucky. Most people wouldn't have their financial statements filled out by then, let alone a trial.

Television tells us that trials are fast, exciting, filled with tough cross-examinations, lying witnesses, surprise alternative theories ("Isn't it actually true, Mrs. Brown, that ...) and the obvious "good person" winning over the obvious "bad person." On television, justice is black and white and no one ever seems to pay the lawyers.

Reality? The process is slow, very slow. Some people wait over a year for their trial (that's a whole TV season, never mind one episode), the process is filled with delays, it's often boring even in the middle of a trial while technical arguments are made, the process is overblown with much posturing and, unlike television, it is tense for you and an even greater burden for your children if they are involved. I think many people justifiably consider a trial to be the most intimidating experience of their lives. You never meet anyone who brags about how great or how interesting or how rewarding their family law trial was. You never hear anyone say, "It was worth every penny." If anything, most people think it was a complete waste of time and money, on top of which it was a tense experience that made them feel vulnerable and out of control.

Having said all that, we cannot simply ignore the trial as a painful lesson in living. Sometimes couples are forced to trial—one person takes an unreasonable position or some aspect of the law is so unclear that a judge's decision is needed. In this chapter I would like to consider the trial from a few different perspectives so that those who simply must go through it can do so with a little more confidence and a little more control.

Before considering any of the technical aspects of a trial we must consider what unfortunately becomes an overriding consideration—the cost. Well in advance of the trial, when it appears that a settlement is unlikely, you and your lawyer should discuss the likelihood of a trial. At that time you should consider preparing and reviewing a new retainer that authorizes the lawyer to conduct the trial on your behalf. At the time the retainer is reviewed the lawyer will undoubtedly inform you that no trial will be possible unless a substantial advance on fees is received before the trial commences. The lawyer will likely explain that the legal fees for a trial are approximately $1,000 to $1,500 per day (minimum), and more if more lawyers are involved on your behalf. It is not unusual for lawyers to request an advance on fees before the trial in the amount of $10,000 or $15,000. It is highly unlikely that you will find a lawyer who will conduct the entire trial on the understanding that he or she will be paid the legal fees out of the eventual recovery of property at the end of the trial. This is particularly so in cases where the dispute is over custody. The lawyer will insist upon his or her fees, in full, in advance and deposited in his or her trust account.

Assuming that the cost of proceeding to trial is not a factor in your decision, let us now consider the physical setting of the proceedings.

THE PHYSICAL SETTING: THE COURTROOM

It is misleading to think of the activity at the courthouse as being confined to the courtroom, although much of the activity does take place there. Important things also occur in the court office, the judge's office (called chambers), the lawyers' lounge and even in the hallways.

The courtroom is laid out in a fairly standard fashion, with the judge at the head of the court, on a platform (usually elevated) called the bench. Immediately in front of the judge's bench is the clerk's table, where exhibits are collected and where the court reporter will sit during the trial.

The court reporter will likely be a different person than the court reporter who assisted at the examinations for discovery. However, their function at a trial is the same; they prepare a transcript of all discussions in the courtroom from beginning to end. A few feet further away from the judge's bench is a long table called "counsel's table." Usually it is two tables, one for each side.

Experienced family law lawyers will often take their clients to the court for a tour in advance of the trial. This is designed to familiarize the client with the layout of the courtroom and to remove any anxiety about the setting in advance of the proceedings.

Let's return to the counsel table. There may be three or four chairs at each table. The lawyers will sit at these tables with their clients, along with any lawyer assisting on the case or, in some circumstances, a witness with whom the lawyer wishes to confer during the proceedings.

On the judge's left is the "witness box," which can be literally a box with a door at the back through which the witness enters and exits. Inside the witness box is usually a Bible for the administering of an oath and a glass of water for the witness.

To the right of the judge will sit the clerk of the court. If the lawyers want to give the judge anything during the course of the trial they will often hand it to the clerk who in turn passes it to the judge. The clerk will also mark exhibits during the trial and provide the judge with any necessary assistance upon entering and exiting the court. You may recall the marking of exhibits at the examinations for discovery. Those same exhibits will now be re-marked during the trial while the entirely new transcript is being prepared.

At the back of the courtroom is a seating area for the public, which may be quite large. The proceedings are open to the public, unless for some special reason (such as protection of a child) they have been closed, but the public is generally free to come and go as it pleases during the course of any proceeding in a courtroom.

Some courthouses use special smaller courtrooms for family proceedings. However, in many, many courthouses, the same courtroom is used for family law trials as for murder trials and other forms of litigation. This means that the courtroom may be equipped with a press box and a jury box. These are often on different sides of the courtroom. The first is reserved for reporters and is generally used only in some of the more spectacular or lurid cases. As mentioned earlier, juries are never used in family law cases.

The courtrooms are often linked by hallways to which only authorized personnel have access. The judges will use these hallways to get to and from their chambers. Court staff and lawyers who have business with the judge will use these hallways as well. In some older courthouses around the country, the judge's office may be in another part of the building, so he or she is escorted from the office through the court hallways to the courtroom. In the judge's chambers, the judge works on judgments, reads the court file, makes telephone calls and dresses in his or her gown in advance of trial. It is important to note that your particular judge has in all likelihood never heard of you or your spouse and has had nothing to do with the case before this day. In some circumstances the judge may have only read the court file a few hours in advance of the trial's beginning.

Generally the judge enters the courtroom through a private door behind the bench itself. A clerk will call out "All rise ..."—with a reference to the particular court in which the trial is taking place—when he or she enters, and everyone in the courtroom stands. The judge carries a large hardcover notebook which he or she will use for the taking of notes during the trial. Some judges take a great many notes, others appear to take notes only on the most important points.

Lawyers have private dressing rooms in the courthouse, too. These are called "Barristers' Lounges" and sometimes look like no more than a locker room. In the locker the lawyer can keep his or her street clothes; lawyers appear in court in gowns. We are all familiar with the flowing black gowns, special white shirts and ties, vests and pants that lawyers wear in court. They slip into these formal outfits in the lawyers' lounge.

It can be quite an experience to be in these lounges. Settlements are negotiated, victories celebrated, losses mourned, war stories and anecdotes traded, and there is a lot of plain old lazing about and fooling around. Of course, clients are not welcome in the lawyers' lounge. It is akin to the local clubhouse in some communities.

When a trial is scheduled to be heard, a lot of time can be spent in the hallways of the courthouse waiting, waiting and waiting. Trials often run overtime, emergency hearings are scheduled, thereby throwing off the judges' plans, judges and court reporters must take breaks, and any number of relatively minor but predictable events can cause delays. While in the halls, lawyers either prepare their witnesses, discuss possible settlements, make telephone calls or just sit and wait. In a busy courthouse the halls can be a fascinating place to spend a few hours. However, those awaiting trial find it less interesting due to the tension of their own impending trial.

THE PAPER CHASE

You will recall that the courthouse maintains a court file with a copy of everything that has happened during your case. All motions, affidavits, claims, petitions, orders, transcripts and so on are in the court file to provide a chronological history of the family dispute. In advance of the trial the lawyers will have prepared a "record," which is a bound collection of all the important court proceedings; the record will be used like a summary book by the judge during the trial. The lawyers will often have duplicates of this summary in front of them so that whenever a reference is made to a particular aspect of the proceedings the judge and lawyers can all refer to the same material at the same time. The lawyers will also prepare copies of important evidence and exhibit books for use during the trial. The financial statements completed by the couple are likely to be out of date by the time the trial arrives, and fresh ones will have been completed and filed for use at trial.

It should be obvious from the above that the court file can be quite a monster by the time the trial has arrived. This is particularly so if litigation has taken place over a couple of years.

The nature of the remaining disagreement between the couple will have an effect on the paperwork in front of the court. If, for example, it is a divorce proceeding which includes a dispute over custody, access, property and the divorce itself, the form of the court proceedings will be dictated by the fact that a divorce is being sought. If some issues have been resolved by the time the trial is to take place—if, for example, only custody is an issue—then the paperwork put before the court may be pared down from the full content of the court file. The bigger the dispute, the bigger the court record and court file used by the judge.

The court file is maintained by court staff and delivered by them to the judge in his chambers. All this work goes on behind the scenes in advance of your case actually being considered by the court.

THE TRIAL ITSELF

The circumstances under which your case is "called for trial" can vary from province to province. Some courts use a "fixed date" method which can add a great deal of convenience to your hearing. By a certain day the lawyer must certify to the court that the particular case is ready for trial. In other words, the lawyer alerts the court to the fact that this case can be called at any time for trial and both lawyer and witnesses will be ready. When judges are ready to book trials they look at the list of cases that are ready (called "the ready list") and start to pick and choose trials that can be heard. This often takes place with just a few dozen lawyers and a judge comparing their schedules over the next few months. Depending on witness availability and the expected length of the trial the cases are slotted into a judge's schedule. Then they are assigned a "fixed date," which means, for example, that Judge Brown will hear *Porter* v. *Porter* on November 20, 1991. Period. This is very convenient for the parties, since they know in advance the date of their trial and can plan accordingly for witnesses to be present and for parties to be available from their place of work.

Another, but far less convenient, method is for the judge just to tell five sets of lawyers to be ready to go to trial "the week of November 20th." The cases are then listed 1 to 5 for that particular week. If case #1 settles, then case #2 must be ready to go. If case #2 settles, then case #3 should be ready, and so on. The judges deliberately overbook and anticipate settlements in such a system. The look of panic on a lawyer's face who finds out on a Friday that he or she is not #10 for the following week but rather #1 on Monday morning is unforgettable. (The list "collapses.") There can be quite a weekend scramble in order to be ready for the trial. Unfortunately, this kind of system also forces some less-than-satisfactory settlements on the parties when the lawyers discover that they are not ready for trial.

Regardless of the method of setting the case for trial, let's assume that your case is going to be called on a particular date. You will need to arrange time off work for the entire trial, which may in some cases be several days, and you will also need to arrange for child care in some circumstances. Your lawyer will be arranging for subpoenas to be served on all the witnesses who will be giving evidence in support of your case. Even friendly witnesses, who have agreed to come to trial, will receive a subpoena and "conduct money" (to cover their expenses travelling to and from the trial; it's not very much). While they will only be needed at the time they actually give their evidence as witnesses, they are required by the subpoena to be available for the *entire trial* unless excused by the judge. This can be quite an inconvenience and requires some sensitivity by the lawyer in ensuring that witnesses do not waste their time sitting around in court on days that they are not giving evidence.

It is not unheard of for everyone to be at the court ready to go and suddenly discover that the judge who is supposed to hear their case is now hearing an emergency injunction application in a labour dispute, for example, or some other urgent matter. The trial co-ordinator tries to explain patiently that the trial cannot go ahead as planned. Sometimes it is put over for a day, sometimes indefinitely. Sometimes the trial begins but is then adjourned. I have even seen cases split in half, with part of the case being heard in November and the rest of the case being heard by the same judge in the new year. The point is, you should not assume that your entire trial will be done in one sitting.

However, let's be optimistic and assume your trial starts when it's supposed to start. It can be divided into five main parts:

(i)   Introduction and Opening Statement
(ii) The Petitioner's (or Plaintiff's) Case
(iii) The Respondent's (or Defendant's) Case
(iv) Summation
(v)   The Judgment.

Let's examine each one separately.

(i) Introduction and Opening Statement

At the opening of the trial, after the judge has been ushered in, the lawyer for the Plaintiff or the Petitioner (I am going to refer to the two opposing people involved as the Petitioner and Respondent in this section; Petitioner and Respondent are used in divorce cases) will stand up and introduce himself or herself and the other client and other lawyer. The lawyer may, for example, begin by saying, "Good morning, Your Honour, my name is Cochrane, initial M. I appear on behalf of the Petitioner, Mrs. Brown. My friend, Mr. Poplata, appears on behalf of the Respondent, Mr. Brown...." This occurs whether the judge knows them or not; it is simply for the record being prepared by the court reporter.

Each lawyer will take turns describing very briefly to the judge by way of a "thumbnail sketch" what the case is all about. They will also tell the judge about anything that has been settled in the case or anything that they may have agreed upon to make the trial more expeditious, such as the preparation of a common exhibit book. The lawyers may even give the judge an idea about which witnesses will be called and when they expect that they will be finished putting evidence before the court. The judge may ask some questions, or may simply say to the Petitioner's lawyer: "Call your first witness."

(ii) The Petitioner's Case

The Petitioner goes first. Basically, the Petitioner tells his or her story in whatever order he or she feels is most logical. The story is told through witnesses; depending upon how complex the case is, it may be told through a few witnesses or several. The rules of evidence, which are quite complex, dictate the type of evidence that may be given by particular types of witnesses. Expert witnesses are given a little more latitude in the types of things that they may testify about. Virtually all other witnesses may only testify about things of which they have actual knowledge. Each witness is handled in the same general way, as follows:

- The witness is called to the witness box by the lawyer or the clerk of the court. If an "order excluding witnesses" has been made, the witness may be waiting in the hallway. These orders are often made at the opening of a trial to keep the witnesses from hearing each other's evidence and tailoring their answers. While in the hall, the witnesses are not allowed to discuss the case with any witness who has given evidence. This has the effect of keeping all witnesses out of the courtroom while the trial is under way.

- Once in the witness box, the witness is sworn in (or affirmed) and asked preliminary questions, such as the witness's name, address and relation to the parties. For example, the witness may disclose that his name is Bob Brown, he lives in Toronto, he is the chartered accountant for the Petitioner and has been for ten years. The lawyer who has called this particular witness then asks the witness "open-ended" questions. By "open ended" I mean that the questions cannot be leading questions. For example, the lawyer could not say to this witness: "Is it true that you have worked for the Petitioner for ten years as a chartered accountant and concluded that his one hundred business shares are worth only one dollar each?" This is a leading question because it suggests the answer to the witness and therefore leads him in a particular direction. The question must be open ended, for example: "How long did you work for the Petitioner?" "Did you calculate the value of his business shares?" "How many shares did he have?" "What method did you use to calculate their value?" "What conclusion did you reach about the value of each share?" The witness is taken step by step through the information he has that is of value to the court and to this particular party's case.

- In advance of the trial the lawyer should spend some time with the client and the witnesses explaining how to give evidence. The evidence should always be given in a clear voice and directed to the judge if at all possible. One should only answer the question that is asked and never guess or speculate about a particular answer. It is particularly useful for a witness to review the transcripts from the examination for discovery in advance of the trial as a way of preparing and refreshing his or her memory about the evidence.

- Once the Petitioner's lawyer's questions are complete, the lawyer for the other side has an opportunity to test the witness's story through cross-examination. In this situation, if the lawyer is doing the job properly, every question will be a leading question requiring only a "yes" or a "no" answer. The conventional wisdom is that a lawyer should never ask a question on cross-examination to which he or she does not already know the answer. Nor should questions ever be open ended during cross-examination. This can mean hours of preparation for even the briefest of cross-examinations.

- One method that a lawyer can use on cross-examination is contradiction of the witness's evidence at trial by demonstrating that the witness made a statement on a previous occasion that is inconsistent with his or her most recent evidence. In other words, the lawyer says to the witness, "What you are telling the court today is not the same as what you told us on a previous occasion under oath." This type of contradiction is called an "impeachment" and is most frequently used against the parties themselves who have had their evidence recorded at the examinations for discovery. In such a case, the lawyer may question the witness as follows:

  Lawyer's question: Is it true that you are telling the court today that the value of your shares is one dollar for each share?
  Witness's answer: Yes.
  Question: Do you remember being asked questions at the examination for discovery and giving answers under oath?
  Answer: Yes.
  Question: Do you remember me asking you the following question at page 190 of the transcript, Question #233: "Could you tell me the value of your shares?" Answer: "The shares are worth seven dollar each." Do you remember me asking you that question, and do you remember giving me that answer?
  Answer: Well ... uh, yes.
  Question: Were you lying then or are you lying now when you tell us that the shares are worth one dollar each?

This example is a little more dramatic than would normally occur in the courtroom, but it does demonstrate that the lawyer is able to challenge a witness at trial with the witness's previous apparently inconsistent statement. So don't forget to review those transcripts in advance of trial.

Once the cross-examination is complete, the Petitioner's lawyer, the lawyer who called the witness in the first place, is given the opportunity to re-examine the witness on any new issue that has arisen during the cross-examination. The lawyer may not ask about something that he forgot to ask about during the direct examination. It must be something new and it must have arisen during the cross-examination. Re-examination does not take place in every case, but it does allow the lawyer who called the witness to tighten up weaknesses of the evidence that may have been established during cross-examination.

Remember that the judge is making notes through all of this evidence. If he or she does not have any questions then the witness is excused and another witness is called to the witness box. The above process is then repeated with the direct examination followed by a cross-examination, followed by a re-examination if necessary and questions from the judge. This applies to the witnesses called and to the Petitioner himself or herself. All witnesses are treated in the same way, although obviously the evidence of some is more important than the evidence of others.

(iii) The Respondent's Case

Once the Petitioner has called all his or her witnesses the Respondent takes over. Sometimes the Respondent will open with a brief statement about the evidence to be called and any other clarifying remarks. The Respondent's lawyer then calls all his or her witnesses and the same procedure described above is repeated with respect to each witness.

As witnesses identify documents, each one is marked and entered as an exhibit. The judge examines each document and make notes about its importance in his or her notebook.

That is the procedure in theory. Now let's add a small dose of reality. While this is underway, consider that the following things may happen:

- A witness who was subpoenaed does not show up and the case is adjourned for a day or the order of witnesses is changed.
- A witness shows up having forgotten to bring important documents and is excused to locate the documents. Again, either an adjournment is triggered or the order of witnesses is changed.
- People are wandering in and out of the court. They may be lawyers waiting to be heard by this judge in another proceeding or students monitoring the court lists so that their bosses don't get a sudden call for trial. There may be university or high-school students on courthouse tours, and even people from other trials may wander in and out of the courtroom.
- Every time somebody walks into the courtroom, the proceeding is disrupted while everyone turns around to take a look. Why? Because the person might be a witness who should be excluded from the proceeding. The judge or lawyers then ask the person why he or she is in the courtroom. Once they are satisfied that it is not a witness who has been excluded, the proceeding gradually returns to normal.
- The trial that was originally estimated to take no more than two days is suddenly at the end of its second day and five witnesses have not yet been heard. The trial is then adjourned for six weeks until

the next time that this particular judge is available to continue hearing evidence.

Returning to the trial process itself, once the Respondent's case is finished the Petitioner has an opportunity to call evidence in "Reply." This is like a re-examination of a witness and means that if something new came up during the Respondent's case that the Plaintiff needs to reply to, he or she can call a witness to provide the court with new information. The Petitioner is not permitted to call a witness who should have been called as a part of the Petitioner's case at the outset, however. The process is then repeated for that witness or those witnesses.

(iv) Summation

After all the evidence is before the court, the lawyers then stand up and take turns (with the Petitioner going first) summarizing their case for the judge. The lawyers trace through the evidence, emphasizing strong points and playing down weak ones, and lace through their summary the relevant law. This will involve pointing out cases or sections of legislation and urging the court in a particular direction favourable to their client. At the end of each summation, the lawyer suggests to the judge the appropriate outcome in very specific terms.

The lawyer for the Respondent repeats this process for his or her client. Once both versions are before the judge the three of them may engage in some detailed discussion of the finer points of the law or the facts of the particular case. The judge will sometimes thank the lawyers for their work and adjourn the case indefinitely. The judge will then pack up his or her notes and the evidence and sit down later to figure out what should happen in this particular situation. Rarely will the judge give a decision on the spot. This adjourning indefinitely while a decision is written is called "reserving judgment." It can put the case on hold for several months.

The people involved leave the courtroom and go back to their lives, the lawyers go on to other cases, and the judge goes on to new trials while everyone waits for a decision.

The lawyers may send their clients reporting letters at this stage, providing a detailed synopsis of what happened and what can be expected in the judge's decision. Sometimes, but not always, the bill is enclosed for the work to date.

(v) The Judgment

Just when you thought things had returned to normal, your lawyer will call to say that the "Reasons for Judgment" are available. This means that the judge has written out—usually typed—the reasons why the case has been decided in a particular way. The judge will often trace his or her reasoning, making it clear that he or she has accepted either the Petitioner's or the Respondent's theory of the case. Sometimes the judge develops his or her own theory. (Surprise!) The Reasons are related to but different from the judgment itself. Out of the Reasons the lawyers identify what the judge has actually decided. For example, the Petitioner gets custody, the Respondent gets access on particular terms, the cottage is divided in a particular way, the shares are valued at a certain amount, and so on and so on. These essentials are extracted by the lawyers from the Reasons (which may refer to cases and the law) and typed into a separate judgment which is then approved by the lawyers and a court official. If they cannot agree on what the judge has decided in the Reasons, they arrange an appointment to see the judge and settle the dispute. Once they have arrived at an agreed form for the judgment, it is recorded at the courthouse and becomes an effective judgment.

The lawyers will then usually make an appointment to see the judge to discuss costs—that is, who will pay the winner's costs and to what extent. This is an important aspect of the case because the offers to settle that were made earlier (see Chapter 10) are now compared with the actual judgment. If the loser rejected a favourable offer to settle, the costs can be considerable.

Once the court decides who must pay whom, a "bill of costs" is prepared in which the winning lawyer sends his or her bill to the losing lawyer for approval. If there is a disagreement about the amount it can be settled by consulting a court official for a taxation or assessment. The court official uses a tariff set by the Rules of Court to decide what is a fair bill from the winner to the loser.

Losing a trial of four or more days can be an expensive proposition. Not only must the person pay his or her own lawyer, but that person must pay the winner's lawyer as well. This is known as "a bitter pill."

Someone out there is undoubtedly saying, "Yes ... but if I win, then the loser pays my legal fees and I'm off the hook." Not quite. The tariff I mentioned, the one that controls the amount of the winner's bill, actually gives the winner only about 50 percent of his or her actual expenses of the trial. So while the loser pays part of the winner's bill, the winner still has to pay his or her own lawyer the other half. This is known as "a smaller bitter pill."

APPEALS

Before leaving this area we should deal briefly with appeals. It is not unusual for the lawyers, upon examining the Reasons for Judgment, to discover what they consider to be an error in law by the judge. In other words, the judge decided the case by using an incorrect principle of law or misinterpreting a section of an Act. It is not unheard of for each lawyer to discover a different mistake and develop two or more reasons as suggested grounds for appeal. These will be pointed out to you in the lawyer's reporting letter. The lawyer will often say that he or she has reviewed the judgment and respectfully feels that the judge "erred in finding as a fact that ..." or "erred in interpreting the law...." It amounts to a difference of opinion. The lawyer is suggesting that if he or she took it to a higher court that court would agree with his or her opinion.

Appeals are not free. In fact, they can be very expensive. The cost of a transcript alone, for a trial of several days, can be thousands of dollars. Something very important or valuable must be at stake to even begin to think about an appeal. It should be treated as seriously as your original decision to begin the case, with emphasis on the costs of the appeal and the likelihood of success. The same rules apply to costs, so the loser will pay the winner's costs again if unsuccessful on the appeal.

Appeals do not occur quickly. Depending on the province and level of court to which you are appealing, they can add several months and in some cases more than a year to the litigation. Ask how long it will take.

The first appeal is not necessarily the last. If the appeal court changes the trial judge's decision, the other side may be able to appeal that new decision to an even higher court. If important new legal concepts are involved, the appeals can go all the way to the Supreme Court of Canada.

You can imagine the dismay felt by the clients who appealed a decision to a higher court on the basis that the trial judge had made an error. The appeal court agreed with them and ordered that *a new trial take place*. They had to repeat the entire process. All the witnesses were called again and all the evidence was resubmitted to a new judge.

The only advantage to appeals is that they occasionally do correct decisions that were made improperly, and they often enable the law to be "stretched" a little to offer fairness to a new situation perhaps not contemplated by the law. For example, Rosa Becker's case went all the way to the Supreme Court of Canada but made a significant new interpretation of the law available to thousands of women. It may have resulted in numerous settlements of cases that were working their way through the legal system across Canada. But Rosa herself, of course, did not benefit in any tangible way from her own appeal.

Another small advantage of the appeal process is that there will be minimal involvement by you in the case. The lawyers take over for appeals and clients need not attend the argument of the appeal at the higher court. They will appear before that court with entirely new, fresh paperwork developed specifically for appeals. An appeal may be presented before as many as three judges, at which time the lawyers will debate the correctness of the law as interpreted by the trial judge. Rarely do the appeal judges give their decision on the spot, so yet another "reserved" decision can be expected. The appeal judges will deliver a complete set of Reasons for their decision, just as the trial judge did. These decisions are considered most important by the lawyers and are often published in legal reporting services so that other lawyers are aware of them. (So much for your privacy.) See Chapter 18 for more information on how to find these reported decisions.

CONCLUSIONS

So, do you still want to go to trial? Are you being forced to go to trial by an unreasonable person on the other side? I don't ask such questions glibly, because the first question you must have answered to your complete satisfaction is, Why must I go to trial? At the outset I noted that people go to trial when they have not settled their differences. Why haven't you settled yours?

Consider the following questions once you have answered that one:

1. Have I received a full written opinion about the case and the issues involved? Does the opinion letter discuss the likely time of trial and expected cost? How long will the trial take? Is it a fixed date? Am I available when the trial is scheduled?
2. What is the theory of the case? How will it be presented to the court? Do I understand the structure of the trial? Have I been briefed in the methods of giving evidence? Have I reviewed the transcripts from the examinations for discovery?
3. Which witnesses will be called?
4. Have I executed a new retainer specifically authorizing the lawyer to conduct the trial?
5. What is the likelihood of success?
6. What Offers to Settle have been made? What effect will they have on costs at the end of a trial?
7. How much of a new retainer will I be required to provide in advance of the trial?
8. If successful, will the retainer cover the costs of collecting the judgment?
9. If custody is an issue, what role will my children play in the proceedings?
10. Do I understand the physical setting of the court? Will my lawyer arrange for a tour of the court in advance?
11. Have all the undertakings been fulfilled and have I done my best to locate any missing pieces of evidence?
12. Have I completed updated financial statements?
13. Do I understand the likelihood of adjournments and delays once the trial is scheduled?
14. What happens if I lose?
15. What is the difference between my likely net on the last settlement offer and my likely net at the end of a trial?
16. If custody and access are the issues, have I considered the use of mediation to resolve that particular dispute?
17. And once again, Why am I going to trial?

12

Alternatives to Court— Mediation and Arbitration

It is fair to say that until recently, we in Canada have had a one-dimensional approach to solving family law problems. Our legal system, as you have seen from previous chapters, requires families to solve delicate issues such as custody of children or division of the family home in the same way that responsibility for car accidents, breached contracts or exploding pop bottles is decided. This adversarial process leads only one place—to the courtroom. It is not a creative process. On the contrary, it encourages lawyers to promote one solution for the entire case and then battle to have their vision prevail.

This approach is particularly unsuited to families undergoing a crisis. Like workers and management in labour disputes, family members must continue to deal with each other after the dispute is finally resolved. It was recognized many years ago that relations between labour and business were important enough that special methods were needed to resolve disputes quickly, inexpensively and without burning every bridge in the process. Mediation and arbitration, techniques well known to those in the labour field, are becoming increasingly popular in family law. In this chapter we will examine these two methods of dispute resolution, with special emphasis on mediation.

In mediation the couple facing a family problem flowing out of separation use a skilled third party to assist them in discussing the issue and to reach a mutually satisfactory agreement on a solution. Instead of having a judge impose a solution, the people design their own. There is no limit on the type of issue suited to mediation: Who should have custody? How should access be structured? Where will we live? How can we divide our furniture and other property?

Mediation's approach is different from the adversarial courtroom approach because the mediator encourages the parties to look at the problem from different angles and to develop an understanding of each person's needs and interests. The goal is not to develop two competing positions but to determine whether everyone's interests—especially the children's—can be met through some creative solution. Who is better able to develop such a solution than the parties themselves?

Mediation is voluntary and non-adversarial and works best when a skilled, impartial mediator guides the discussion. Not surprisingly, those who have used mediation note that it provided them with new negotiation skills that permitted them to resolve subsequent disagreements about matters affecting the family. In a nutshell, mediation seems to be faster, less expensive and makes people happier with the agreement, to the point that we find them more likely to comply with it. Sounds great? It has the potential to be the most important development in family law in decades.

Before looking at mediation in more detail we should understand what it is not. It is not marriage counselling, which is designed to help a couple sort out difficulties in their relationship with a view to staying together or easing the emotional strain of ending it. Mediation is also not therapy, which is designed to help an individual sort out a personal, emotional or psychological problem that affects that person and his or her relationships with others. There may be moments when they appear to be working toward the same goal—easing the strain and pain of separation—but they have distinct roles.

Assuming a decision to separate has been made, mediation can offer a family a more humane method of tackling any issue—no matter how big, no matter how small. Its goal is joint planning for the future, not argument over the past.

Mediation has become more popular in Canada over the last decade through a combination of word of mouth and encouragement of its use by legislation. The federal *Divorce Act*, for example, was amended in 1986 to place a positive duty upon lawyers to advise clients of the advisability of negotiating support and custody issues and of the availability of mediation services in their community. This provision has resulted in lawyers encouraging clients to try mediation for these issues.

To assist lawyers in advising clients about the availability of these services, the federal Department of Justice has assembled a directory of mediators across the country. At the end of this chapter I have provided a list of all the mediation associations in Canada by province.

Provincial laws also encourage the use of mediation. For example, section 11 of Saskatchewan's new *Children's Law Act* (in force as of December 1990) now mirrors the *Divorce Act* and requires lawyers involved in custody and access disputes governed by provincial law (you will recall that this happens when the couple is not seeking a divorce but still needs help with custody matters) to inform their clients about mediation facilities that might be able to assist in negotiating a solution. As in the case of the *Divorce Act*, the lawyer must certify that he or she has complied with this requirement.

Ontario's provincial family laws, the *Children's Law Reform Act* and the *Family Law Act, 1986*, do not require lawyers specifically to inform clients about mediation but they do facilitate the use of mediation by allowing the court to order the parties to use it when they both consent. (These provisions are contained in section 31 of the *Children's Law Reform Act* and section 2 of the *Family Law Act, 1986*.)

Almost every province has such a provision in its provincial family laws, and every province is governed by the *Divorce Act*. So, at the very least, husbands and wives who are divorcing and need assistance with custody and access will have mediation drawn to their attention.

Let's look more closely at the actual mediation process.

Family mediators are not regulated in any way by either federal or provincial legislation. There are national and provincial associations, however, which organize the membership through voluntary guidelines, accreditation levels, continuing education and so on. There is no requirement that a mediator join these associations prior to offering services to the public, so you must be cautious in selecting a mediator who is experienced and qualified.

An ongoing debate concerns whether mediators need any special educational background in order to assist a family with a problem. Some "mediators" seem to have no other qualification than having gone through a bad divorce themselves. They may be empathetic but they are not qualified. Many of the best family mediators are lawyers, social workers (M.S.W.) or psychologists. Near the end of this section we will look at how to find a good mediator, but for now you should understand that the neutral third party who will conduct the mediation should be a qualified professional who brings some special skills to the dispute resolution process.

The mediator's role includes a variety of functions and obligations. He or she must:

- be impartial: both of you are clients
- control the mediation; the mediator will act more as a chairperson than anything else and will never impose a decision
- keep the discussion on track
- work out a schedule for the meetings
- co-ordinate the sharing of information between the couple (such as financial information related to support)
- keep the process confidential
- be vigilant to ensure that you get help from other professionals as needed (therapists, accountants)
- be careful to act only as a mediator and not, for example, give legal advice (if he or she is also a lawyer) or psychiatric advice (if also a doctor)
- promote co-operation by helping to build good-will and reducing tension
- help you to develop your own negotiating skills
- ensure that domestic violence is not present
- compensate for subtle differences in the bargaining positions and abilities of the parties
- stay in touch with your respective lawyers to keep them up-to-date on developments.

Within these general parameters, the mediator leads the couple through the mediation process.

Do mediators exclude the need for lawyers? In a word—no. Even if the mediator you have selected is also a lawyer you should still each have your own independent legal advice from your own individual lawyers. The mediator is not there to provide legal advice. He or she facilitates the discussion and helps discover solutions and options. Your lawyer (so carefully selected at the outset, remember?) is there to make sure you understand your rights and obligations under federal and provincial law. He or she will also advise you on the merits of any agreement reached with the help of the mediator. It has been said that people negotiate "in the shadow of the law." This means that people should negotiate a settlement based in part on what would happen if the matter went to court. Lawyers make sure that a fair deal is achieved, one that will hold up over time.

The lawyer's role, therefore, also includes a number of functions and obligations. He or she must:

- meet the obligations imposed by the *Divorce Act* and, in some cases, provincial law with respect to available mediation services
- keep up-to-date on qualified mediators and their professional qualifications and accreditation
- explain to clients the relative advantages and disadvantages of mediation
- be cautious to ensure that clients unable to negotiate effectively are not placed at an unfair disadvantage in negotiation with their spouse
- stay in close contact with the mediator and client once mediation begins
- be careful not to undermine the mediator's work; the lawyer must scrutinize the agreement to protect the client, but also protect the consensus that was achieved.

As you can see, the lawyer and mediator must work together closely to ensure a fair and lasting agreement. You may recall my suggestion about retaining a lawyer who is well versed in the area of mediation.

Assuming you have found a mediator, perhaps through a recommendation from your family lawyer, and both you and your spouse are willing to give mediation a try, the mediation process will generally move through three or four stages: identifying the issues, developing options and choices, making choices, developing the agreement and recording it after receiving legal advice on its fairness.

At the outset, the mediator will begin by helping you identify and list the issues which need to be resolved. This is an important "sorting out" phase. Once they have been sorted, the mediator may suggest tackling them in a particular order.

The mediator will also ask whether you would like to have the mediation "open" or "closed." The choice is yours and it is an important one. You may wish to discuss it with your lawyer before deciding, since the decision affects the use to which things said during mediation can be put later in court. If the mediation is open, then statements made in mediation may be admissible later in court if the mediation fails to achieve an agreement. Some people feel that if the mediation is open the people using it will be less willing to speak openly—something that is essential.

Closed mediation is the opposite: nothing said in the sessions is capable of being used in court—it is all confidential (unless, of course, it relates to evidence of child abuse, which provincial law requires be reported).

Mediators report that open mediation does not seem to inhibit the discussions and that people speak freely regardless of whether it is open or closed. Consider the choice carefully and discuss it with your lawyer and spouse.

One case I am aware of involved a husband and wife who were separating because the husband had developed a relationship with a woman he met through a new church he had joined. There were two children involved, boys aged seven and ten, and they were justifiably anxious about what was happening. The father wanted joint custody of the boys while the mother, who was quite angry, felt she should have sole custody. (See Chapter 7, "The Children," for an explanation of these terms.) To complicate matters, the father wanted the boys to convert to his new faith, while the mother vigorously opposed any further disruption in their lives. Child support was of course linked to custody. The mother wanted to move to her home town to be nearer her family. Unfortunately, that was two thousand miles away and the father opposed any move away from his good job and new church. A tough, but not unusual, problem.

The mediator helped this husband and wife to organize these issues into a logical agenda that could be discussed without losing sight of the children's interests. That is exactly where they began, with a discussion of past child-care routines and parenting for the boys. The husband's new faith was explored so that the wife understood his new needs. The need for a move was examined, again with the focus on the children and their existing routine.

They agreed to postpone the move for the time being and entered into a joint custody arrangement. This freed the mother to retrain to develop job skills with support from the husband. The boys continued in their regular church but received some exposure to the father's faith with a view to letting them make their own decision further down the road. And so step by step the mediation progressed.

The couple learned that it is possible to settle the problems without having one win and the other lose. The mediator kept track of the developing agreement and prepared a written memorandum of the final decision. The mediator's memorandum formed the basis of a more detailed separation agreement which was prepared by the lawyers in consultation with the couple and the mediator.

Why, you may ask, did the couple not just sign the agreement prepared by the mediator? This is because often there are technical matters that the lawyers need to build around the clients' basic agreement. The mediator may not have discussed with the couple matters such as the precise wording of releases concerning property claims, and so on.

The lawyers will ensure that the agreement is legally correct, fair and what you want.

The advantages of mediation seem clear:

- You make the decisions, not the court.
- The discussions are private and confidential.
- The process is faster than waiting for court dates.
- The solution is tailor-made for your circumstances.
- It can be less expensive than going to court.
- The agreement can be renegotiated if circumstances change.
- The process can teach you new negotiating skills that will help resolve disputes in the future.
- You still have the benefit of a lawyer scrutinizing your agreement to ensure fairness and legality.
- It is a dispute resolution method that leaves its users feeling better about themselves and happy about their agreement.

Having said that mediation holds great potential for families that are separating, I must add that it is not for everyone. It is a process suited to people who are in a relatively equal negotiating position. If one spouse is at a clear disadvantage, mediation will not produce a fair result.

We examined domestic violence early in this book. Women who come from homes where there has been violence are unlikely to be able to negotiate with the spouse who has beaten or harassed them. So violence that puts one spouse in fear of the other and unable to negotiate should be a decisive argument against using mediation.

Similarly, if for any reason one spouse does not wish to mediate, it is not the appropriate method of dispute resolution. It must be voluntary and undertaken in good faith.

Finally, where child abuse is present the mediator will be unable to honour the traditional need for confidentiality. All provinces require persons learning of child abuse to report it to authorities so that an intervention can be made to protect the child.

A brief word should be said about those who oppose mediation in family law. Some women's groups, some feminists and related groups oppose the use of mediation in family law. They argue that mediators promote joint custody of children, that mediation is a method of taking women out of the public court system to deprive them of hard-earned rights in private, and that many women are in an inherently weak bargaining position vis-à-vis their spouses (in many cases as a result of violence). Their concerns about violence are legitimate; great strides have been made to get the message out that mediation is not suited to those rendered incapable of bargaining as a result of violence in the home. But to suggest that mediation not be available for those who wish to use it and are capable of negotiating is, I believe, very unfair. It would deprive many men and women of a most humane method of solving family problems.

Not every province delivers mediation services in the same way. Some provinces have made publicly funded mediation services available for free. Other provinces and territories only have private mediation services on a fee-for-service basis paid in full by the parties. Still others have a combination of free public services and private mediators.

In Quebec, for example, free mediation services are available in Montreal and Quebec City. In Montreal the mediation is comprehensive, that is, available for all issues the family faces. In Quebec City the service is there to mediate only issues relating to the children. To use the service the couple simply make an appointment at the courthouse. In addition, couples are free to use private mediators at their own expense.

In Ontario there is a mix of public and private. Toronto has some public services available. Hamilton is the site of an important pilot project for mediation that was undertaken recently. This project implements the recommendations of the Ontario Attorney General's Advisory Committee on Mediation in Family Law (which I had the pleasure of chairing for a little over a year). This service will provide free mediation services for the community before, during and after legal proceedings have been commenced. Other provinces will be watching this project closely to see mediation's full potential in family law.

The Ontario Legal Aid program will now provide a legal aid certificate to pay for the cost of mediation services in family law cases. The client must still qualify for legal aid in the normal way. To find out whether the cost of mediation is covered, contact your provincial legal aid plan. (You can find the list of addresses for legal aid offices mid-way through Chapter 3.)

While mediation is generally available in each province, it is difficult to say community by community whether a qualified and experienced mediator is close at hand. You have a couple of options when searching for a mediator. First and foremost, if you have selected a good family law lawyer he or she should have experience with local mediators. Lawyers should have a list of three or four from whom you can choose, and will likely provide a recommendation.

You should ask your friends for suggestions. Word of mouth is a valuable recommendation if it is based on personal experience. Stay away from the Yellow Pages.

Towards the end of this chapter I have set out a list of provincial mediation associations that would be happy to assist you in finding a mediator suited to your needs. It is important to find someone that both you and your spouse are happy with.

When you finally have a list of names to pick from and are meeting with mediators do not hesitate to ask probing questions about the mediator's background, qualifications, experience and specialties. Some mediators do not do financial matters, some will only do custody and access, while still others prefer to do comprehensive mediation, tackling all the issues facing the family. Remember, the mediator is also anxious to see if the "chemistry" is right, so take full advantage of the meeting, which is often free of charge.

You will want to discuss costs again. Most mediators charge an hourly rate ranging between $50 and $150. The cost is often much less than a lawyer's fee because the process is faster and less protracted by paperwork and court dates. Most mediators will have an agreement with the couple at the outset about who will pay, how, and how much.

Usually the cost is split equally and billed directly to the clients. In some cases the mediator may send the bill on to the lawyers who in turn pass it on to the clients.

I recommend spending as much thought hiring the mediator as you did hiring the lawyer (or at least as much as I hope you did!).

The following questions should help you decide about mediation and the mediator for you.

1. Do I understand the purpose of mediation?
2. Can I distinguish it from marriage counselling and personal therapy?
3. Would I participate willingly and in good faith?
4. Am I capable of negotiating with my spouse?
5. Has there been violence between my spouse and me that would prevent me from negotiating effectively?
6. Has there been child abuse in my home?
7. Does my lawyer feel I am suited to mediation? Is he or she supportive?
8. Will I use an independent lawyer to double-check the agreement and advise me during negotiations?
9. Will the mediation be open or closed?
10. Are public (free) facilities available?
11. Will legal aid cover the mediation?
12. Is the mediator qualified and experienced? What training has he or she had?
13. Is the mediator a member of a mediation association?
14. Does the mediator have a specialty?
15. What are the hourly rate and billing arrangements?
16. Will the mediator stay in contact with the lawyers and report to them as well as me?
17. Will the mediator prepare a memorandum of understanding of any agreement reached and work with the lawyer to see it implemented in a separation agreement?
18. What kind of schedule does the mediator propose for meetings?
19. What references do I have for this mediator?
20. Have I contacted the provincial mediation association?
21. Do I like the mediator? Does the chemistry feel right?

CANADIAN MEDIATION ASSOCIATIONS

Mediation Development Association of British Columbia
P. O. Box 3381
Vancouver, British Columbia V6B 3Y4
(604) 261-9429

Alberta Family Mediation Society
405 - 918 - 16th Ave. N.W.
Calgary, Alberta T2M 0K3
(403) 284-3351

Family Mediation Saskatchewan
c/o 5th Ave. Family Mediation Clinic
215 5th Ave.
North Saskatoon, Saskatchewan S7K 2P2
(306) 933-6104

Family Mediation Manitoba
P. O. Box 2369
Winnipeg, Manitoba R3C 4A6
(204) 949-1312

Ontario Association for Family Mediation
c/o 123 Woolwich St., 2nd Floor
Guelph, Ontario N1H 3V1
(416) 366-3776

Association de Médiation Familiale du Québec
C.P. 354
Place d'Armes
Montréal, PQ H2Y 3H1
(514) 842-9225

Family Mediation New Brunswick
222 Chamin Mountain Road
Moncton, New Brunswick E1E 1V8
(506) 856-2305

Nova Scotia Association for Divorce and Family Mediation
P. O. Box 3154
South Halifax, Nova Scotia B3J 3H5
(902) 494-3760

Family Mediation Association
c/o Family Court, P. O. Box 2290
Charlottetown, P.E.I. C1A 8C1
(902) 892-7667

Family Mediation Newfoundland and Labrador
c/o Unified Family Court
21 Kings Bridge Road
St. John's, Newfoundland A1C 3K4
(709) 753-5873

Yukon Family Mediation Association
c/o Yukon Public Legal Education
Yukon College, P. O. Box 2799
Whitehorse, Yukon Territory Y1A 5K4
(403) 667-5797

Family Mediation Association of the Northwest Territories
P. O. Box 262
Yellowknife, N.W.T. X1A 2N2
(403) 873-3770

ARBITRATION

A few words should be added about arbitration, which has been available for hundreds of years in commercial matters but has only recently found its way into family law. It is another alternative to going to court and is not unlike the use of a private judge. The parties select a private individual, often an experienced lawyer or a retired judge, to hear their dispute in private. After the hearing the arbitrator renders a decision, sometimes within thirty days.

Arbitration is attractive for a variety of reasons. It is completely private. The public and press (if that is a concern) do not have access to your private affairs. It can be significantly faster and more predictable than the public courts, which are busy and subject to delays such as summer breaks, adjournments and other interferences.

Proponents of arbitration also point to the desirability of being able to select the "judge" and to be able to have someone preside who is truly interested in a family law matter. This is not the case in the public courts where judges are assigned to all sorts of cases, family law being about the least popular. Many judges are as devoted to family law cases as any other, but many are not and assignments can be quite random.

The expense of arbitration is its weakness. The parties are still paying for two lawyers, and now pay the judge on top of it. In the public courts the judge is "free"—tax dollars pay the judge's salary. A private judge can cost between $2,000 and $3,000 per day for each day of a hearing. This cost is not covered by legal aid and must be shared by the parties themselves. But for those who can afford it, the privacy and speed of the arbitration process can be attractive.

13

Enforcing Family
Law Orders

Obtaining a court order for custody, access, support, property division or any other aspect of family law is one thing—enforcing the order can be another experience altogether. You cannot assume that the other person will simply abide by the order of the court. Remember, that person may have "lost" in court; this order is an unwanted imposition. When faced with a spouse who refuses to comply, the spouse with the order may wonder, after having gone through all the expense and tension, what was the point of the court proceeding.

In this chapter we will examine each of the family orders from the perspective of enforcement.

CUSTODY ENFORCEMENT

In the late 1970s a Mr. Kosowan and his wife were living in Manitoba with their five children. One day after the entire family and their belongings had been loaded into the family van, Mr. Kosowan suggested to his wife that she go to the store for some last-minute groceries. When she returned, her husband and children were gone. He eventually left Canada for the United States and only later returned to live in Quebec, having told the children that their mother had died.

The lengths to which people will go to hurt each other seem to know no limit. Mrs. Kosowan did not even have a court order which could be enforced on her behalf. Many months later, Mr. Kosowan was arrested and returned to Manitoba, charged with having abducted his own children. Through a quirk in the law that has since been amended, he was never convicted because Mrs. Kosowan did not have a custody order and he, as a parent, could not therefore be considered to have abducted his own children.

Canadian criminal law, in the form of both the Canadian Criminal Code and the civil law, provides remedies for the enforcement of custody orders. The prime goal of these remedies is the location and return of the child. Punishment of the abductor is a secondary consideration.

Criminal Law Custody Enforcement

It is a criminal offence in every part of Canada to abduct a child who is under the age of fourteen and who is the subject of a custody order. If the child is taken from the custodial parent with the intention to deprive that parent of the child, then the abducting person (95 percent of abductions are by non-custodial parents) may be found guilty and punished with up to ten years in jail.

This is the case whether the parent has a custody order or not, except that when the parent does not have a custody order charges cannot be laid unless the Attorney General of the province gives his or her permission.

When the child is the subject of a custody order it can be either a sole custody order or a joint custody order. The court will look at the terms of the order and decide whether there was an intention to deprive the other parent of custody at a time when that parent was entitled to it.

In the Kosowan case, where the mother did not have a custody order when the father abducted the children, he was not convicted. At the time the case came to court, the Canadian Criminal Code did not apply to situations where no custody order had been made. However, in response to the outcome of that case the Canadian Criminal Code was amended to cover the situation where no order had yet been made but one parent intended to deprive the other of the child.

A "no order" situation can arise in cases like Kosowan, where the parents simply separate; it can arise where they have separated and agree that the child will live with one of them, but they never obtain a order from the court; and finally, it can apply to situations where there is a court order for custody but it was not made by a Canadian court. A Wisconsin father who abducted his children to Winnipeg after the Wisconsin court had ordered that the mother should have custody was charged under this part of the Canadian Criminal Code and the children were returned to their mother. Again, these children had been told that their mother was dead. We can only imagine the consequences for them upon learning the truth.

If the custody order was made by a Canadian court it can be enforced immediately anywhere in Canada through the abduction provisions of the Canadian Criminal Code. However, it should be noted that if caught, the abducting parent may have a couple of defences available. First, no conviction will be obtained where the person with custody consented to the child's being removed by the other person. It is not uncommon for parents to live in direct contravention of the court's custody order. In other words, the order may say that the mother is to have custody, but the child actually lives with the father. This could happen if circumstances change and, for example, the mother became ill and could not care for the child. There may have been little reason at the time to amend the court order if the intention was that the child would eventually return to the mother's custody. However, if the father decided to move out of the province the mother would have difficulty alleging that the child was being abducted if she had originally consented to the child's being in the father's custody.

It is also a defence to an abduction charge if the child was taken to protect him or her from "imminent harm." This situation would arise where the non-custodial parent discovers that the custodial parent is mistreating the child. I heard of a case where the father had custody but lost his job and began to drink heavily. He could not care for the child, and the mother refused to return the child after an access visit for fear that the child might meet with harm. No abduction conviction would be likely in such a situation.

It is, however, no defence to a charge of abduction that the child consented or suggested that the change in custody take place.

The benefit of the Criminal Code provisions is that once a charge is laid a Canada-wide warrant for the abductor's arrest will be issued to all police forces. The criminal enforcement route is faster that the civil law, which is critical when the person may be attempting to flee the jurisdiction.

Many provinces have adopted a standard protocol for responding to an abduction of a child once the parent has contacted the police (which should be done immediately). In most if not all cases, the custodial parent will require a lawyer's assistance. A necessary starting point is, of course, the custody order itself. A good, certified (if possible) copy of the order should be kept in a safe, accessible place at all times. One of the issues addressed in the standard protocol concerns domestic violence. How can the police and a Crown Attorney (who would be called upon to lay the charges) distinguish between an abduction and the case of a parent who is fleeing domestic violence and is simply taking the children with her? Such determinations are made on a case-by-case basis.

Even if the abducting parent is located with the child and criminal charges are laid, it can be difficult to arrange the return of the child. The warrant only brings the abductor back. It is often necessary to involve the local child-care or child-protection agencies which can take custody of the child until the custodial parent or his or her designate can arrive. The best solution, of course, is for the police to co-ordinate their arrest of the abductor with the presence of the custodial parent.

Parents faced with abductions should also contact ChildFind (Canada) at 1-800-387-7962. It is a non-profit organization which locates missing and abducted children, and it will assist in reuniting the child and the custodial parent. ChildFind has offices in British Columbia, Alberta, Saskatchewan, Manitoba, Ontario, Nova Scotia, P.E.I. and New Brunswick.

Via Rail will provide free transportation to children who are being reunited with their parents if the parents cannot afford the cost of the transportation. However, Via Rail will only respond to a request from ChildFind. Despite Via Rail's declining network, their offer is a generous one and should be taken advantage of if at all possible.

Civil Justice Enforcement of Custody Orders

The civil justice system will also attempt to respond to a parental child abduction in its own special way. Not every case is a clear-cut abduction, and in some circumstances the custody order simply needs to be enforced in another jurisdiction. The provinces (except Quebec) and territories have all passed laws to speed enforcement of each other's custody orders. These laws attempt to prevent the re-hearing of custody cases in their own jurisdiction. The goal is to enforce, with minimal fuss, the other province's custody orders and return the child to the jurisdiction that made the order. One province enforces the other province's orders as if they were its own. This discourages the "abducting parent" from trying to have the other province's order reconsidered in the new province. There are exceptions, of course. If the court thinks the first order was made by a jurisdiction to which the child did not have a strong connection, or if everybody is now present in a new jurisdiction and a review is appropriate, the court may reconsider the whole matter of custody.

Also, if the child might meet with harm if the custody order were enforced, then the court may choose to substitute its own order for the other province's order.

Only Nova Scotia requires "reciprocity" before it will enforce another province's custody order. In other words, "We'll enforce yours if you enforce ours." Everywhere else the courts simply enforce the other province's order without conditions.

The two primary considerations in a civil enforcement case are the child's welfare and the fair and proper administration of justice. Each province has attempted to adopt rules and procedures that facilitate the achievement of these two goals. For example, all Canadian provinces have implemented the Hague Convention on the Civil Aspects of International Child Abduction. This Convention, which has been accepted by many countries, attempts on an international scale to secure the prompt return of children wrongfully removed to, or retained in, a country that has signed the Convention. It also attempts to ensure that rights of custody or access under the law of a country are respected by other countries. It applies to children who are under the age of sixteen years.

The following is a summary of major jurisdictions and their position on the Hague Convention on the Civil Aspects of International Child Abduction:

1. Contracting States (by ratification or accession)

(A contracting state will enforce a custody order when a child has been abducted.)

State	Entry into Force for Canada
Australia	January 1, 1987
Austria	October 1, 1988
Belize	September 1, 1989
Canada	December 1, 1983
British Columbia	December 1, 1983

Alberta	February 1, 1987
Saskatchewan	November 1, 1986
Manitoba	December 1, 1983
Ontario	December 1, 1983
Quebec	January 1, 1985
New Brunswick	December 1, 1983
Nova Scotia	May 1, 1984
Prince Edward Island	May 1, 1986
Newfoundland	October 1, 1984
Yukon	February 1, 1985
Northwest Territories	April 1, 1988
Federal Republic of Germany	December 1, 1990
France	December 1, 1983
Hungary	April 1, 1988
Luxembourg	January 1, 1987
Netherlands	September 1, 1990
Norway	April 1, 1989
Portugal	December 1, 1983
Spain	September 1, 1987
Sweden	June 1, 1989
Switzerland	January 1, 1984
United Kingdom (England, Wales, Northern Ireland and Scotland)	August 1, 1986
United States (Extends to Puerto Rico, Guam, U.S. Virgin Islands, American Samoa and Northern Marianas)	July 1, 1988

2. Signatories

(If a country has signed but not yet ratified the Convention, it is not a contracting state and the Convention is not applicable.)

The following countries do *not* offer enforcement of the Hague Convention:

Belgium
Greece
Ireland
Italy

3. Countries which are not yet contracting or signatories

Argentina	Japan
Czechoslovakia	Surinam
Denmark	Turkey
Egypt	Venezuela
Finland	Yugoslavia
Israel	

Of special note is Ontario's *Support and Custody Orders Enforcement Act, 1985,* which offers parents assistance with the enforcement of child custody orders and agreements. The Support and Custody Enforcement Office treats custody problems in three different categories: minor overholding (where the non-custodial parent is late returning a child), major overholding (where the non-custodial parent is very late in returning the children), and abductions (where it is known to be an abduction or is likely, regardless of whether the ultimate location of the children is known). The Enforcement Office after completing a "Custody Inquiry Report" will co-ordinate the civil and criminal enforcement of the order, link up with other enforcement agencies, and cause to be undertaken a search for information that may help to track down the abductor. Basically, everything a lawyer would do is done by the Enforcement Office, including putting the custodial parent in touch with ChildFind.

The form presented here is Support and Custody Orders Enforcement's "Custody Enquiry Report." It is reproduced here because, regardless of the province in which you may need to enforce a custody order, it will be necessary for you to provide this information in the event of an abduction.

Support and Custody Enforcement Program
CUSTODY ENQUIRY REPORT

Date: _____

Caller: _____ Phone Number: _____

Address: _____

1. Do you have an order? _____

2. Is the order/agreement filed with the director? _____
   _____

3. Are there any court proceedings scheduled at this time?_____
   _____

4. What are the terms of the order? _____
   _____

5. To the best of your knowledge, have any other court orders been granted with respect to the child? _____

6. Have any specific informal arrangements been made with respect to the custody of, or access to, the child? _____
   _____

7. How long has the child been missing? _____
   _____

8. Do you know where the child is? _____
   _____

9. When did the child leave and when was he/she supposed to be returned? _____

10. What were the intended plans, i.e., what were the non-custodial parent and child going to be doing or where were they going? _____
    _____

11. Have you made inquiries as to where the child is? _____
    _____

12. Have you contacted the police? _____
13. Have you contacted a lawyer? _____
14. Who was the lawyer who represented you at the time the court order was obtained? _____
15. Is this the first time the child has been taken and not returned? _____
    _____
16. If no, how many times? _____
17. By whom? _____
18. Who has a passport for the child? _____
    _____
19. Do you have reason to believe that the non-custodial parent is about to leave? _____
20. What is the child's age (over 12, child's view is relevant)? _____
    _____
21. Does the child have any special medical needs? _____
    _____
22. Is the child where he/she is supposed to be; i.e., has the child's usual routine been disrupted, e.g., is the child attending school? _____
    _____
23. How long has the non-custodial parent lived where he/she is presently living? _____
    _____
24. Have you and the non-custodial parent had a fight or disagreement recently?_____
    _____
25. Do you perceive that the child is in danger? _____
    _____
26. Do you have a recent photograph of the child? _____
    _____
27. Is there a propensity for violence (alcohol or drug abuse) by the non-custodial parent? _____
    _____
28. Names and Birthdates of the Children
    Name:_____ D.O.B. _____
    Name:_____ D.O.B. _____
    Name:_____ D.O.B. _____
29. Have any charges been laid against your spouse? _____
    Date   Charge   Prov/State who issued
    _____
30. Non-custodial Parent
    Name:_____ D.O.B. _____
    Address: _____
    _____
    Previous names (alias): _____
    Occupation:_____Vehicle: _____
    Driver lic. # _____
    Citizenship/Passport: _____
    Lic. plate:_____

Friends: _____

If you have an Ontario custody order and wish to enforce it in Ontario, complete the Support and Custody Orders Enforcement filing package which is available free of charge from any Support and Custody Orders Enforcement Office.

More on Abductions

If faced with the abduction of a child, consider the following:

- It may be necessary to hire a private investigator to locate the child. They can be very effective and often have sources of information available to them that others do not. In some provinces legal aid will pay for the cost of the private investigator if the need for one is reasonable in the circumstances.
- Provincial law often provides for an order requiring others to assist in the search for a child. This can enlist the help of other enforcement agencies such as a local sheriff's office.
- It is a criminal offence to obtain a Canadian passport falsely listing a child as one's own contrary to a custody order. Sometimes a parent will forge the custodial parent's signature in order to spirit the child out of the country. The penalty for such an offence is two years in jail.
- While the custodial parent may be able to recover costs of locating and recovering the child, he or she cannot sue for damages for emotional distress that may have been suffered as a result of the abduction.
- The federal government has enacted the *Family Orders and Agreements Enforcement Assistance Act, 1986,* which will help a custodial parent trace an abducted child through the federal information banks. However, private individuals have no direct access and a provincial enforcement agency must request the information. This is done for reasons of confidentiality.

One final word about child abduction, a topic I raise with great reservation. It concerns the issue of "self-help" or "kidnapping back." The whole thrust of legal changes in this area of family law has been to discourage kidnapping, but what does a parent do when faced with an opportunity to snatch a child he or she is rightfully entitled to by a custody order? Lawyers are naturally reluctant to discuss this option with their clients, but if all else fails and to have the child back would undoubtedly fulfil the child's best interests, "self-help" or "kidnapping back" must be given serious consideration.

This is as good an opportunity as any to provide advice to parents who have considered abducting their own children. First, as praiseworthy as you may think your motives are, the courts will take an extremely dim view of the abduction. If caught—and there is a strong likelihood that you will be caught—the court will be under great pressure to make an example of you to discourage other parents from carrying out similar abductions. Few people will see you as a martyr if you are imprisoned for abducting your own children.

Secondly, barring some life-threatening situation, it is next to impossible to characterize the abduction as being in your child's best interest. Robbing a child of the other parent can be catastrophic. Lying about the other parent's death or whereabouts will seriously undermine your credibility and the child's confidence in people in authority. Abduction is very rarely a realistic option.

ACCESS ENFORCEMENT

The news with respect to access enforcement is mostly bad. To begin with, most non-custodial parents have orders that entitle them to "reasonable," "liberal" or "generous" access. When access is denied these terms are virtually impossible to enforce. The parent holding such an order will be required to return to court to have the access converted into something more specific.

Once the specific access is denied the non-custodial parent is in a position to try to enforce the order.

When access is denied, the non-custodial parent has one remedy—that is to request a finding of contempt of court against the custodial parent. This means that the non-custodial parent must convince the court that the denial of access is a wilful interference with the non-custodial parent's entitlement to access.

The police will rarely, if ever, assist with the enforcement of an access order knowing that there are civil remedies available for the enforcement of the order.

In a recent court decision in British Columbia, however, a father who had a custody order concerning his son was convicted of child abduction under the Criminal Code when he deprived the boy's mother of her access rights. The father had moved to Toronto in search of work and took his son with him. The case is unusual, but may set a precedent for future situations where one parent denies another parent access to a child.

The standard of proof required on a contempt hearing is higher than in normal civil proceedings. The non-custodial parent must prove the wilful denial beyond a reasonable doubt. If successful, the court has two options available to it—jail or a fine for the custodial parent. Neither is appropriate in most cases, since the fine will only deprive the family of much-needed money and the jail sentence is often out of proportion to the access denial itself. The result is that neither penalty is imposed and the access denial goes unpunished. In some provinces (such as Manitoba and Ontario) the court has permitted custodial parents to avoid punishment for contempt by giving them an opportunity to purge their contempt through the provision of "makeup time" with the child. Makeup time involves making up for the time that was lost by simply giving it back on another occasion. If this is done, the contempt is ignored and no penalty is imposed.

However, with a few exceptions, access enforcement is not effective in Canada. The contempt power is slow, expensive (one motion can cost as much as $3,000) and burdensome, and those who use it must seek penalties the court is reluctant to impose.

Saskatchewan and Newfoundland have enacted an access enforcement procedure developed in Ontario. This procedure gives the non-custodial parent quick access to court when access is denied. Once there, if the court agrees that access was denied without reason, it can order that the time lost be given back, that the non-custodial parent be reimbursed for expenses, that mediation be explored if the parties consent or that supervision of the access take place. If these remedies fail, the court could then turn to the use of its contempt power.

Manitoba has developed a unique scheme entitled the "Access Assistance Program." This child-oriented program assists parents in resolving disputes over access. The counsellors will assess the family's needs and help them to develop an access plan that can work. The service is voluntary, but if access does not occur as outlined in a specific court order and the counsellors are of an opinion that the access should occur, the matter is then referred to a lawyer for enforcement. The enforcement can take the form of seeking a contempt order.

Ontario enacted in 1989 the access enforcement method now in place in Saskatchewan and Newfoundland. This procedure was approved by both the Federal/Provincial/Territorial Committee on Family Law Policy and the Uniform Law Conference of Canada. However, the law was never proclaimed in Ontario due to pressure from women's groups, lawyers, shelters for battered women and other groups. The area is under review.

Two unfortunate consequences of poor access enforcement concern child support and custody order compliance. The courts of three Canadian provinces have now made orders suspending child support orders until access orders are complied with. In these cases, the court, frustrated by a custodial parent's refusal to permit access, orders the non-custodial parent not to pay child support. This, of course, is a double punishment for the child. Poor access enforcement has long been an excuse used by non-custodial parents for the non-payment of support. This connection may become stronger as non-custodial parents turn to support withholding as a means of access enforcement.

The other issue that is more difficult to assess is custody order compliance. There is little or no research available on why non-custodial parents abduct their children. Some theorize that it is an act of anger designed to punish the custodial parent for his or her perceived failings in the relationship. There is no doubt that it is harmful to the child; a non-custodial parent is hard pressed to justify any abduction of a child. Some people are now asking whether poor access enforcement influences the non-custodial parent's decision to abduct the children. In doing so, they note that parents who are satisfied with access are not likely to abduct. Good access enforcement provisions in provincial laws certainly would not hurt the situation.

Those faced with access denial should not withhold support from the family unless a court has so ordered. Similarly, those with custody should not withhold access because support has not been paid. Consider the following:

- Avoid access orders that provide only for "reasonable/liberal" or "generous" access. Have an access entitlement specified, right down to the days, times and specific holidays to which you and the child are entitled. The parents can always agree to more access, but at the very least set out a minimum amount of access for reasons of certainty.
- Consider calling the arrangement "joint custody" rather than "access" if the access is extensive. The provisions can be the same but the change in terminology can result in easier enforcement, should difficulties arise.

Another concern is with respect to the custodial parent's entitlement to access enforcement. What can be done about the non-custodial parent who does not come to see the child in accordance with the terms of an order made by the court? There are many parents who are entitled to see their children, many children who are entitled to see parents and many courts that have decided that such access is in the child's best interest. Yet these parents do not exercise their right to time with the child. A part of the remedy developed in Ontario and in place in Manitoba, Saskatchewan and Newfoundland assists custodial parents and children to see the non-custodial parent who does not visit. If the court has ordered a visit and the person does not use it, then the court can order reimbursement of expenses incurred as a result of the failure to exercise the access, impose supervision on the access or, if the parties consent, order them into mediation. This can be important in the situation where a custodial parent has planned a ("well-earned") two-week vacation and the non-custodial parent cancels his or her scheduled summer access at the last minute. In such a case, with this new remedy, the court could order reimbursement of the expenses incurred by the custodial parent.

As you can see, the enforcement of access orders is a difficult undertaking, to say the least. Let's now take a look at an area of enforcement that has seen a great investment of time, energy and money yet has still yielded little compliance—support enforcement.

SUPPORT ENFORCEMENT

In a word? Pitiful. Compliance with support orders is a relatively rare event in many provinces. Numerous studies have been done which suggest that non-payment of support orders ranges from 50 to 80 percent. Non-payment includes paying the order late, not paying the full amount or not paying the order at all. A quarter to one-third of all support payors *never make any court ordered payments*. The consequences this has for the family awaiting the support can be overwhelming. As tens of thousands of marriages break down every year and tens of thousands of new single-parent families, usually headed by women, are formed, nearly 60 percent of them live below the poverty line.

So why don't they pay? Studies suggest it has nothing to do with their ability to pay. One study found that 80 percent of separated or divorced spouses had a disposable income sufficient to discharge their obligations to their spouse and child. So why don't they pay? It would seem that they do not pay because they do not have to pay. Virtually all provinces and territorial governments, with support from the federal government through complementary legislation, have established "support enforcement programs." These programs have been established at a cost of tens of millions of dollars to provide support creditors (by "support creditor" in this chapter I mean a spouse who is awaiting either spousal support or child support, and by "support debtor" I mean the person who is supposed to be paying either the spousal support or the child support) with free enforcement of their orders. The governments have an obvious stake in this service, because those who do not receive support tend to rely on public assistance at a cost of tens of millions of dollars to taxpayers. The justice system is also drawn into disrepute when its orders are considered unenforceable by both husbands and wives.

Before examining some of the individual features of the provincial and territorial services, we should consider the techniques the services themselves use to enforce support orders. These techniques may vary slightly from province to province but they are all basically the same.

An order of support is most often an order for the monthly payment of an amount of money. We saw in Chapter 8 how that amount is calculated; you may wish to take a moment to review that chapter. It is important to note, however, that some provinces define "support order" to include many things other than money, for the purpose of enforcement. Ontario, for example, has the most comprehensive definition in its support and custody orders enforcement legislation. The definition includes exclusive possession of the matrimonial home, repairs, maintenance, legal costs and even the irrevocable designation of a life insurance policy in favour of a spouse or child. We are most concerned, however, with the monthly support payment which is treated by the justice system like other money debts. It can be collected in the same way that a small business collects a debt owed to it by a customer.

The most popular method of enforcing a support order is through the attachment or garnishment of wages. The court in this situation allows the deduction of a fixed amount from the pay of the support debtor on a continuing basis. The amount requested is remitted to the Support Enforcement Office which then sends the cheque on to the support creditor.

Many people are under the mistaken impression that the Support Enforcement Office issues a cheque each month to the support creditor for the full amount of the support order. This is not the case. The Support Enforcement Office sends a cheque for any amount actually collected. If nothing is collected, then nothing is sent. If half the amount owed is collected then that amount is remitted to the support creditor. The attachment or garnishment of wages can be an effective method if the support debtor has a regular job and, as a result of recent innovations, the garnishment needs to be done only once for ongoing effectiveness, which means that a deduction is made from every subsequent paycheque.

All employees are subject to garnishment of wages, although federal public servants have been covered only since the early 1980s. Civil servants, Senators, MPs, federally appointed judges, the RCMP and members of the Canadian Armed Forces are all subject to garnishment. Most jurisdictions place a limit on the amount of wages that can be taken through this method (usually a maximum of 50 percent). This leaves the support debtor with money to live on while at the same time allowing him to meet his obligations to the family.

Another method of enforcement is the "Writ of Execution" or "Warrant of Distress." These writs are essentially orders of the court to the local sheriff to seize any land or property owned by the support debtor. Once it is seized it can be sold to pay the debt owed to the support creditor. This applies to land, furniture, cars, bank accounts and so on. It is effective only against property in the particular province that is enforcing the court order. Few debtors are foolish enough to let property be lost in such a way. Even fewer seem to have property available against which the writ can be executed.

The court has the power to imprison a support debtor for non-payment, but this is rarely used unless the debtor can clearly pay but wilfully refuses.

Other techniques for collection of support orders include ordering the support debtor to post security that would then be forfeited if he or she does not pay as ordered. Some provinces now permit the support order to be registered on title to property owned by the support debtor. This could, for example, block a refinancing of the property until a support order is paid and could ultimately force the sale of the property to meet the support debt.

Ontario plans to implement a new method of enforcement that will have the amount of support deducted directly by the employer of the support debtor but this legislation has not yet been passed.

British Columbia, Manitoba and Ontario through their various support enforcement offices have the power to arrange for the appointment of a Receiver for the support debtor's property or business in order to facilitate payment. But as you can see, the above remedies are only effective when the person actually has property or money. If support enforcement is to be effective, support enforcement offices will need to be able to seize wages quickly and efficiently to impress upon a support debtor the need to pay. Only tough enforcement will form the habits necessary for ongoing compliance.

The Support Enforcement Offices

The unifying features of support enforcement services are that support enforcement is automatically initiated, monitoring and tracing are available, and government computers and lawyers are available to track down and enforce the support order at no cost to the support creditor. The exact type of system may vary from province to province. For example, Ontario, Manitoba, Saskatchewan and Alberta have a system by which all support orders made by the court are automatically entered on the system for enforcement. The support creditor need not do anything other than get the support order in the first place. In Ontario, every order made by the court is required to have a direction in it to the Director of the Support Enforcement Office.

By contrast, British Columbia has an "opt-in" system which requires the support creditor to take the support order to the office and ask that it be enforced. It is the only privately run support enforcement office in Canada.

Regardless of which system is used, it is always open to creditors to opt out and enforce the order themselves with the help of a lawyer in private practice. They do so at their own expense, of course, and would only consider doing so if the support enforcement office were failing to respond to their immediate needs.

Once in the system, the support debtor must make all payments to the support enforcement office, which in turn remits the amount collected to the support creditor. As you might have guessed, computers play a large role in this type of system and payments are recorded as they are made. If one is missed, the computer notifies the enforcement personnel who respond with the most appropriate enforcement procedure—usually a garnishment or wage assignment. In some cases, a "show cause" is needed whereby the support debtor is summoned before the court to explain his failure to pay the order. The support debtor must, in other words, show the cause of his failure to pay.

An important function of the support enforcement office is its tracing ability. Provincial and federal data information banks can be searched to locate a support debtor's address, place of work, sources of income and other important information. These tracing powers were put in place with great emphasis on the protection of privacy. The information obtained may be used only for the purposes of enforcing a support order or custody order and nothing else.

At the federal level, the Canada Pension Plan data banks and Canada Employment and Immigration Commission data banks are available for searching. Provincially, driver's licence information, health insurance data and other provincial benefits can be searched if they will assist in the location of a support debtor.

Assuming the search of federal data banks turns up some information, federal monies that may be owing can be garnished to satisfy the support order. Money that can be seized includes:

- income tax refunds
- UIC benefits
- interest on Canada Savings Bonds
- Canada Pension Plan benefits
- Old Age Security benefits, and
- a variety of agricultural benefits payable to farmers.

At the provincial level, similar benefits have been identified for diversion if the support debtor is not meeting support obligations. In Ontario, a large lump sum payment to a doctor under the provincial health insurance plan was intercepted for non-payment of support. (Yes, even doctors don't pay their support.)

One would think that with so much effort support orders must surely now be paid routinely. No such luck. The reality is that most of these services are overburdened and cannot begin to enforce as vigorously or as effectively as they would wish.

Ontario's service, which is by far the busiest in the country, reports no more than a 30 percent rate of compliance with support orders, even though it has been enforcing them at taxpayers' expense for over three years. In many cases, support creditors must seriously consider removing their support orders from the enforcement service and taking the matter to court themselves if they want to have immediate attention paid to their needs.

Clients of these services should be scrupulous in filling out the necessary forms and be certain that all information in the possession of the enforcement services is up-to-date ... and then they must wait.

PROPERTY ENFORCEMENT

The litigation over the family property may produce a judgment in favour of one spouse for a significant amount of money if the family assets were of considerable value. As we saw in Chapter 6, "Dividing the Family's Property," some potentially large assets are now subject to division on marriage breakdown. Pensions, homes, cottages, bank accounts, GICs, cars, boats and other assets are all available for division. Judgments can be in the hundreds of thousands of dollars—but again, the judgment is of little use if it cannot be enforced.

For spouses who are legally married this can be a relatively easy exercise if the family property is still in existence. Most provincial family laws permit the court to order, at the time of judgment, the method by which the judgment is to be paid (or "satisfied," as lawyers like to say). So, for example, if the wife at judgment is owed $250,000, then the court can order that certain pieces of property be transferred to her in order to pay that debt. The husband may be ordered to transfer his interest in the matrimonial home to her in satisfaction of the judgment. This method is very practical and saves the couple further time and trouble with the enforcement of the judgment.

Unfortunately, this power is not available for common-law spouses. Its absence was in part responsible for the difficulties Rosa Becker had in enforcing her judgment.

Assuming that property is not transferred at the time of judgment, a spouse who is entitled to money may use a number of different enforcement procedures. These procedures include a Writ of Execution which is registered on title to land owned by the debtor spouse, garnishment or attachment of wages and, if no assets are readily available, the lawyer acting for the creditor spouse can arrange for an examination in aid of execution. This is sometimes known as a "judgment debtor exam." In this procedure, the lawyer summons the debtor spouse into an inquiry that is not unlike a discovery. The lawyer is given an opportunity to examine the debtor spouse under oath as to his or her ability to pay the judgment. A transcript is prepared, and the debtor's assets can be pursued with the information obtained during the examination.

Each step can be expensive and time-consuming. This type of enforcement should not be undertaken unless the creditor spouse has had a detailed discussion with his or her lawyer about why they are in this predicament (of having a judgment and no property to seize), what the expected cost of the enforcement will be and what the likelihood of success is considered to be in the circumstances.

The "judgment and no property to execute against" issue raises an important aspect of property enforcement that begins long before the judgment itself is obtained. It is known as the "restraining" or "preservation order." At any point in the legal proceedings, a person concerned about a particular piece of property that is in dispute may ask the court for an order restraining the owner of the property from dealing with it in any way. For example, a husband who owned a valuable coin collection could be restrained by court order from selling that coin collection until the trial is finished and a judgment has been rendered. This preserves the property in case it is needed to satisfy the judgment or in case the property itself is ordered transferred to the other spouse.

A restraining order may go beyond a prohibition of selling it to include even barring its use as security. So, for example, a wife could be prohibited from increasing the amount of a mortgage registered against a cottage that was in her name alone.

Another type of family law order that relates to property is the order for exclusive possession of a matrimonial home. This type of order does not affect ownership of the home, but determines who may possess it or live in it during the period leading up to a trial (and in some cases afterwards, too). The criteria may vary a little from province to province but the goal is the same—to leave in possession of the home the spouse who needs shelter and could not find alternative accommodations. It is not uncommon for the parent who is given interim custody of the children also to be given possession of the matrimonial home until the case is decided once and for all.

The order for possession of the home prohibits the other spouse from being on the property until further order of the court. In Ontario, for example, the breach of an order for exclusive possession is a provincial offence punishable by a fine and/or a jail sentence of considerable length. Subsequent offences are punished even more severely. To enforce such an order, the spouse in possession should always have in hand a certified copy of the order for possession of the home and proof that it has been served on the other spouse. If that spouse then appears at the home in contravention of the order the police will know in an instant that he or she is aware of the order and can be arrested and removed from the property. In Ontario, the officer may even arrest the offender without a warrant. The order for exclusive possession is considered to be an important tool for the protection of spouses where there has been violence in the home.

PERSONAL RESTRAINING ORDERS

A restraining order of a different kind is the type that restrains not the disposition of property but a person from doing something. This type of order may restrain one spouse from "molesting, annoying or harassing" the other spouse and children if necessary. It can be a blanket prohibition of contact or a more specific prohibition of contact at all times except those specified in the order. In the latter case the order may prohibit contact except on Friday evening at 7:00 P.M., for example, so that a father may speak with his children.

In Ontario, this type of order is enforced the same way as the order for exclusive possession. The breach of the order is treated as a provincial offence punishable by fine or jail and places the offender in a position of being arrested without a warrant.

In jurisdictions where a specific punishment is not prescribed, the court may enforce such orders for possession of the home or restraint of a person through the use of its contempt power.

CONTEMPT

Television has familiarized everyone with the concept of "contempt of court." Usually a misbehaving lawyer is being warned by the judge about some courtroom antic. Again, reality is quite different. The power to find someone in contempt of court is the court's way of controlling its own process, of making sure that day by day, people follow the rules of the court whether big or small. This type of enforcement is necessary to ensure the smooth and respectful functioning of our courts. If a person using the court process shows a wilful disregard for the court's rules then the court can punish that contempt in an appropriate way, through a jail sentence or a fine, or through denial of access to the court's remedies. Most provinces have given the court this power through specific legislative provisions or through the Rules of Court themselves. Some courts are considered to have this power inherently; their judges may invoke the power on their own but usually only do so if one of the parties before the court has urged a finding of contempt against the other spouse.

Regardless of the source of the power of contempt, it is a potent method of enforcing the court's orders because the judge ultimately has the ability to jail someone he or she considers to be wilfully disregarding the court process.

Because someone's freedom may be at stake, the courts have developed very rigorous standards for making a finding of contempt. If a motion is brought asking the court to find someone in contempt because that person has ignored a court order, the person asking for the finding of contempt must follow these standards closely. Consider the following:

- The motion must be served on the person personally, not through a lawyer.
- The conduct complained of must be clearly wilful; any confusion will prevent a contempt finding.
- All the facts must be disclosed to the court at the very outset.
- It must be proved beyond a reasonable doubt—as if a crime had been alleged.
- There must be no other appropriate way of punishing the conduct.

This power is used rarely, and only to protect the administration of justice as a last resort.

Jail sentences and fines are rarely appropriate in family cases and are saved for the most blatant misconduct. Judges, however, have an equally effective method of controlling the process when relatively smaller types of misconduct occur: they can refuse to let the offending person do anything else in the case until the conduct complained of has been remedied. For example, if a husband undertook at the discoveries to produce copies of his income tax returns for the previous three years but has failed to do so, then the court can deny him any court orders until he has produced the income tax returns as promised. If he still refuses to produce them then the court can strike out his case completely (claims and defences) and simply give his wife judgment for her claim. In this way the court controls the case before it.

CONCLUSION

As can be seen from the foregoing, obtaining the family law order is sometimes less than half the battle. Enforcement can be just as time-consuming and just as expensive. An essential early step in any family law case is the discussion with one's lawyer about the likelihood of recovery and the best methods of recovering any final judgment. In other words, discuss with your lawyer the likelihood of compliance with an order made by the court. Don't let someone tell you "We'll cross that bridge when we come to it." Orders that can't be enforced are of no value. Concrete plans can be made right at the outset of a case to ensure compliance with any order that is finally made by the court.

14

Grandparents and "Other Interested Persons"

In the fall of 1989 I was invited to speak to the Toronto chapter of the GRAND Society. It was my second meeting with this group and like the first, it fell on a beautiful, sunny, fall afternoon at their meeting place on Spadina Avenue near Bloor Street. The GRAND Society is a support group for grandparents who wish to maintain contact with grandchildren after their own children have divorced or, in some cases, after they have been denied access to grandchildren who are members of an intact family. On this particular afternoon I estimated the number in attendance to be approximately fifty people. They had come from all across Ontario and some from as far as the United States. Their stories underscore the sometimes forgotten consequences of marriage breakdown or the ending of a common-law relationship. If we remember that there are approximately 100,000 divorces a year affecting over 75,000 children, we can safely estimate that there are tens of thousands of grandparents who are affected in some way.

Grandparents, of course, are not the only ones unexpectedly caught in the legal difficulties of couples separating; aunts, uncles, brothers, sisters and others all can be drawn into the dispute over children. In this chapter, I intend to examine the special aspect of family law that pertains to them. Even though it is actually a part of custody and access considerations, it merits separate treatment.

GRANDPARENTS

The special role of grandparents in a child's upbringing has long been taken for granted in our society. No doubt their role has changed over the years with the increasing mobility of families and the frequency of divorce, but their special status remains.

In many communities grandparents play a significant role as daycare providers for their grandchildren. They should also provide an important source of heritage and continuity to a family. However, this is not always the case, and many grandparents have found themselves cut off from their grandchildren by divorce or some other family dispute. The grandchild can become a weapon that is wielded in a dispute, or a prize or reward to be withheld or granted if the grandparents "behave properly." I have heard of cases where couples have actually "extorted" so-called loans from their own parents by withholding access to the grandchild.

This is not to suggest that all grandparents have some divine right to be with their grandchildren. I have also heard of equally disturbing cases where grandparents have attempted to use access to a grandchild as a means of disrupting their children's marriage. These people have placed their children (the parents) in a position of choosing between them and their own children. But, however the conflict may have arisen, in some cases the grandparent is left with no alternative but to seek an order from the court for access to the child or in a few cases even custody.

The federal *Divorce Act, 1986* and various provincial family laws acknowledge this issue by permitting persons other than the parents themselves to bring or participate in legal proceedings affecting a child. Depending on whether the family is undergoing a divorce or is intact, different rules will apply. Let's consider the situation of a couple divorcing where custody and access to their child are in dispute.

It can be difficult to watch from the sidelines as a son's or daughter's marriage goes sour. This is particularly so if the parents had doubts about the "wisdom" of the union in the first place. Rarely does the problem surface suddenly; more often than not the marriage's difficulty is known to everyone in the family circle well in advance. Opinions and advice may already have been offered, with the parents of the couple being drawn into the dispute and being asked to take sides.

If the couple is on acrimonious terms and a custody dispute looms, the grandparents may be on pins and needles wondering whether their role with the grandchild can be maintained and whether picking any sides, other than the child's, is advisable. Special questions occur to grandparents: What if the son-in-law gets custody and moves back west? What if the daughter-in-law gets custody, remarries, and the child has a new stepfather? Will there be step-grandparents? A whole new world awaits the child, and adjustments for the family circle will be inevitable.

The *Divorce Act, 1986,* as we have seen, applies only when a couple that was legally married is divorcing. It does not apply to "intact" families or separating common-law spouses. The Act provides for persons other than the parents to apply for custody of or access to a child of the marriage in the divorce action itself. It does not use the word "grandparent" specifically, but the words "other person" clearly include grandparents. So any person, including a grandparent, may apply, but the Act also provides that the person must first get the court's permission to intervene. This means that if a couple separated and filed for a divorce the grandparents could, with the help of their own lawyer, apply for permission to intervene in the divorce action. If permission is granted, the grandparents may ask for custody of or access to the child.

In deciding whether to grant permission, the court will examine the past connection between the child and the grandparents. Is there a real connection between them? Why is the grandparent applying to intervene? What is in the child's best interest? Once permission to intervene is granted, the request for custody or access is decided like any other, by asking simply, What is best for this child in this family? (You can find a detailed discussion of the child's best interests in Chapter 7, "The Children.")

A special consideration will be the obvious constraints on the child's time. There is only so much time to be parcelled out to the parents, the grandparents (on both sides) and any others who have an interest in this child's life. The issue becomes how much time, realistically, does this child have for all of these people? The court will strive to maintain as much continuity as possible in the child's life while the parents try to build a new life for themselves.

Even when the grandparents obtain an order of custody or access, remember that they will face the same enforcement problems as others, as described in Chapter 13.

What if the family is not divorcing? Perhaps the marriage or relationship is intact but the grandparents are being denied contact with the child for a particular reason, good or bad. The problem could be one of remarriage. Some grandparents have described situations where their child had passed away or left a relationship and the child's new family unit was denying contact with the grandchild. In these situations, the *Divorce Act* would not permit an opportunity to intervene. However, most provincial family laws offer some recourse to grandparents in this position.

Provincial custody and access laws also contemplate "other persons" applying for an order with respect to children. These laws do not necessarily speak in terms of marriage breakdown or divorce and may thus be used by a grandparent faced with an intact family or a common-law relationship which has ended.

Ontario's *Children's Law Reform Act*, for example, provides that a parent of a child or "any other person" may apply to a court for an order respecting custody or access to a child. This provision has been used by grandparents seeking access to children in intact families. Again, the best interests test applies and the court considers all the needs and circumstances of this particular child. In Ontario, the best interests test includes a consideration of the relationship by blood between the child and each person who is party to the application.

In a British Columbia decision the judge commented that "any person" in that province's family law might include blood relatives, relatives by marriage, grandparents, aunts, uncles (including in-laws), babysitters, foster parents or daycare workers who have developed some relationship with the child.

Attitudes vary from province to province about the degree of latitude in the use of these provisions. A lawyer should be consulted to determine whether or not a particular province's law has been applied on behalf of grandparents. Legal remedies do exist for grandparents to attempt to obtain access to or custody of grandchildren, and these remedies have been used successfully.

A word of warning, however. Grandparents have applied for access to grandchildren and lost. The court will only do what is best for the child.

There has been one highly publicized case in Ontario in which the grandparents came under considerable criticism by the court as being unsuitable for contact with the grandchild. In that case, these grandparents were ordered to pay their son's legal costs in defending their unsuccessful claim for access to a grandchild.

This raises some important considerations for grandparents: the advisability of legal proceedings, alternatives to court and the expense of legal proceedings.

The advice in Chapter 3 about hiring a lawyer who specializes in family law applies equally to grandparents who would consider such an application to the court. The commencement of legal proceedings should be seen as an absolute last resort. If the relationship between the grandparent and the child is beyond the point of no return, the court will do little if anything to salvage it. I recommend family counselling in such cases and, if possible, the use of mediation to sort out the underlying problems that have created the barrier to contact between the child and grandparent.

Legal fees can be considerable in these proceedings. They should be reviewed, in detail, with the lawyer at the outset. Discuss the likelihood of success based on cases that have been undertaken in your own province. If there are none, you may find that you are the test case. In these situations much depends on the circumstances of the particular case. I think a reasonable place to begin is for the parents of the child and the grandparents to have a private conversation, either all together or individually, but most certainly in the absence of the grandchildren themselves. The purpose of the meeting should be to assure the parents of three things:

1. that you as grandparents do not sit in judgment of their decision to separate or of their parenting abilities;
2. that you as grandparents have had a role in the grandchild's life that has been positive and that you want that role to continue;
3. that the overriding consideration in the situation should be what is best for the child and that you want to develop a plan that allows you to contribute to some cushioning for the children.

The point of this meeting should be to have the parents of the child appreciate that you want to understand their decision to exclude you from the child's life and find out why they think that that decision is best for the grandchild.

Do not threaten to sue, to withdraw financial support, to eliminate inheritances, to cut out new partners or to penalize the couple in any way. To do so suggests, perhaps even proves, that you are not actually interested in the child's best interests after all. If you feel strongly about inheritances and other financial relations between yourself and the couple you are free to make whatever arrangements you wish, but I believe it is a mistake to connect them to spending time with the child.

If the meeting is refused or is unproductive, it is at that time that you should seriously consider obtaining legal advice from an experienced family law lawyer about your likelihood of success in a court application under either the *Divorce Act* or provincial family law.

"OTHER PERSONS"

As I mentioned at the outset, there may be more than grandparents interested in the children at marriage breakdown. Dozens of cases across Canada have tested the applicability of the expression "other person" in custody and access applications. Consider the following who have applied—not always successfully—for custody of or access to a child:

- a man who claimed he was the father of a child but his paternity had not yet been established
- a child's stepfather
- a former common-law partner of the child's mother
- a grandmother and an aunt together
- the child's natural mother after she had given the child up for adoption
- the child's natural father after the child's natural mother had given the child up for adoption
- a former adoptive father
- a babysitter
- foster parents
- a stepsister and her husband
- a friend of a twelve-year-old girl.

The same considerations with respect to the advisability and cost of legal proceedings apply for anyone in these categories.

These cases, whether they involve grandparents or other family members, serve as a serious reminder of the ripple effect of divorce and marriage breakdown. More than the child's parents and the child himself or herself are affected—the child's whole world has an interest.

15

Marriage Contracts and Cohabitation Agreements

In this chapter we will examine two other kinds of domestic contract—the marriage contract and the cohabitation agreement. In Chapter 10 we studied the most common type of domestic contract, the separation agreement. It has a very different purpose than either the marriage contract or cohabitation agreement. It is designed to settle a dispute that has arisen over property, custody, access and so on. Marriage contracts and cohabitation agreements are designed to avoid disputes well in advance by setting out the couple's agreed intentions about important things like property division or support. They serve the same purpose, but for people of different legal status: marriage contracts are for those who are married or intend to marry, while cohabitation agreements are for those who are living together or intend to live together.

In looking at these areas we should never lose sight of the fact that these arrangements are contracts and nothing more. They are contracts designed to deal with a specific issue the same way a contract to purchase a car or house is a written record of an agreement reached. There is no more magic in a marriage contract than in the car purchase.

Every province's family law contemplates couples making such agreements, and the technical requirements are not that difficult to meet. Just as in the case of separation agreements they must be written, signed by the parties and witnessed. They can be signed before or after the marriage or cohabitation commences.

With this in mind, let's examine each type of contract in more detail with a view to finding out why they are needed and how they are made—and how they are broken.

MARRIAGE CONTRACTS

A marriage contract is an agreement entered into by a man and a woman who are married to each other or intend to marry, in which they agree on their respective rights and obligations under the marriage or on separation, on the annulment or dissolution of their marriage or on death.

No one is quite sure how many couples are turning to marriage contracts as a planning device for their marriage, but one thing seems clear: more couples are exploring the possibility and in some cases actually signing them. Lawyers report that they are often consulted about them but that many are left unsigned when the issues touch nerves at home.

The need for a marriage contract seems to arise in two circumstances—in anticipation of the marriage or after the marriage has taken place and some new circumstance has arisen. They can produce dramatically different situations for the couple.

You will recall the incident I described at the beginning of this book where a bride-to-be was presented with a marriage contract at her wedding rehearsal. She was told rather sheepishly by her fiancé to take the contract to a lawyer and have it signed—before the wedding. The message was clear, if unspoken: If it's not signed there will be no wedding.

She had arrived at my office, with her parents, teary eyed, surprised but feeling she had no choice. After all, the wedding was in two days and ... and ... the honeymoon.... More tears. Her parents had shelled out thousands of dollars on the wedding and the photographer, the church was booked, and the reception hall, the meal was being prepared, bars were being stocked—a big wedding was planned. I suggested that the parents go home and prepare a list of expenses with supporting receipts. It should include *every* related expense. They rushed off enthusiastically to do their part and I reviewed the contract with their daughter. It became clear after a few minutes that the contract had more to do with the groom's parents' wedding gift (a $25,000 contribution to a downpayment on a house) than anything else. The parents wanted to ensure that if the marriage did not last, then the daughter-in-law would not benefit from the gift. It was, I guess, a conditional gift, conditional on staying married.

We discussed a few things—the need for the house, the need for the downpayment, their relationship, his parents and even the honeymoon. I asked a few key questions: Would she get married if they could not buy the house? Yes. Would she decline the gift and therefore the house and still get married if necessary? Yes. Would she sign the contract as is, if push came to shove? Yes. Would she like to see what her future husband was made of? Pause—Yes.

Who made the honeymoon arrangements? I did, she replied, and quickly recited the details of their trip to San Francisco. I dialled the hotel operator.

"My name is Michael Cochrane and I'm calling on behalf of my client, a Ms Bride, who has reservations for her honeymoon at your hotel." A quick check, and the operator confirmed that the reservations were intact. I continued, "We're having a little problem with the groom's friends who have been playing practical jokes on him all week. Now they are trying to find out where the honeymoon is, and we think they might try to call you to, you know, cancel or fiddle with the reservations. If anyone other than myself or Ms Bride calls, please tell them that no reservation has been made there and if they push, tell them the bride cancelled the reservation. But, of course, we'll know they haven't been cancelled. Could you do that?" "Certainly—it's a pleasure to help out. We've had that kind of problem before...."

"Oh yes," I continued. "If anyone inquires about the reservations, would you let me know? Here is my number...."

The parents returned, and we faxed the total bill for the wedding ($40,000) to the other lawyer, with a note that we were considering the contract but in the event the wedding was cancelled we expected a cheque for the full amount.

The phone rang within twenty minutes. The lawyer laughed and speculated that we were bluffing and that she would sign the contract as is.

I said, "Don't be too sure. She left here very upset and said something about San Francisco. What do you make of that?" He put me on hold while he spoke to his client. When he came back on, he said that the honeymoon was planned for San Fran. His voice changed as he put two and two together. I told him that I would wait for his call. Wait we did until the phone rang about fifteen minutes later.

"Mr. Cochrane? It's the hotel. You called just in time. We just had an inquiry from a man who insisted he was the groom. I told him it was cancelled and that was that. He tried to get me to re-book it! Do you believe those characters?"

"Yeah, they are something else. Thanks," I replied.

A few more minutes and the phone rang again. It was the lawyer on the other side. "She won't sign it," I said. "Sorry."

"Never mind, throw it out, he's reconsidered. So has the family. Don't ask me why, I have no idea."

The wedding was held as scheduled. (Is the story true, you ask. That's my secret.)

That is probably the best example of the worst way to handle a marriage contract. The outcome of this situation was lucky. In fact, weddings have been cancelled—or worse, contracts have been signed under circumstances of virtual blackmail. What a way to start a marriage!

In negotiating a contract before the wedding, people are usually attempting to do one of two things—exempt some specific property (a home, pension, business) from division in the event of separation and divorce, or opt out completely from the province's scheme for division of property and instead provide their own scheme. Rarely would you see a couple opt out completely after the marriage has taken place.

In discussing the proposed exclusion of an asset from division, a fair question to ask is "Why should this asset not be shared? Is there some emotional, financial or other reason to exempt this asset?" The most common example would have to be the case of the person entering a second marriage and bringing a home. Perhaps the home was inherited or is the chief asset from the property division after the first marriage. The person's concerns may be quite legitimate, and can probably be met with some creative alternatives.

If the goal of property division at the end of a marriage is to ensure that the fruits of the marriage are shared equally or that one spouse is not left disadvantaged because the other spouse holds all the property, then special assets can be protected through the provision of some alternative security. Perhaps the spouse with the home can take out an irrevocable life insurance policy payable to the other spouse, or perhaps some other asset will not be divided equally in order to provide balance. The possibilities are limited only by the assets available and your imagination.

Perhaps one of the most difficult marriage contracts to negotiate is one whose need arises after the marriage has taken place. For example, in Ontario all assets, including business interests, are shareable on divorce. This means that if a business person's marriage fails, his or her interest in a company, a partnership or other business is at risk of division in the family property dispute. The business partners or the person's bank may not wish to expose themselves to the risk of the business's being tied up or devalued. In these circumstances business partners have sent each other home to obtain marriage contracts from their respective spouses. In such a contract the spouse is asked to release any claim he or she may have to an interest in the business. This may be necessary to obtain a line of credit at the bank or other form of financing.

Sometimes the release can be obtained by substituting a full interest in some other equivalent asset. For example, the wife releases the husband's business and he releases any interest in the matrimonial home or her pension. Naturally, values would need to be fairly equivalent. If a separation occurred he would keep the business and she would keep the house.

This example is relatively simple. Situations can be more difficult if the business is the only asset.

Another matter that is often provided for in marriage contracts is spousal support. In the contract the couple agree in advance with respect to how support would be handled if a divorce took place. They may simply agree not to ask for support from each other if the marriage ends, or they may agree to an actual monthly amount and a fixed term (perhaps $500 per month for eighteen months), depending on how long the marriage lasted and the need.

Lower down on the scale of importance, some spouses have felt the need to provide for the division of household cleaning and child-care responsibilities. Personally, I feel that if you need to put such things in a contract you have bigger problems than you think.

On the other side of the coin, there are some things that you cannot put in a marriage contract—or if you do put them in they will not be binding on anyone or the court. For example, a couple is not permitted to provide for custody of or access to their children in advance of separation. The child's best interests cannot be ascertained in advance, so such provisions are not binding. Similarly, attempts to fix or avoid child support are not binding.

It is permissible to agree to "childrearing methods," such as method of education, religious instruction and so on. So parents could agree in advance of marrying that any children born will be given a Catholic education, for instance, or will be bar mitzvahed.

In Ontario, where spouses are given special rights to ask for possession of a matrimonial home at the time of separation regardless of ownership of the home, any attempt to give up the right to ask for possession in a marriage contract is not binding. This is designed to protect people from putting themselves in a very vulnerable position without knowing what circumstances they could face when separating.

As should be clear by now, these contracts can have important consequences for one's entitlement to support and property at the end of the marriage, so they should not be entered into lightly or in the absence of independent legal advice. Circumstances will change. Children may be born. Career choices may be made, property sold, illnesses develop, and so on. Couples who simply agreed to have separate property at the outset of the marriage have found themselves in an awkward situation fifteen years later when one has given up a career to raise children. The contract is still binding on them and will have accomplished little if it only produces a patently unfair result for one of them. At the end of this chapter is reproduced a sample marriage contract. It contains a relatively straightforward agreement and some more sophisticated terms for your consideration.

In conclusion, when negotiating a marriage contract be cautious, be fair, get legal advice, and think about your future and the need for the contract. An unfair contract will haunt you both.

COHABITATION AGREEMENTS

A cohabitation agreement is a contract entered into by a man and a woman who are cohabiting or intend to cohabit and who are not married to each other, in which they agree on their respective rights and obligations during cohabitation, or on ceasing to cohabit or on death.

As with marriage contracts, we have no accurate estimate of how prevalent these contracts are among cohabiting couples. Based on discussions with lawyers I feel they are still relatively rare. Many more people consult lawyers about them than actually sign them.

The purpose of the cohabitation agreement with respect to property is to provide a property division scheme where none exists. You will recall from Chapter 9 that one of the difficulties a common-law couple faces when their relationship ends is the reconstruction of their financial or other contribution to property jointly acquired. It is necessary for them to prove who acquired which property for what purposes and with whose money. A cohabitation agreement can avoid that type of historical review of the relationship by providing for a particular method of division. Options include:

(A) SEPARATE PROPERTY SCHEME

This method involves each spouse keeping what he or she acquired in his or her own name. If something is registered in his name, such as the car, it is his. If a piece of property is not registered in any way (such as a piece of furniture) then whoever paid for it keeps it.

(B) COMMUNITY OF PROPERTY SCHEME

This is actually the opposite of (a) because under this scheme *all* property, regardless of registration or source of payment, is divided equally.

(C) FAMILY ASSET SCHEME

In this scheme the couple identifies types of property that will be considered "family assets" and therefore divided equally regardless of registered title or source of payment (home, savings, furniture, vehicles, cottage). Other property would be divided on the basis of a separate property scheme (business, pensions, personal investments).

(D) PROVINCIAL PROPERTY SCHEME

In this method the couple simply opts to be treated as if they were legally married and therefore covered by the provincial family law for property division.

These are the general options available, but the couple is free to develop whatever scheme they wish.

Cohabitation agreements may also provide for spousal support in the same way as a marriage contract. That is, they may waive support or fix it according to their wishes. The same restrictions apply to provisions dealing with custody, access and child support. The court never considers itself bound where children are affected. However, as in a marriage contract, the couple can agree to educational and religious training of the child in advance of cohabitation.

Other matters of importance include the following:

- Marriage will turn a cohabitation agreement into a marriage contract.
- Amendments to either a marriage contract or cohabitation agreement are made the same way the contract itself is made. They are written, signed and witnessed.

SETTING ASIDE DOMESTIC CONTRACTS

No matter how good one's intentions or how clever one's lawyer, these contracts (and here I include separation agreements) can be set aside by the court. It is fair to ask, "Why enter into them at all, seeking predictability, if the court will just set them aside?" While the court has the power to set them (or provisions in them) aside, it will not use that power lightly and will, therefore, do so in very limited circumstances.

The court may set aside a valid domestic contract for the following reasons:

- the failure of one person to disclose an important asset or liability
- the finding that one party did not understand the nature of the contract
- any other reason acceptable in the general law of contract.

Let's consider briefly each one of these reasons.

Failure to Disclose

No one would like the idea of signing a contract and discovering afterwards that the other side had failed to disclose an important fact. Since the key to the domestic contract is most often financial or property arrangements, everything related to the calculations or property division scheme must be revealed. Most lawyers will not allow clients to sign domestic contracts unless each person provides a *sworn* financial statement setting out all of his or her assets and liabilities. (See the Financial Statement reproduced in the Appendices.)

These financial statements are not normally used for property division by common-law spouses because they do not have property rights under any legislation, but modified versions can be developed or they can act as a guide.

The court will usually act to set aside an agreement where the failure to disclose relates to a significant asset or liability that existed when the contract was made. The meaning of "significant" will vary from case to case depending on the full asset liability picture for the couple. The failure to disclose need not be a deliberate attempt to mislead; accidental failures are still valid grounds to set aside the whole agreement or just those parts affected by it.

Failure to Understand

If one of the people signing the domestic contract did not understand the nature or consequences of the agreement, the court may set it aside. This ground is very difficult to establish if both people have received independent legal advice and have signed statements to the effect that they understand what they are doing and are doing so voluntarily. You will recall the affidavits and statements signed at the end of a separation agreement that set out the fact of the lawyer's independent legal advice or the availability of it. These same affidavits are attached to marriage contracts and cohabitation agreements if they have been prepared by a lawyer.

In one case a man had his wife sign a handwritten summary of how they would like to have a marriage contract prepared. In it they summarized their assets and liabilities and exempted some of his property from sharing if they split up. They both signed it and had a friend witness it. When the husband took it to the lawyer he was told that technically it was already a marriage contract. The wife thought that it would be used as a starting point for negotiating between the lawyers. She didn't appreciate that this was a contract (its nature) and that she was giving up property rights (its consequences). The lawyers eventually agreed that the court would probably set it aside so they started over.

Contractual Failures

You will recall my statement at the outset that domestic contracts are just that, contracts. The general law of contract therefore applies to them, and any available ground for setting aside a contract will apply to a domestic contract. These grounds include such things as mistakes, fraud or public policy reasons. If the couple make a serious mistake about the law or their assets when negotiating the contract the court may set it aside. For example, if the couple thought that neither of them was entitled to support after their common-law relationship ended they would have both made a mistake about the law that in all likelihood affected their agreement.

If one deliberately deceived the other to the extent that the contract was actually an attempt to defraud the other, the court will intervene. In one case I learned of, a young man had moved in with an older woman and, over time, tried to defraud her of her life savings. He had an agreement prepared that he asked "a friend" to witness for them so he could have control over some of her assets. It was a form of cohabitation agreement. No lawyers were involved—until the woman's family found out and stopped the fraud.

There is a general ground available in contract law that allows the court to ignore contracts or parts of them that are "against public policy." This means that if the court considers a particular term offensive it will ignore it. For example, if a woman promised never to have children for the rest of her life or if someone agreed to be a virtual slave to another person, the court would refuse to enforce it. The meaning or extent of "public policy" can vary from time to time.

Ontario's *Family Law Act, 1986* has a unique provision in it that may be adopted by other provinces and is being considered as a potential amendment to the federal *Divorce Act*. It concerns Jewish divorces and a curious and unfortunate practice that has arisen within the Jewish community when marriage breakdown occurs.

Briefly, in order for Jews to divorce the husband must give and the wife must receive what is known as a *get*. It amounts to a contractual release from the religious marriage. Without it, Jews cannot remarry within their faith. The husband has been under no obligation to provide it, and in some cases it has been used to pressure women unfairly into inadequate settlements. Typically, the subject of the *get* would arise during the discussion of the separation agreement. The husband would give the *get* in exchange for an unequal division of the property in his favour or if he were given custody or generous access rights, and so on.

Ontario has short-circuited this process by giving the court the power to set aside any agreement in which the giving of the *get* was a factor. The language of the provision in the *Family Law Act* is general and does not refer specifically to the *get*. It speaks in terms of "the removal by one spouse of barriers that would prevent the other spouse's remarriage within that spouse's faith."

The application to non-Jews is considered to be minimal or nonexistent but it should be considered by all faiths as possible grounds for setting aside domestic contracts.

The following checklist is designed to flag some of the important questions that should be asked when dealing with marriage contracts or cohabitation agreements.

1. Do I really need one? What event has prompted the discussion of a contract?
2. What are my rights and obligations *without* the contract? Why change?
3. Am I being pressured to sign? Is there time to discuss this thoroughly?
4. What are the alternatives to a contract? Not marrying? Not cohabiting?
5. What effect will the discussion have on the relationship? Can it withstand the negotiations?
6. What are my expectations—and my partner's—if there is a death or separation?
7. Do we both have access to independent legal advice?
8. Has there been full financial disclosure?
9. Is the proposal fair? Will one of us resent the agreement?
10. Do we understand the nature and consequences of this contract?
11. Since a contract is being discussed, is there anything else that could be put in it that does not relate to property?
12. How will assets acquired in the future be covered?
13. Have we considered a contract that will expire by its own terms on a certain date?
14. Have the technical requirements been met?
15. Do I have a copy on the contract in a safe place?
16. Have I considered independent legal advice?
17. Have I considered independent legal advice again?

An Example of a Marriage Contract

THIS IS A MARRIAGE CONTRACT made on September   , 1991.
B E T W E E N:

MICHAEL GEORGE BLACK

- and -

NATALIE TANYA WHITE

1. INTERPRETATION
   (1) In this contract
      (a) "Black" means Michael George Black who is party to this contract;
      (b) "White" means Natalie Tanya White who is a party to this contract;

      (c) "Family Law" means the Provincial Family Law

      (d) "property" means property as defined in the appropriate provincial Family Law

      (e) "family residence" means the buildings and lot located at [address] in [City/Prov.], but does not include any other buildings or lot acquired in substitution for them;

      (f) "breakdown of the marriage" means

          (i) the separation of the parties with no reasonable prospect that they will resume cohabitation;

         (ii) the dissolution of their marriage; or

       (iii) the annulment of their marriage.

  (2) An Act of the Legislature or Parliament referred to by name will mean that Act in force at the material time and includes any amendment or any successor Act which replaces it.

2. BACKGROUND
The following items set out some of the background information to this contract.

  (1) _____

  (2) _____

  (3) Black and White have cohabited from time to time during a period of approximately _____ years preceding the making of this contract.

  (4) They intend to marry each other on _____.

  (5) They intend to live in the family residence.

  (6) The family residence is owned by White and is subject to a mortgage in the amount of ($87,000) with XYZ Trust.

3. PURPOSE OF CONTRACT
Each party intends by this contract

      (a) to avoid any rights and obligations relating to property which arise or which may in the future arise at law or in equity from their marriage;

      (b) except as specifically provided by this contract, to elect and affirm that none of the property of either party will be divided between them except according to ownership; and

      (c) if there is a breakdown of the marriage, to make specific provision for the division after the breakdown of any increase in value of the family residence accruing between the effective date of this contract and the date of the breakdown of the marriage.

4. AGREEMENT
Each party agrees with the other to be bound by the provisions of the contract.

5. EFFECTIVE DATE OF CONTRACT
This contract takes effect on the date the parties marry.

6. DOMESTIC CONTRACT

This is a marriage contract entered into (pursuant to relevant provincial law) and is a domestic contract which prevails over the same matters dealt with in provincial law.

7. FINANCIAL PROVISION

The responsibility for making financial provision for the family during cohabitation under the marriage will be assumed jointly by the parties in proportion to their respective financial abilities as may be agreed upon from time to time.

8. SUPPORT AFTER BREAKDOWN OF MARRIAGE

If there is a breakdown of the marriage, each party will have such rights to receive financial support from the other and will be under such obligations to provide financial support to the other as are given or imposed upon each party by the (provincial law) or the Divorce Act.

9. FAMILY PROPERTY

Under no circumstances will any property owned by either party, or by them together, be divided pursuant to (appropriate provincial law).

10. RIGHTS OF OWNERSHIP GOVERN PROPERTY DIVISION

Each party waives all rights pursuant to provincial law and in lieu thereof each with the other provides by this agreement that

(a) rights of ownership govern the division of property between them, and there shall be no division of property except according to ownership,

(b) neither of them will be entitled to property rights arising out of their marital relationship,

(c) neither of them will be entitled to a division of property owned by the other,

(d) neither of them will be entitled to the _____ family properties,
and

(e) neither of them will be entitled to a share of any property or the value of any property owned by the other,

notwithstanding

• they are cohabiting,
• they are married,
• one party is improvidently depleting or may improvidently deplete his or her net family property,
• they are separated,
• a divorce is being, or has been granted,
• the marriage is being, or has been declared a nullity, or
• one party has died leaving the other surviving.

11. WAIVER AND RELEASE

Each party

(a) waives all rights and entitlement, and

    (b) releases and discharges the other and his or her estate from all claims, that he or she has on the effective date of this contract or may later acquire under the provincial family law or under the laws of any jurisdiction

    (c) to a division of property or the value of property owned by the other,

    (d) to the equalization of their net family properties or other sharing of their net family property, and

    (e) to any property or value of property owned by the other,

on any basis notwithstanding the fact that

- they are cohabiting,
- they are married,
- one party is improvidently depleting or may improvidently deplete his or her net family property,
- they are separated,
- a divorce is being, or has been granted,
- the marriage is being, or has been declared a nullity, or
- one party has died leaving the other surviving.

12. DEEMED OWNERSHIP

Subject to an appropriate instrument in writing, the rule of law applying a presumption of resulting trust shall not apply in questions of ownership of property between the parties, and

    (a) property transferred from one party to the other party shall be deemed to be owned by the party to whom the property is transferred;

    (b) property held in the name of one party shall be deemed to be owned by that party;

    (c) property held in the name of both parties as joint tenants shall be deemed to be owned by both parties as joint tenants; and

    (d) money on deposit in the name of both parties shall be deemed to be in the name of the parties as joint tenants.

13. NO OWNERSHIP UNLESS LEGAL OWNERSHIP

Except as provided by this contract, each party

    (a) waives all rights and entitlement, and

    (b) releases and discharges the other and his or her estate from all claims, that he or she has on the effective date of this contract or may later acquire,

- in equity by way of constructive, implied or resulting trust, or by way of any other doctrine in equity, and
- at law under the provincial family law and the laws of any jurisdiction to compensation, and
- any interest in property or the value of property owned by the other, by reason of
- the transfer of property to the other without any or any adequate payment or other consideration,
- work, money or moneys worth contributed to the acquisition, management, maintenance, operation or improvement of

property, or
- any other fact or circumstance creating a beneficial interest in property.

14. RIGHT TO DEAL WITH SEPARATE PROPERTY

Except in the case of the family residence, each party may dispose of or encumber or otherwise deal with his or her property as he or she deems fit, free from any claim by the other as if he or she were unmarried.

15. FAMILY RESIDENCE

(1) Each party acknowledge that the family residence is owned by White and each agrees with the other that it will remain her separate property.

(2) If there is a breakdown of the marriage, White will pay Black a sum equal to one-half of any increase in the market value of the family residence accruing between the effective date of this Agreement and the date of the breakdown of the marriage as determined under the next section of this Agreement.

(3) The sum will be payable within thirty days after the amount is determined.

(4) The right of Black to share in the increase in value is an ownership interest in the family residence to the extent of the value realized by that right.

16. INCREASE IN MARKET VALUE

(1) The increase in market value of the family residence will be the increase accruing between
   (a) the effective date of this contract, and
   (b) the date of the breakdown of the marriage.

(2) The market value on the effective date of this contract is $270,000.00.

(3) The market value on the date of the breakdown of the marriage will be the value determined by
   (a) the agreement of the parties; or
   (b) the opinion of a single qualified appraiser selected by both parties; or
   (c) the agreement of a qualified appraiser selected by Black and a qualified appraiser selected by White; or
   (d) if the two appraisers selected in (c) cannot agree, by the opinion of a third qualified appraiser selected by the two appraisers.

(4) If within 30 days from the date of the breakdown of the marriage
   (a) the market value as of the date of the breakdown has not been determined, and
   (b) arrangements have not been made to pay Black a sum equal to one-half of any increase in the market value,
   either party may apply under the provincial family law for sale of the family residence.

(5) Any order for sale made under the provincial family law must provide for

(a) a reference to the court to determine the interests of the parties as set out in this contract;

(b) the right of each party to purchase the interest of the other; and

(c) such other directions as may be necessary for the expeditious realization of the respective interests of the parties.

17. RIGHTS RELATING TO MATRIMONIAL HOME

Nothing in this contract restricts or modifies the rights of either party with respect to the possession, disposition or encumbrance of the family residence _____ or any other matrimonial home as defined under the provincial family law, but each of the parties intends that if there is a breakdown of the marriage, Black will give White vacant possession of the family residence as of the date of the breakdown, although he is not and cannot be bound by this contract to do so.

18. CONTENTS OF FAMILY RESIDENCE

If there is a breakdown of the marriage of the parties, the contents of the family residence or any successor residence will be distributed between the parties according to ownership whether that ownership arises by way of purchase or gift, including gifts from the other party.

19. RELEASE AGAINST BUSINESS INTERESTS

Without restricting the generality of the other waivers and releases given under this contract, except for any interest that is expressly granted by an instrument in writing,

(a) Black releases and discharges White from all claims that he may have on the effective date of this contract or may later acquire, to all interests in _____ and any business of _____, and any other business carried on by her;

(b) White releases and discharges Black and any partnership and any company and any business in which he may acquire an interest, from all claims that she may acquire to any interest in the partnership and the corporation and any business of the partnership and the corporation, and any other business carried on by him.

20. RELEASE AGAINST THE ESTATE OF THE OTHER

Without restricting the other waivers and releases in this contract, and subject to transfers or bequests that may be made, each party

(a) waives all rights, and

(b) releases and discharges the other and his or her estate from all claims that he or she has or may in the future acquire under the laws of any jurisdiction, and particularly under the (provincial law), entitling him or her upon the death of the other

- to a division of property owned by the other or to one-half the difference between their net family properties or to any other share of this difference, or to any share of the property of the other;

- if the other party dies leaving a will, to elect against taking under the will in favour of receiving an entitlement equalizing their net family properties, or in favour of any other benefit;
- if the other party dies intestate, to elect to receive an entitlement in intestacy or to receive an entitlement equalizing their net family property;
- if the other party dies testate as to some property and intestate as to other property, to elect to take under the Will and to receive an entitlement in intestacy, or to receive an entitlement equalizing their net family properties;
- to share in the estate of the other under a distribution in intestacy in any manner whatsoever;
- to receive support as a dependant from the estate of the other in any manner whatsoever; and
- to act as executor or administrator of the estate of the other.

21. TRANSFER OR BEQUEST OF PROPERTY TO OTHER PARTY
Either party may, by appropriate written instrument,
   (a) convey or transfer during his or her lifetime, and
   (b) devise or bequeath for distribution after his or her death any property to the other, or appoint the other as executor of his or her estate. Nothing in this Contract will limit or restrict in any way the right to receive any such conveyance, transfer, devise or bequest from the other, or, if so appointed, the right to act as executor or administrator of the estate of the other.

22. FINANCIAL DISCLOSURE
Each party
   (a) has fully and completely disclosed to the other the nature, extent and probable value of all his or her significant assets and all his or her significant debts or other liabilities existing at the date of this contract, and in addition to this disclosure,
   (b) has given all information and particulars about his or her assets and liabilities that have been requested by the other,
   (c) is satisfied with the information and particulars received from the other, and
   (d) acknowledges that there are no requests for further information or particulars that have not been met to his or her complete satisfaction.

23. AMENDMENT OF CONTRACT
Any amendment of this contract will be unenforceable unless made in writing and signed by each party before a witness.

24. GOVERNING LAW
This contract will be governed by the law of the Province of
_____.

25. SEVERABILITY

The invalidity or unenforceability of any provision of this contract will not affect the validity or enforceability of any other provision, and any invalid provision will be severable from this contract.

26. CONTRACT TO SURVIVE DIVORCE

If a divorce is granted, or if the marriage is declared a nullity, the terms of this contract will survive the event and continue in force.

27. CONTRACT TO SURVIVE DEATH

This contract is intended to survive the death of a party or the parties and will be binding on the heirs, administrators, executors and assigns of the deceased party or parties.

28. INDEPENDENT LEGAL ADVICE

Each party acknowledges that he or she

    (a) has had independent legal advice,

    (b) understands the nature and the consequences of this contract, and

    (c) is signing this contract voluntarily.

TO EVIDENCE THEIR AGREEMENT, each of the parties has signed this contract under seal before a witness.

SIGNED, SEALED AND DELIVERED)

)

)

_____)

Witness as to the   )

signature of:)   _____

)   MICHAEL GEORGE BLACK

)

)

)

_____)

Witness as to the   )

signature of:)   _____

                          NATALIE TANYA WHITE

CERTIFICATE AND AFFIDAVIT OF SOLICITOR

I,_____, of the City of _____ in the Municipality of _____, Barrister and Solicitor, MAKE OATH AND SAY:

    1. I am the solicitor for Michael George Black and a subscribing witness to this contract, and I was present and saw it executed at the City of _____ the said Michael George Black.

    2. I believe that the person whose signature I witnessed is the party of the same name referred to in the contract.

    3. I have advised the said Michael George Black with respect to the within contract and I believe that he is fully aware of the nature and

consequences of the contract on and in light of his present and future circumstances and is signing it voluntarily.

SWORN BEFORE ME at the City)
of _____, in the)
Municipality of _____) _____
on December _____, 199 .)

_____

A Commissioner for Taking Affidavits.

Note: Natalie's lawyer would sign a similar affidavit and both would be attached to the contract.

Caution: Please do not attempt to adapt this contract to your situation without the advice of a lawyer. Many of the clauses are alternatives to each other and would not necessarily be applicable to every case. It is reproduced here as an example or guide only.

16

Family Law and Your Will

In this chapter I would like to examine briefly in the context of family law some of the considerations you should keep in mind when making a will. It is not my intention here to provide you with a blueprint for will making or estate planning. I'll leave that job to others. However, there are some special considerations that should be kept in mind when making a will, or when separating or divorcing.

MAKING A WILL

The most valuable piece of advice I may be able to offer in this chapter is simply to go out and make a will. Thousands of people avoid this essential bit of financial planning. However, the fact remains the same: If you care about your hard-earned money and about protecting your family then you should make an appointment with a lawyer who has experience with estate planning and have a will prepared. Not having a will means that your estate would be considered an "intestacy," which in turn means considerable delay, the hiring of lawyers and the wasting of your estate's resources in finding someone to distribute the estate for a fee. Most law offices have word processors and computers that will produce the necessary clauses; the whole exercise takes very little time. In fact, it is one of the most reasonably priced pieces of legal work available from a law firm.

The point of making the will is to plan the distribution of your property after your death. The vast majority of wills provide simply that the property goes entirely to the surviving spouse or to the surviving spouse and the children of the marriage, in particular portions.

Family law commonly expresses two concerns here: first, the possible effect of family law property-division rules on the planned distribution of the estate, and second, the effect of a marriage breakdown upon an inheritance that a spouse has received during his or her marriage.

The first concern about the impact of family law property-division rules is of great interest in Ontario. The *Family Law Act, 1986* provided a unique Canadian solution to the potentially inequitable treatment of one spouse upon the death of the other spouse as opposed to upon separation. As we have seen, family law provides for the equitable division of property upon marriage breakdown and divorce. It strikes most people as patently unfair that a husband, for example, could upon his death leave everything to his children, but if he had separated he would have had to share the property with his spouse. In other words, why should separating spouses be treated more fairly than widows and widowers?

Ontario sought to address this problem by providing the surviving spouse with a choice (called an "election") when the other spouse died. The survivor could either take the inheritances in the will or take what he or she would have received had they separated. If the surviving spouse elected to take what was given in the will, then the estate would be distributed as planned. However, if the survivor chose to take what he or she would have received if they had separated, then the estate plan could be thrown into turmoil. For example, if the will has left the surviving wife only 10 percent of the total property value in the estate when she would have received 50 percent upon separation, then the transfer of the extra 40 percent will upset the other gifts in the will. Everyone else will have to accept less. In most cases, these beneficiaries would be the testator's children, perhaps children from a previous marriage.

At the present time, Ontario, Alberta, Newfoundland, Nova Scotia, Saskatchewan and Quebec have provisions in their family law that state that the death of a spouse has an effect on the division of family property. Each province is a little different, but the point is a simple one, for our purposes: When making a will it is now necessary to keep in mind the possible effect of provincial family property division rules upon the estate. An estate plan that is turned upside down by an unhappy surviving spouse is worthless.

This has led to lawyers using marriage contracts and wills in conjunction. The estate plan actually comes in two parts—the will, which sets out the intended inheritances to beneficiaries; and the marriage contract, by which the spouses release any interest in particular pieces of property and agree to accept the will without challenge. The releases are often given in exchange for the substitution of some other property or something else of value. In many cases the spouses make what are known as "mutual wills" and "mutual marriage contracts" by which they simultaneously agree to honour each other's will and develop a joint estate plan through the use of their wills and marriage contracts.

A second aspect of wills in the context of family law concerns the effect of a person's divorce upon his or her inheritance. It is not uncommon for a parent, when giving a lawyer instructions for a will, to ask whether the inheritance given to his or her child can somehow be protected from that child's spouse in the event the child's marriage breaks down. For example, a father may wish to leave the family business to his son, but wonders whether the business would be jeopardized if his son's marriage broke down. These concerns are not unlike those mentioned by parents who want to give large wedding gifts to their children, but only so long as the marriage works out.

Eight provinces (British Columbia, Manitoba, New Brunswick, Newfoundland, Nova Scotia, Ontario, Prince Edward Island and Saskatchewan) have provided in their family property-division rules exemptions for gifts and inheritances. Generally, a person who receives a gift or inheritance during the marriage will not have to share that asset with the other spouse at marriage breakdown. In some cases, such as Ontario, any income earned by the gift or inheritance after it is received can also be shielded from division with a spouse. However, the inheritance must specifically state that the income is not to be shared. This means that in Ontario, if a father wishes to pass on a family business, then it will be critical also to state in the will that income earned by the business is not to be included in the son's family property should the son's marriage break down.

Therefore, when consulting a lawyer about a will, two important considerations are:

1. the ability of the surviving spouse to set aside the estate plan if he or she is dissatisfied with the inheritance in the will; and
2. the advisability of protecting a child's inheritance from his or her spouse in the event their marriage should break down after the inheritance is received.

DIVORCE AND YOUR WILL

Assuming you had the foresight to have a will prepared but now find yourself divorcing or separated, an important consideration is the effect of your separation agreement upon your will. Most separation agreements have standard form releases by which the husband and wife release any interest in each other's estate. (See the Separation Agreement in the Appendices.) This may put the will and your separation agreement in direct contradiction. You should undertake to make a new will with a new beneficiary at the same time that you draft the separation agreement.

Another consideration at the time of separation or divorce is whether any support orders made in the context of the divorce will be binding on the estate of the person paying support. Several provinces now provide that the support will continue to be paid by the support payor's estate. This should be specifically discussed at the time a separation agreement or court order for support is drafted.

In conclusion, while I have not set out a detailed overview of all the aspects of estate planning for a family, I have identified a number of considerations—both at the time a will is drafted and at the time of separation—that are of special interest to the family law issues that arise in Canada.

17

How to Complain

My guess is that despite all of the advice, forewarning and caution set out herein, you will still probably be disappointed in some way by a part of the system. Experience tells us that one or more of the following things will give you cause to complain:

(i) your lawyer
(ii) the judge
(iii) the court system
(iv) your mediator
(v) the official guardian
(vi) the law
(vii) your spouse.

(I) LAWYERS

All lawyers practising law in Canada are subject to regulation and discipline by their provincial law society. Each law society has a committee established specifically to inquire into complaints made by the public about that province's lawyers. Complaints should therefore be sent in writing to the attention of the "Discipline Committee" of the appropriate law society. Here are their addresses:

The Law Society of Alberta
344-12th Avenue South West
Calgary, Alberta
T2R 1P3
403-229-4700

The Law Society of British
Columbia
300 - 1148 Hornby Street
Vancouver, B.C.
V6Z 2C4
604-669-2533

The Law Society of Manitoba
201-219 Kennedy Street
Winnipeg, Manitoba
R3C 1S8
204-942-5571

The Law Society of New
Brunswick
305 - 1133 Regent Street
Fredericton, New Brunswick
E3B 3Z2
506-458-8540

The Law Society of Newfoundland
P.O. Box 1028
Baird's Cove
St. John's, Newfoundland
A1C 5M3
709-722-4740

Barreau du Québec
Maison du Barreau
445, boulevard Saint-Laurent
Montréal, Québec
H2Y 3T8
514-866-3901

The Law Society of the Northwest
Territories
P.O. Box 1298
Yellowknife, N.W.T.
X1A 2N9
403-873-3828

The Law Society of Saskatchewan
201 - 2208 Scarth Street
Regina, Saskatchewan
S4P 2J6
306-569-8242

The Nova Scotia Barristers' Society
Keith Hall
1475 Hollis Street
Halifax, Nova Scotia
B3J 3M4
902-422-1491

The Law Society of Upper Canada
Osgoode Hall
130 Queen Street West
Toronto, Ontario
M5H 2N6
416-947-3300

The Law Society of Prince Edward
   Island
P.O. Box 128
Charlottetown, P.E.I.
C1A 7K2
902-892-9131

The Law Society of Yukon
201 - 302 Steele St.
Whitehorse, Yukon
Y1A 2C5
403-668-4231

If your complaint concerns the amount of your bill, please refer to Chapter 3, "Taking a Look at Lawyers," which discusses assessment of a lawyer's fees.

(II) JUDGES

This is a more sensitive area, and we must make a distinction between complaining about the judge and complaining about the judge's decision. In the latter case the method of complaint is called an appeal. There are specific grounds and procedures upon which to challenge a decision.

If the complaint is about the judge himself or herself, the correct place to lodge the complaint will depend on whether the judge was a federal appointee or a provincial appointee. As a general rule of thumb, judges of the highest courts are all federally appointed judges. A complaint against such a judge should be directed in writing to the following body:

Canadian Judicial Council
112 Kent Street, Room 450
Ottawa, Ontario K1A 0W8

In the case of provincially appointed judges the complaint should be lodged, again in writing, with the appropriate provincial judicial discipline body for judges.

Refer to the Ministries of the Attorney General addresses listed below, except for these:

Judicial Council of Quebec
Court House, Room 7.45
1 Notre Dame St. East
Montreal, Quebec H2Y 1B6

Ontario Judicial Council
Osgoode Hall
130 Queen St. West
Toronto, Ontario M5H 2N5

Alberta Provincial Judicial Council
402 Law Centre
University of Alberta
Edmonton, Alberta T6G 2H5

(III) THE COURT SYSTEM

The court system is notoriously slow and in most cases overburdened. Cases often fall between the cracks. This does not mean, however, that anyone should accept delays in having his or her case heard.

Each province has responsibility under our Constitution to care for and manage the "administration of justice." This means providing the rules and regulations, the court structures and the staff of the court system. Generally the provinces leave that responsibility in the hands of the respective Ministries of the Attorney General. Their addresses are set out below. Don't worry about writing to the appropriate civil servant; write to the Attorney General himself or herself. You will receive, in most cases, a prompt personal response. You should also consider providing your provincial member of the legislature with a copy of your letter.

Minister of Justice and Attorney
   General of Canada
3rd Floor Justice Building
239 Wellington Street
Ottawa, Ontario
K1A 0H8
613-992-4621

Attorney General of Alberta
Room 423
Legislative Building
Edmonton, Alberta
T5K 2B6
403-427-2339

Attorney General of British
   Columbia
Room 232
Parliament Buildings
Victoria, B.C.
V8V 1X4
604-387-1866

Minister of Justice and Attorney
   General of Saskatchewan
Room 355
Legislative Building
Regina, Saskatchewan
S4S 0B3
306-787-5353

Minister of Justice and Attorney
    General of Manitoba
104 Legislative Building
Winnipeg, Manitoba
R3C 0V8
204-945-3728

Attorney General of Ontario
11th Floor, 720 Bay St.
Toronto, Ontario
M5G 2K1
416-326-4000

Minister of Justice and Attorney
    General of Quebec
1200, route de l'Église
Saint Foy, Québec
G1V 4M1
418-643-4210

Attorney General and Minister of
    Justice of New Brunswick
Room 416
Centennial Building
P.O. Box 6000
Fredericton, N.B.
E3B 5H1
506-453-2583

Minister of Justice and Attorney
    General of P.E.I.
P.O. Box 2000
Charlottetown, P.E.I.
C1A 7N8

Attorney General of Nova Scotia
10th Floor
5155 George Street
P.O. Box 7
Halifax, Nova Scotia
B3J 2L6
902-424-4044

Minister of Justice
P.O. Box 8700
St. John's, Newfoundland
A1B 4J6

Minister of Justice
P.O. Box 2703
Whitehorse, Yukon
Y1A 2C6

Minister of Justice
P.O. Box 1320
Yellowknife, N.W.T.
X1A 2L9

(IV) MEDIATORS

Mediators are not regulated to the same extent that lawyers are regulated.
As of publication, no provincial association of mediators stands capable of
disciplining its members. Nor does the national association, Family
Mediation Canada. However, complaints should be forwarded to the
appropriate provincial body. Their addresses are reproduced at the end of
Chapter 12, "Alternatives to Court."

You should also send a copy of your complaint to Family Mediation
Canada.

(V) OFFICIAL GUARDIANS

Many provinces have created divisions within their Attorney General's
Department to investigate the interests of children in divorce proceedings
or other family law matters. For example, in Ontario it is known as the

Office of the Official Guardian and is a part of the Ministry of the Attorney General.

The "O.G.'s" office will investigate the child's interests and report to the court. In some cases they will even arrange for the children to have their own separate lawyer to advocate the child's best interests throughout the proceedings.

Parents are not always pleased with these investigations. Complaints should be directed to the Ministry of the Attorney General (Attention: Attorney General) and your local representative in the legislature. If you have a lawyer, he or she should also be notified of the complaint and may assist you in preparing it.

(VI) THE LAWS

No one said you had to like the laws that have been passed by the federal and provincial governments with respect to family law. If you are unhappy with the philosophy of a particular law, a particular provision's effect on you and your family or the law's failure to address your needs, then write to those who can make a change—the provincial Attorney General or the federal Minister of Justice.

The addresses are set out in section (iii) above.

For those interested in more specific and concerted efforts to bring about law reform, consider lobbying for change. The word "lobbyist" has a certain pejorative sound to it but it really means no more than an individual or group pressing for specific changes to the law. In many cases lobbying involves no more than writing to the appropriate politicians and public servants with a suggestion for change. Even pointing out an unfair result can trigger a policy person's interest and result in reform.

During my years at the Ministry of the Attorney General in Ontario I often saw letters from ordinary laypeople pointing out shortcomings in our laws. Their opinions were valuable and were saved until an opportunity for reform arose. This brings me to my point on reform of family laws. In most provinces, and certainly federally, the basic legal structures are already in place. If reform is to take place it will most likely be in the form of amendments to existing laws. Reform will occur through the passage of amending bills. Like any new law, these bills move through the first, second and third reading stages, followed by royal assent and proclamation.

Those interested in lobbying for change will be most interested in what happens between second and third reading. If members of a legislature feel that public input or comment is called for on a proposed reform, they may refer a bill to a "standing committee" for detailed discussion in between second and third reading.

A standing committee of the legislature is simply a group of politicians from all parties. Each committee has its own area of expertise—justice, economics, social affairs and so on. Most family law matters are dealt with in the justice committee. In Ontario it is known as the Standing Committee on Administration of Justice. At the federal level, the committee is called the Standing Committee on Justice and it would consider, among other things, amendments to the *Divorce Act*.

The standing committees will often call for public submissions when a family law amendment is being considered. This gives interested groups and individuals an opportunity to comment or propose further changes. It is not a difficult process. You simply contact the clerk for the particular committee and ask for an opportunity to be heard. A spot on the agenda will be reserved for you or your group, and when the appointed day arrives you simply show up and make your views known.

If you have the time to prepare one, a written version of your remarks should be delivered to the committee, as it will help you make a lasting impression. It is not essential, however.

I also suggest that anyone who appears before such a committee *not* simply read his or her written submission. Committee members would rather hear your remarks. Talk directly to them and do your best to answer their questions. Remember, they may know little more than you about the subject—and often less.

During the standing committee's consideration of Ontario's *Family Law Act* (known at that time as Bill 1) in November and December of 1985, I saw many very thoughtful submissions from individuals, representatives of women's groups, fathers' groups, the insurance industry, lawyers, grandparents, individual parents and many others. Each was received politely, patiently and gratefully by committee members. Most important, many submissions resulted in changes to the draft legislation.

(VII) YOUR SPOUSE
How should you complain about your spouse? You already know how to do that.

CONCLUSION

One of the most difficult aspects about complaining is that it is time-consuming and forces you to continue to think about a part of your life that you would just as soon put behind you. In many situations your complaint may not change the outcome of your own case. So, why do it?

Your efforts may save someone else from a similar experience. For example, there was an incident in a court in one of the Atlantic provinces concerning a family law judge who made inappropriate remarks to a woman one day. She did something about it by launching a complaint. No sooner was it public than several other women came forward to say that they too had been victimized in the same way. Her courage in coming forward saved many others who followed her from similar humiliation.

Complaining is hard work—but it's often worth it.

18

Other Things to Read

It may be hard to believe, but for all the details we have covered in the preceding chapters we have only scratched the surface. Many of you may want to do further reading on the various subjects I have covered and I encourage you to do so by all means. In this chapter I have collected a list of materials you may find useful. I put them all in one chapter, as opposed to at the end of each chapter, so that you would have one easy reference.

Some of the books will be available at the local public library, some are available in university or law school libraries and some are available for free from the provincial, territorial or federal governments. On some materials I have included short comments and a little information.

Before going any further I shall add a short note for those who might be adventurous enough to try a law school library. Every province has a law school (Ontario has six) and you should feel free to use them—your tax dollars have paid for every one of them. Having said that, I think you should note that law students can be a tense bunch—especially around exam time. I know, because I have taught at the University of Ottawa Law School and in Carleton University's Department of Law, and some days it was just better to steer clear of them. The staff at the various libraries, on the other hand, I have found to be universally co-operative. They will be more than happy to help you use the indexing system (now computerized at some schools) and locate the appropriate book on the shelf (sometimes called "in the stacks"). Once you have located the book, find a nice quiet spot away from the fuss of studying students and settle in for a read. You cannot remove a book without a library card which is only issued to registered students.

The law books often contain case citations—codes to help locate actual reported decisions in cases that have been to court. These cases are likely to be located right there in the library and can be found with a little help and some digging. Not all cases are reported, but the most significant ones are routinely published. (Remember those "Reasons for Judgment.")

The following are the more popular sources of actual family law cases as reported:

- Ontario Reports (O.R.)
- Reports on Family Law (R.F.L.)

- Dominion Law Reports (D.L.R.)

A typical case citation would be as follows:

Pettkus v. *Becker*   (1980), 117 D.L.R. (3d) 257 or
(1980), 19 R.F.L. (2d) 165

The names are, of course, the names of the people involved, and the year refers to the year in which it was reported (not necessarily the same as the year in which it was decided). The next number is a reference to the volume of the particular services (for example, volume 117 of the Dominion Law Reports or volume 19 of the Reports on Family Law). These volume numbers are printed on the spine of the book near the name of the service. The next bit of information describes which edition of the service carries the case. All editions are filed chronologically. Be careful you don't pick up the right volume number but the wrong edition. The last number is the page reference.

Usually the case names are the same, *Brown* v. *Brown*, *Porter* v. *Porter* and so on, but not always. Try locating the following volumes if you want some experience locating family law decisions in a law library:

- *Andris* v. *Andris* (1984), 40 R.F.L. (2d) 315 (Sask.)
- *Brockie* v. *Brockie* (1987), 5 R.F.L. (3d) 440 (Manitoba)
- *Moss* v. *Moss* (1916), 5 R.F.L. (3d) 62 (Nfld.)
- *Murdoch* v. *Murdoch* (1975), 13 R.F.L. 185 (Alta.)
- *Pelech* v. *Pelech* (1987), 7 R.F.L. (3d) 225 (Ontario, but the decision is from the Supreme Court of Canada)

[Note: When asking for a case describe it as Andris *and* Andris not Andris *versus* Andris.]

I have included in the following list of books and materials some popular legal textbooks on family law. They are probably available in your university or law school library as well.

Good luck—it can be a lot of fun in a law library. If you get bored with family law cases, try the Canadian Criminal Cases (C.C.C.)—you won't want to go home until you have registered for law school!

A Selected Bibliography

by Subject Area

DOMESTIC VIOLENCE
- *Understanding Wife Assault: A Training Manual for Counsellors and Advocates*, by Deborah Sinclair, M.S.W., C.S.W. (© 1985). This book is an excellent one, and I relied on it preparing my chapter on domestic violence. It is available from the Ontario Government Bookstore, 880 Bay Street, Toronto, Ontario M7A 1N8. It was developed and published with funding from the Ontario Ministry of Community and Social Services, Family Violence Program.

- *Children of Battered Women*, by Peter Jaffre, David Wolfe and Susan Kaye Wilson, vol. 21 of *Developmental Clinical Psychology and Psychiatry* (Sage Publications © 1990). This is another exceptional book by three Canadian authors.

THE LEGAL PROFESSION
- *Court Jesters* (three volumes), by Peter V. MacDonald, Q.C. (Stoddart). Lawyers don't mind laughing at themselves and their clients. These books can be a bit of fun.
- *Lawyers*, by Jack Batten (Penguin Books © 1987).
- *Judges*, by Jack Batten (Macmillan of Canada © 1988).

DIVORCE
- *Divorce Law: Questions and Answers*, published by the Federal Minister of Justice and Government of Canada. For free copies contact Communications and Public Affairs, Department of Justice, Canada, Ottawa, Ontario K1A 0H8.
- *Divorce Law for Counsellors*, published by the same people as above and available free from the same address. It is more detailed than the above pamphlet.
- *The Divorce Revolution: The Unexpected Social and Economic Consequences for Women and Children in America*, by Dr. Lenore Weitzman (The Free Press, A Division of Macmillan Inc. © 1985). This book traces the impoverishing effect of no-fault divorce laws upon women and children in the United States.
- *The Complete Guide for Men & Women Divorcing*, by Melvin Belli and Mel Krantzler (St. Martin's Press © 1988). This book deals with U.S. law and experience.
- *Current Demographic Analysis, New Trends in the Family, Demographic Facts and Features*, by Bali Ram for the Ministry of Industry, Trade and Technology c 1990. Available from Statistics Canada, Ottawa, Ontario K1A 0T6 ($25.00). Cat. 91-535E.
- *Families in Canada, 1986 Census of Canada*, by Thomas Burch c 1990. Available from Statistics Canada, Ottawa, Ontario K1A 0T6 ($10.00). Cat. 98-127.
- *Consultation with Family Law Lawyers on the Divorce Act, 1985*, by James MacDonald (May 1989). Available from the Department of Justice, Canada, Bureau of Review.
- *Review of Support Factors and Objectives in Case Law Decided under the Divorce Act, 1985*, by Carol J. Rogerson (February 1990). Available from the Department of Justice, Canada, Bureau of Review. This is an exceptionally good review of support obligations written by a professor at the University of Toronto, and I am grateful for having had access to it.
- *Divorce: Law and the Family in Canada*, Statistics Canada, Research and Analysis Division (Ministry of Supply and Services Canada © 1983) ($12.00). Cat. 89-502E.

FAMILY PROPERTY

- *The New Family Law*, by Lorne Wolfson (Random House © 1987). This book deals just with Ontario and has a financial impact emphasis.
- *Spousal Property Rights under the Ontario Family Law Act*, by Julian Payne (Butterworths © 1987). This book draws on Canadian cases, not just Ontario, and is particularly good.

CUSTODY AND ACCESS

- *Beyond the Best Interests of the Child*, by Joseph Goldstein, Anna Freud, and Albert J. Solnit (The Free Press © 1973).
- *Surviving the Breakup: How Children and Parents Cope with Divorce*, by Judith Wallerstein and Joan Kelly (Basic Books © 1980).
- *Two Homes: A Parent's Guide to Joint Custody in Canada*, by Laurie Coulter (HarperCollins c 1990).
- *Where Do I Stand? A Child's Legal Guide to Separation and Divorce*, published by the Ministry of the Attorney General of Ontario and available free of charge. This is a great little book for children.

MEDIATION

- *Family Mediation Handbook*, by Barbara Landau, Mario Bartoletti, and Ruth Mesbur (Butterworths © 1987).
- *Family Mediation: Theory and Practice of Dispute Resolution*, by Howard H. Irving and Michael Benjamin (Carswell © 1987).
- *An Inventory of Divorce Mediation and Reconciliation Services in Canada*, available free from the Communications and Public Affairs Division of the Department of Justice, Canada, Ottawa, Ontario K1A 0H8.
- *Family Mediation: Consumer's Guide*, published by Family Mediation Canada (free). See the addresses in Chapter 12.
- *Another Way, Mediation in Divorce and Separation*, published by Department of Justice Canada, Ottawa, Ontario K1A 0H8 (613) 957-4222 (free).

ENFORCEMENT OF FAMILY LAW

- *Challenging our Assumptions*, materials from the 1990 meeting of the Association of Family and Conciliation Courts; and in particular, two papers, one by Robyn Moglove Diamond (now Madam Justice Diamond of Manitoba Queen's Bench) called "Enforcement of Custody and Access Orders," and the other, Freda Steel's article, "An Overview of Provincial and Federal Maintenance Enforcement Legislation."
- *Child Finder*, by Colin Maxwell and Allan Gould (Prentice-Hall Canada © 1989).

GRANDPARENTS

- *Between Parents and Grandparents,* by Arthur Kornhaber, M.D. (St. Martin's Press © 1986).

MARRIAGE CONTRACTS

- *Marriage Contracts,* by Evita Roche and David Simmonds (Carswell and the Law Society of Upper Canada © 1988). This book is for lawyers, but it is so well written that non-lawyers can easily understand most of it.

MISCELLANEOUS

- *On Death and Dying,* by Elizabeth Kübler-Ross (Macmillan © 1970).
- *Splitting Up: The Yukon Law on Separation,* by Lynn Gaudet; available from the Yukon Public Legal Education Association, Yukon College, Box 2799, Whitehorse, Yukon Y1A 5K4. This book is excellent. If every province published a book like this one you wouldn't need mine.
- *Family Law in Ontario: A Practical Guide for Lawyers and Law Clerks,* by Michael G. Cochrane (Canada Law Book c 1990). I wrote this book for people in Ontario, but a great deal of the information is valid in all provinces. It's available from Canada Law Book, 240 Edward Street, Aurora, Ontario L4G 3S9 (416) 841-6472 ($65.00). It describes how lawyers analyse family law problems and get ready for trial, among other things.
- The Research Facility, Ontario Legal Aid Plan, 200-481 University Ave., Toronto, Ontario. This facility produces excellent up-to-the-minute legal research for lawyers in Ontario, free of charge for lawyers who do legal aid. I am indebted to the facility, which has shared its research memoranda with me.
- *Family Law, Reference Materials,* by Philip Epstein, Q.C. (Law Society of Upper Canada © 1990). Available from the Law Society, 130 Queen Street West, Toronto, Ontario M5H 2N6. I am indebted to these materials, which are probably the best in Canada.

Appendices

Mountains of paper will be exchanged in family law cases, everything from letters between lawyers, faxes, pleadings, evidence, offers to settle and affidavits, to separation agreements and divorce judgments. I wish I could provide you with an example of each one but space considerations simply won't permit it. Instead, I have selected several key documents for your consideration. Before each one I have provided a brief annotation about its purpose and where in the text you can find more information about its role.

I have also included a glossary of common family law terms.

(i) The Retainer

This is your contract with your lawyer. In it, he or she should describe the work that will be done on your behalf and the estimated (or maximum) cost of the work. These retainers vary from lawyer to lawyer but they should have, as a minimum, the amount of detail contained in the following sample forms. You should *always* have a written retainer with your lawyer. For more information on retainers read Chapter 3 and see the definitions in the Glossary. Retainer #1 is the best of the three, I think.

RETAINER FORM #1

I,   , of the City of   in the Regional Municipality of   hereby retain and employ Messrs. Cochrane & Cochrane, Toronto, Ontario as my solicitors and hereby authorize them to [purpose] and to take such actions and conduct such proceedings as they may consider necessary or proper for the conduct of such action on my behalf.

DATED this   day of   , 19 .

Witness: _____
[Signature of client]

Fees and Disbursements Policy

For the information of clients, the firm's policy in regard to fees and disbursements is as follows:

1. All services performed by lawyers and students on behalf of a client are ordinarily recorded on a time occupied basis and charged against the client on that basis at rates ranging from $150 per hour down to $25 per hour. The hourly rates are reviewed on an annual basis. Time in court may be charged in certain cases at rates in excess of $1,000 per day depending upon the nature of the case, its complexity, and the lawyer or lawyers involved.
2. Most matters require the disbursement of money by the firm on the client's behalf. These disbursements will be billed regularly to the client as they are incurred on an interim statement of account entitled "Disbursements Only".
3. In most litigious and other matters, clients will be requested to provide an advance on accounts of fees and disbursements, which sum will be held in the firm's trust account to the client's credit to be applied towards such disbursements and fees incurred in connection with the matter.
4. It is recognized by this firm that many clients are unfamiliar with the manner in which lawyers bill and further, are unfamiliar with the amount of fees that may be owing from time to time during the course of a particular proceeding. In the circumstances, clients are encouraged to feel free to discuss fees at any time with any representative of the firm and in particular, to discuss the method of billing when the firm is originally retained.

Note to a Litigant

In view of the fact that   practice involves a great deal of court work, he/she may be out of his/her office, or on occasion, out of the City and thus sometimes unavailable on an immediate basis for appointments or reception of telephone calls. On those occasions,   secretary and other members of the firm who are familiar with your case will be of as much assistance to you as possible.

M   will, of course, attend to your problem at his/her earliest opportunity.

> Barristers & Solicitors
> Toronto, Canada
> Tel. (416) 000-0000

RETAINER FORM #2

NOTE TO CLIENT RE LEGAL FEES AND DISBURSEMENTS

Legal fees are sums charged for a lawyer's services. Disbursements are the sums paid by a lawyer on your behalf for actual expenses, e.g., filing court documents, long distance telephone charges.

In an uncontested court action, e.g., a divorce action where there are no issues in dispute between the spouses, it is possible to quote accurately the cost of legal fees and disbursements since the length of time and the results can be predicted precisely.

Your case is not an uncontested court action since there are unresolved disputes between you and your spouse. Accordingly, in your case, it is impossible to exactly estimate the length of time or the results. Therefore, it is impossible to predict precisely the legal fees and disbursements.

From time to time you will be sent interim accounts. Such interim accounts do not necessarily represent the value of legal services performed to-date but are merely interim payments on account of the final legal fees and disbursements.

The following matters must be taken into account in determining what is a reasonable legal fee:

(a) The time expended by the solicitor;
(b) The legal complexity of the matters dealt with;
(c) The degree of responsibility assumed by the solicitor;
(d) The monetary value of the matters in issue;
(e) The importance of the matters to the client;
(f) The degree of skill and competence demonstrated by the solicitor;
(g) The results achieved;
(h) The ability of the client to pay.

When your file is closed, a detailed account for professional services rendered listing all disbursements will be delivered to you.

If you have any questions concerning the above, please do not hesitate to ask.

I HAVE READ AND UNDERSTAND THE ABOVE.

[Date] _____ [Signature] _____

RETAINER FORM #3

I, _____, hereby retain and instruct Messrs. _____ to advise me and to act on my behalf with respect to all aspects of the matrimonial and financial issues outstanding between myself and my spouse, including the negotiation of a domestic contract and, if necessary, the instituting of:

(a) proceedings under the Family Law Act, 1986 [or relevant provincial law] and any other statutes affecting matrimonial property;
(b) divorce proceedings;
(c) proceedings for support for myself;
(d) proceedings for custody of and support for the children of the marriage;
(e) proceedings in any court that may be necessary to enforce or retain any rights I may have.

Generally, I retain and instruct this law firm to conduct the above matters on my behalf in all respects.

I understand that Messrs. _____ will render accounts to me mainly on the basis of time spent on my file on my behalf however that time may be spent; that such time will include telephone calls; and that the hourly rates charged are as follows:

Students............................ $ _____.
Lawyer 1........................... $ _____.
Lawyer 2........................... $ _____.
Lawyer 3........................... $ _____.

I understand that Messrs._____ may render interim accounts to me from time to time and that the above hourly rates may be increased on written notice to me.

I understand that, in addition to the fees charged in interim accounts, there will be a final account in which the complexity of the issues and the result obtained will also be taken into consideration in fixing the amount of the final fee.

I agree that accounts paid more than thirty days after their date will bear interest at ____ per cent per annum from their date.

I acknowledge receipt of a copy of this form of instructions.

Dated at _____ this _____ day of _____, 19___.

_____   _____
      Lawyer's name   Client's name

(ii) The Petition for Divorce

The requirements for a divorce are set out in the federal *Divorce Act*. The standards are therefore the same in every province and territory. The Petition is the formal document that starts the divorce case's journey through the legal system. It is prepared in the lawyer's office, signed by the person asking for the divorce (the petitioner) and his or her lawyer, issued at the courthouse (meaning it is checked over by court staff and authorized by them to proceed) and then served on the other spouse (the respondent). Whether the divorce is contested, uncontested or a joint petition for divorce, it is always started by petition, and it ends with a judgment unless settled in some other way.

For more information see Chapter 5, "Divorce," and the definition in the Glossary.

Three documents are reproduced here:

- Petition for Divorce
- Joint Petition for Divorce
- Divorce Judgment

PETITION FOR DIVORCE—S.C.O.
(Form 70A under the Rules)
AMENDED JULY 1, 1989

DYE & DURHAM CO. LIMITED
Form No. 906

Court file no.

SUPREME COURT OF ONTARIO

(The parties should be identified in the title of the proceeding as "husband" and "wife" in addition to their formal designation as "petitioner" and "respondent". When this is done, the parties may be referred to in the body of the document as "husband" and "wife" alone.)

BETWEEN:

(Court seal)

and

PETITIONER

(   )

RESPONDENT

(   )

PETITION FOR DIVORCE

TO THE RESPONDENT

A LEGAL PROCEEDING FOR DIVORCE HAS BEEN COMMENCED AGAINST YOU by the petitioner. The claim made against you appears on the following pages.

IF YOU WISH TO DEFEND THIS PROCEEDING, you or an Ontario lawyer acting for you must prepare an answer in Form 70D prescribed by the Rules of Civil Procedure, serve it on the petitioner's lawyer(s) or, where the petitioner does not have a lawyer, serve it on the petitioner, and file it, with proof of service, in this court office, WITHIN TWENTY DAYS after this petition is served on you, if you are served in Ontario.

If you are served in another province or territory of Canada or in the United States of America, the period for serving and filing your answer is forty days. If you are served outside Canada and the United States of America, the period is sixty days.

Instead of serving and filing an answer, you may serve and file a notice of intent to defend in Form 70J prescribed by the Rules of Civil Procedure. This will entitle you to ten more days within which to serve and file your answer.

If this petition for divorce contains a claim for support or division of property, you must serve and file a financial statement in Form 70K prescribed by the Rules of Civil Procedure within the time set out above for serving and filing your answer, whether or not you wish to defend this proceeding. If you serve and file an answer, your financial statement must accompany your answer.

IF YOU FAIL TO SERVE AND FILE AN ANSWER, A DIVORCE MAY BE GRANTED IN YOUR ABSENCE AND WITHOUT FURTHER NOTICE TO YOU, JUDGMENT MAY BE GRANTED AGAINST YOU ON ANY OTHER CLAIM IN THIS PETITION AND YOU MAY LOSE YOUR RIGHT TO SUPPORT OR DIVISION OF PROPERTY. IF YOU WISH TO DEFEND THIS PROCEEDING BUT ARE UNABLE TO PAY LEGAL FEES, LEGAL AID MAY BE AVAILABLE TO YOU BY CONTACTING A LOCAL LEGAL AID OFFICE.

NEITHER SPOUSE IS FREE TO REMARRY until a divorce has been granted and has taken effect. Once a divorce has taken effect, you may obtain a certificate of divorce from this court office.

Date ....

Issued by ....
Local registrar

TO:

Address of court office

(Name and address of each respondent.)

Page 2—PETITION FOR DIVORCE—S.C.O.
(Form 70A under the Rules)
AMENDED JUNE 1, 1986

DYE & DURHAM CO. LIMITED
Form No. 906

<u>**CLAIM**</u>

1. The petitioner claims:

*(State precisely
everything you want
the court to include in
the judgment. If you
claim support or a
division of property,
set out the nature
and amount of relief
claimed and the
amount of support
claimed for each
dependant. If you
want to include
provisions of a
separation agreement
in the judgment, refer
to the specific
provisions to be
included.)*

(a) a divorce;

(b) under the *Divorce Act,*

    (i)

(c) under the *Family Law Act,*

    (i)

*(If relief is claimed
under any other Act,
refer to the Act in the
claim.)*

Page 3—PETITION FOR DIVORCE—S.C.O
(Form 70A under the Rules)
AMENDED JUNE 1, 1986

DYE & DURHAM CO. LIMITED
Form No. 906

GROUNDS FOR DIVORCE—SEPARATION

*(Strike out
inapplicable
paragraphs.)*

2. (a) The spouses have lived separate and apart since   The spouses

date

have resumed cohabitation during the following periods in an unsuccessful attempt at reconciliation:

Date(s) of cohabitation
(If none, state "none".)

GROUNDS FOR DIVORCE—ADULTERY

2. (b) The respondent spouse has committed adultery. Particulars are as follows:

GROUNDS FOR DIVORCE—CRUELTY

2. (c) The respondent has treated the petitioner with physical or mental cruelty of such a kind as to render intolerable the continued cohabitation of the spouses. Particulars are as follows:

Page 4—PETITION FOR DIVORCE—S.C.O.
(Form 70A under the Rules)
AMENDED JUNE 1, 1986

DYE & DURHAM CO. LIMITED
Form No. 906

RECONCILIATION

3. There is no possibility of reconciliation of the spouses.

(Give details. Where no efforts have been made, state "None".)

4. The following efforts to reconcile have been made:

DETAILS OF MARRIAGE

(Where possible, copy the information from the marriage certificate.)

5. Date of marriage:...

6. Place of marriage:...
(municipality and province, state or country)

7. Wife's surname immediately before marriage:...

8. Wife's surname at birth:...

9. Husband's surname immediately before marriage:..

10. Husband's surname at birth:..

11. Marital status of husband at time of marriage:..
(never married, divorced or widower)

12. Marital status of wife at time of marriage:...
(never married, divorced or widow)

13. Wife's birthplace:...
(province, state or country)

14. Wife's birth date:..

15. Husband's birthplace:..
(province, state or country)

16. Husband's birth date:..

(Check (a), (b) or (c) and complete as required.)

17. (a) ☐ A certificate of ☐ the marriage
☐ the registration of the marriage

of the spouses has been filed with the court.

(b) ☐ It is impossible to obtain a certificate of the marriage or its registration because:

(c) ☐ A certificate of the marriage or its registration will be filed before this action is set down for trial or a motion is made for judgment.

Page 5—PETITION FOR DIVORCE—S.C.O.
(Form 70A under the Rules)
AMENDED JUNE 1, 1986

DYE & DURHAM CO. LIMITED
Form No. 906

RESIDENCE

18. The petitioner has resided in:...

since..
(municipality and province, state or country)
(date)

19. The respondent has resided in:...
(municipality and province, state or country)

since..
(date)

20. The respondent's current address is:...

....

21. The ☐ petitioner has habitually resided in Ontario for at least one year immediately preceding the
☐ respondent

commencement of this proceeding.

CHILDREN

22. The following are all the living children of the marriage as defined by the *Divorce Act:*

Full name	Birth date	School and grade or year	Person with whom child lives and length of time child has lived there

The children ordinarily reside in:...
(municipality and province, state or country)

(Be sure that this paragraph agrees with the claim on page 2.)

23. (a) The petitioner seeks an order for custody or joint custody of the following children on the following terms:

Name of child	Terms of the order

The respondent ☐ agrees
☐ does not agree with the above terms.

Page 6—PETITION FOR DIVORCE—S.C.O.
(Form 70A under the Rules)
AMENDED JUNE 1, 1986

DYE & DURHAM CO. LIMITED
Form No. 906

(Strike out if not applicable.)

(b) The petitioner is not seeking an order for custody and

☐ is content that a previous order for custody remain in force

☐ is attempting to obtain an order for custody in another proceeding

(Give name of court, court file no. and particulars of the order or proceeding.)

full particulars of which are as follows:

(Strike out if not applicable.)

(c) The petitioner seeks an order for access (visiting arrangements) and is content that the respondent have an order for custody of the following children on the following terms:

Name of child	**Terms of the order**

The respondent ☐ agrees
☐ does not agree with the above terms.

Page 7—PETITION FOR DIVORCE—S.C.O.
(Form 70A under the Rules)
AMENDED JUNE 1, 1986

DYE & DURHAM CO. LIMITED
Form No. 906

24. (a) The following are the existing visiting arrangements (access) for the spouse who does not have the children living with him or her:

(Give details such as days of the week, hours of visit and place of access.)

Page 8—PETITION FOR DIVORCE—S.C.O.
(Form 70A under the Rules)
AMENDED JUNE 1, 1986

DYE & DURHAM CO. LIMITED
Form No. 906

*(If not satisfactory,
give reasons and
describe how the
arrangements should
be changed.)*

(b) The existing visiting arrangements (access) are ☐ satisfactory
☐ not satisfactory.

25. The order sought in paragraph 23 is in the best interests of the children for the following reasons:

26. The following material changes in the circumstances of the spouses are expected to affect the children, their custody and the visiting arrangements (access) in the future:

Page 9—PETITION FOR DIVORCE—S.C.O.
(Form 70A under the Rules)
AMENDED JUNE 1, 1986

DYE & DURHAM CO. LIMITED
Form No. 906

27. (a) The existing arrangements between the spouses for support for the children are as follows:

Amount paid	Time period (weekly, monthly, etc.)	Paid by (husband or wife)	Paid for (name of child)

(If not being honoured, specify how much is unpaid and for how long. If you seek an order for payment of part or all of the unpaid amount, be sure to include it in the claim on page 2.)

(b) The existing support arrangements ☐are being honoured
☐are not being honoured.

(Be sure that this paragraph agrees with the claim on page 2.)

(c) The petitioner proposes that the support arrangements for the children should be as follows:

Amount to be paid	Time period (weekly, monthly, etc.)	To be paid by (husband or wife)	To be paid for (name of child)

(If not being met, give particulars.)

28. The educational needs of the children ☐ are being met.
☐are not being met.

Page 10 – PETITION FOR DIVORCE—S C O
(Form 70A under the Rules)
AMENDED JUNE 1, 1986

DYE & DURHAM CO LIMITED
Form No 906

OTHER COURT PROCEEDINGS

(Give the name of the court, the court file no , the kind of order the court was asked to make and what order, if any, the court made If the proceeding is not yet completed, give its current status.)

29. The following are all other court proceedings with reference to the marriage or any child of the marriage:

DOMESTIC CONTRACTS AND FINANCIAL ARRANGEMENTS

(Indicate whether the contract or arrangement is now in effect, and if support payments are not being paid in full, state the amount that has not been paid.)

30. The spouses have entered into the following domestic contracts and other written or oral financial arrangements:

Date	Nature of contract or arrangement	Status

COLLUSION, CONDONATION AND CONNIVANCE

31. There has been no collusion in relation to this divorce proceeding.

(Strike out this paragraph if the divorce is sought on the ground of separation only.)

(Where there has been condonation or connivance, strike out the previous sentence Give details and set out the facts relied on to justify a divorce in the circumstances.)

32. There has been no condonation of or connivance at the grounds for divorce in this proceeding.

Page 11   PETITION FOR DIVORCE - S C O
(Form 70A under the Rules)
AMENDED JUNE 1, 1986

DYE & DURHAM CO LIMITED
Form No 906

MATTERS OTHER THAN DIVORCE AND CUSTODY

*(Set out in separate,
consecutively
numbered paragraphs
the material facts
relied on to substan-
tiate the claims.)*

33. The grounds for the relief sought in paragraph 1, other than a divorce or custody, are as follows:

Page 12—PETITION FOR DIVORCE—S.C.O.
(Form 70A under the Rules)
AMENDED JUNE 1, 1986

DYE & DURHAM CO. LIMITED
Form No. 906

TRIAL

34. The petitioner proposes that if there is a trial in this action, the trial be held

(Where a claim is made for custody of a child who ordinarily resides in Ontario, the place of trial must be in the county where the child ordinarily resides.)

at   before

       (place)

☐ a High Court judge.

☐ a local judge.

☐ either a High Court judge or a local judge.

DECLARATION OF PETITIONER

35. I have read and understand this petition for divorce. The statements in it are true, to the best of my knowledge, information and belief.

Date ....

                                                  Signature of petitioner

STATEMENT OF SOLICITOR

(Strike out this paragraph if you do not have a lawyer.)

(Where in the circumstances it would clearly not be appropriate to discuss the matters in section 9 with the applicant, set out the circumstances.)

36. I,   , solicitor for the petitioner, certify

to this court that I have complied with the requirements of section 9 of the *Divorce Act*.

Date ....

                                                Signature of solicitor

                               Name, address and telephone number of petitioner's solicitor or petitioner

(Short title of proceeding)

PETITIONER ( )

and

RESPONDENT ( )

Court file no

SUPREME COURT OF ONTARIO

Proceeding commenced at

PETITION FOR DIVORCE

(Form 70A under the Rules)

DYE & DURHAM CO. LIMITED—Form No. 906

Name, address and telephone number of petitioner's solicitor or petitioner:

ACKNOWLEDGMENT OF SERVICE

I,

am the respondent named in this petition. I acknowledge receipt of a copy of this petition. My address for service of documents in this divorce proceeding is

Date ....

....
Signature of respondent

....
Signature of witness

I,

served this petition personally on the respondent.

☐ The respondent completed and signed the acknowledgment of service above in my presence and I signed it as witness.

or

☐ The respondent declined to complete and sign the acknowledgment of service.

....
Signature

DYE & DURHAM CO. LIMITED
Form No. 929

Court file no.

ONTARIO COURT (GENERAL DIVISION)

HUSBAND

(Court seal)   and

WIFE

JOINT PETITION FOR DIVORCE

Date..   Issued by...
                                                                            Local registrar

Address of court office

JOINT PETITION

(State precisely everything you want the court to include in the judgment. Everything you want to include must have been agreed to by both spouses. If you want to include provisions of a separation agreement in the judgment, refer to the specific provisions to be included.)

1. The husband and wife jointly seek:

   (a) a divorce;

   (b) under the *Divorce Act,*

      (i)

210   Family Law

DYE & DURHAM CO. LIMITED
Form No. 929

(c) under the *Family Law Act,*

　(i)

*(If relief is claimed on
consent under any
other Act, refer to the
Act in the claim.)*

GROUNDS FOR DIVORCE—SEPARATION

2. The spouses have lived separate and apart since　　　　　　　　**The spouses**
date

have resumed cohabitation during the following periods in an unsuccessful attempt at reconciliation:

Date(s) of cohabitation
(If none, state "None".)

DYE & DURHAM CO. LIMITED
Form No. 929

RECONCILIATION

3. There is no possibility of reconciliation of the spouses.

(Give details. Where no efforts have been made, state "None".)

4. The following efforts to reconcile have been made:

DETAILS OF MARRIAGE

(Where possible, copy the information from the marriage certificate.)

5. Date of marriage:..

6. Place of marriage:..
(municipality and province, state or country)

7. Wife's surname immediately before marriage:...................................

8. Wife's surname at birth:...

9. Husband's surname immediately before marriage:............................

10. Husband's surname at birth:...

11. Marital status of husband at time of marriage:...............................
(never married, divorced or widower)

12. Marital status of wife at time of marriage:....................................
(never married, divorced or widow)

13. Wife's birthplace:..
(province, state or country)

14. Wife's birth date:..

15. Husband's birthplace:...
(province, state or country)

16. Husband's birth date:..

(Check (a), (b) or (c) and complete as required.)

17. (a) ☐ A certificate of ☐ the marriage
☐ the registration of the marriage

of the spouses has been filed with the court.

(b) ☐ It is impossible to obtain a certificate of the marriage or its registration because:

(c) ☐ A certificate of the marriage or its registration will be filed before this action is set down for trial or a motion is made for judgment.

RESIDENCE

18. The wife has resided in:...
(municipality and province, state or country)

....since..
(date)

19. The husband has resided in:...
(municipality and province, state or country)

....since..
(date)

20. The husband's current address is:...

....

The wife's current address is:...

....

21. The ☐ husband has habitually resided in Ontario for at least one year immediately preceding the
☐ wife

commencement of this proceeding.

CHILDREN

22. The following are all the living children of the marriage as defined by the *Divorce Act:*

Full name	Birth date	School and grade or year	Person with whom child lives and length of time child has lived there

The children ordinarily reside in:...
(municipality and province, state or country)

(Be sure that this paragraph agrees with the claim in paragraph 1.)

23. (a) The spouses seek an order on consent for custody or joint custody of the following children
on the following terms:

Name of child	Terms of the order

DYE & DURHAM CO. LIMITED
Form No. 929

(Strike out if not applicable.)

(b) The spouses are not seeking an order for custody and

☐ are content that a previous order for custody remain in force

☐ are attempting to obtain an order for custody in another proceeding

(Give name of court, court file no. and particulars of the order or proceeding.)

full particulars of which are as follows:

(Be sure that this paragraph agrees with the claim in paragraph 1 or strike out if not applicable.)

(c) The spouses seek an order on consent for access (visiting arrangements) to the following children on the following terms:

Name of child   **Terms of the order**

JOINT PETITION FOR DIVORCE—Page 6 of 11
(Form 70B under the Rules)
Amended 1990

DYE & DURHAM CO. LIMITED
Form No. 929

(Give details such as days of the week, hours of visit and place of access.)

24. **(a)** The following are the existing visiting arrangements (access) for the spouse who does not have the children living with him or her:

DYE & DURHAM CO. LIMITED
Form No. 929

(If not satisfactory, give reasons and describe how the arrangements should be changed.)

(b) The existing visiting arrangements (access) are   ☐ satisfactory
☐ not satisfactory.

25. The order sought in paragraph 23 is in the best interests of the children for the following reasons:

26. The following material changes in the circumstances of the spouses are expected to affect the children, their custody and the visiting arrangements (access) in the future:

JOINT PETITION FOR DIVORCE—*Page 8 of 11*
(Form 70B under the Rules)
Amended 1990

DYE & DURHAM CO. LIMITED
Form No. 929

27. (a) The existing arrangements between the spouses for support for the children are as follows:

Amount paid	Time period (weekly, monthly, etc.)	Paid by (husband or wife)	Paid for (name of child)

(If not being honoured, specify how much is unpaid and for how long. If you agree on an order for payment of part or all of the unpaid amount, be sure to include it in paragraph 1.)

(b) The existing support arrangements ☐ are being honoured.
☐ are not being honoured.

(Be sure that this paragraph agrees with the claim in paragraph 1.)

(c) The spouses propose that the support arrangements for the children should be as follows:

Amount to be paid	Time period (weekly, monthly, etc.)	To be paid by (husband or wife)	To be paid for (name of child)

(If not being met, give particulars.) **28.** The educational needs of the children ☐ are being met.
☐ are not being met.

DYE & DURHAM CO. LIMITED
Form No. 929

OTHER COURT PROCEEDINGS

(Give the name of the court, the court file no., the kind of order the court was asked to make and what order, if any, the court made. If the proceeding is not yet completed, give its current status.)

29. The following are all other court proceedings with reference to the marriage or any child of the marriage:

DOMESTIC CONTRACTS AND FINANCIAL ARRANGEMENTS

(Indicate whether the contract or arrangement is now in effect, and if support payments are not being paid in full, state the amount that has not been paid.)

30. The spouses have entered into the following domestic contracts and other written or oral financial arrangements:

Date	Nature of contract or arrangement	Status

NO COLLUSION

31. There has been no collusion in relation to this divorce proceeding.

DYE & DURHAM CO. LIMITED
Form No. 929

DECLARATION OF SPOUSES

32. (a) I have read and understand this petition for divorce. The statements in it are true, to the best of my knowledge, information and belief.

    (b) I understand that I have the right to seek independent legal advice concerning this proceeding and to retain my own separate counsel.

    (c) I understand that I may lose my right to make a claim for division of property after the divorce if I do not make the claim at this time.

Date ....
                                                        Signature of husband

Date ....
                                                        Signature of wife

STATEMENT OF WIFE'S SOLICITOR

(Strike out this paragraph if you do not have a lawyer.)

(Where in the circumstances it would clearly not be appropriate to discuss the matters in section 9 with the wife, set out the circumstances.)

33. (a) I,   , solicitor for the wife,

    certify to this court that I have complied with the requirements of section 9 of the *Divorce Act.* I also certify that I have advised the wife that she has the right to seek independent legal advice and retain separate counsel in this proceeding.

Date ....
                                                        Signature of solicitor

                                                Name, address and telephone number of solicitor:

STATEMENT OF HUSBAND'S SOLICITOR

(Strike out this paragraph if you do not have a lawyer.)

(Where in the circumstances it would clearly not be appropriate to discuss the matters in section 9 with the husband, set out the circumstances.)

33. (b) I,   , solicitor for the husband,

    certify to this court that I have complied with the requirements of section 9 of the *Divorce Act.* I also certify that I have advised the husband that he has the right to seek independent legal advice and retain separate counsel in this proceeding.

Date ....
                                                        Signature of solicitor

                                                Name, address and telephone number of solicitor:

(Short title of proceeding)

HUSBAND

and

WIFE

Court file no.

ONTARIO COURT (GENERAL DIVISION)

Proceeding commenced at

JOINT
PETITION FOR DIVORCE

(Form 70B under the Rules)
Amended 1990

DYE & DURHAM CO. LIMITED—Form No. 809—Page 11 of 11

Name, address and telephone number of solicitor. If no solicitor, addresses
and telephone numbers of husband and wife.

DIVORCE JUDGMENT (ON JOINT MOTION)—S.C.O.
(Form 70S under the Rules)
JUNE 1, 1986

DYE & DURHAM CO LIMITED
Form No 995

Court file no.

SUPREME COURT OF ONTARIO

(Name of judge)   THE HONOURABLE   19

(day and date judgment given)

(Name only the spouses in title of proceeding unless an order is also made against another person.)

BETWEEN:

HUSBAND

(Court seal.)   and

WIFE

DIVORCE JUDGMENT

THIS MOTION made jointly by the spouses for judgment for divorce was heard this day

at

(place)

The spouses jointly petitioned for divorce.

(Refer to any other material filed, such as the Official Guardian's report dated (date)); (where oral evidence was heard, add and on hearing the evidence presented by the spouses.)

ON READING the petition, the notice of motion for judgment, the affidavit dated

(date)

of the husband and the affidavit dated   of the wife filed in support of the

(date)

(Where the divorce is to take effect earlier than the thirty-first day after it is granted, add: and since this court is of the opinion that by reason of special circumstances the divorce should take effect earlier than the thirty-first day after the day this judgment is granted, and since the spouses have agreed and undertaken that no appeal from the judgment will be taken.)

motion and

Page 2—DIVORCE JUDGMENT (ON JOINT MOTION)—S.C.O.
(Form 70S under the Rules)
AMENDED JULY 1, 1989

DYE & DURHAM CO. LIMITED
Form No. 995

1. THIS COURT ORDERS AND ADJUDGES that

(names of spouses)

who were married at

(place)

on   are divorced and that the divorce takes effect on

(date)   *(date)*

*(Delete if inappli-
cable; or, where the
court also grants
judgment for other
relief, add: "under
the Divorce Act" (or
as may be), that . . .)*

*(In a judgment for the
payment of money on
which postjudgment
interest is payable,
add: "This judgment
bears interest at the
rate of   per
cent per year
commencing on
(date).")*

2. THIS COURT ORDERS AND ADJUDGES

_____

*(In a judgment that provides for payment of support, set out the last known address of the support creditor
and debtor.)*

**THE SPOUSES ARE NOT FREE TO REMARRY UNTIL THIS JUDGMENT TAKES EFFECT, AT WHICH
TIME A CERTIFICATE OF DIVORCE MAY BE OBTAINED FROM THIS COURT. IF AN APPEAL IS TAKEN
IT MAY DELAY THE DATE WHEN THIS JUDGMENT TAKES EFFECT.**

(Short title of proceeding)

and
HUSBAND

Court file no.

WIFE

SUPREME COURT OF ONTARIO

Proceeding commenced at

DIVORCE JUDGMENT
(ON JOINT MOTION)

(Form 70S under the Rules)

DYE & DURHAM CO. LIMITED—Form No. 995

(iii) A Notice of Motion

This document is simply a way of giving the court and the other side notice of the fact that, now that a court case is under way, one of the parties intends to ask the court to make a particular order. The order sought can range from the significant issues of custody or possession of the home to small technical issues such as amending a pleading or determining whether a piece of evidence needs to be shared. For more information see Chapter 4, "Taking a Look at the Process."

NOTICE OF MOTION

Court File No.

BETWEEN:

(Wife's name)
Applicant

and

(Husband's name)
Respondent

NOTICE OF MOTION

THE (Applicant)   will make a motion to a local judge, on
day,   , 19 , at   , or as soon
after that time as the motion can be heard, at   Ontario.

THE MOTION IS FOR:

1. Interim custody of the child of the marriage, namely, [child's name and birthday].
2. Interim support for the child of the marriage.
3. Interim support for the applicant.
4. Temporary exclusive possession of the matrimonial home known municipally as [address of home].
5. An order restraining the respondent from molesting, annoying or harassing the applicant and the child in her lawful custody and requiring the respondent to enter in the recognizance that the court considers appropriate.
6. An order restraining the depletion of the property of the respondent.
7. An order for the possession, delivering up, safekeeping and preservation of the property of the respondent.
8. An order requesting the leave of the court in abridging the time for service of this notice of motion and filing of the record.
9. Costs on a solicitor-and-client basis.
10. Such further and other relief as this Honourable Court deems just.

THE GROUNDS FOR THE MOTION ARE:

(1) The applicant claims interim custody of the child of the marriage pursuant to ss. 21 and 28 of the Children's Law Reform Act, R.S.O. 1980, c. 68, as amended by 1982, c. 20, [or relevant provincial law] on the following grounds:
  (a) The applicant has been the primary caretaker of the child since birth.
  (b) The child has resided with the applicant since the date of separation.
  (c) The respondent is not able to care for the child.
  (d) It would be in the best interests of the child if the applicant was awarded custody of the child.

(2) The applicant claims interim support for the child of the marriage and for herself pursuant to ss. 33 and 34 of the Family Law Act, 1986, [or relevant provincial law] on the following grounds:
  (a) The applicant is in need of such support for the child and herself.
  (b) The respondent is receiving income and is able to provide support for the child and the applicant.

(3) The applicant requests an order for interim exclusive possession of the matrimonial home pursuant to s. 24 of the Family Law Act, 1986, [or relevant provincial law] on the following grounds:
  (a) It would be in the best interests of the child if the applicant was granted exclusive possession of the matrimonial home having regard to the possible disruptive effects on the child of a move to other accommodation and the child's views and preferences.
  (b) There is an existing order under Part I and an existing support order.
  (c) The respective financial position of the applicant and respondent.
  (d) There is a written agreement between the applicant and respondent with respect to exclusive possession.
  (e) No other suitable or affordable accommodation is available.
  (f) The respondent/defendant has been violent to the applicant/plaintiff and the child.

(4) The applicant requests an order restraining the respondent from molesting, annoying or harassing her or the child in her lawful custody, pursuant to s. 46 of the Family Law Act, 1986, [or relevant provincial law] or from communicating with the applicant or child except as this court considers appropriate, on the following grounds:
  (a) The respondent has been violent in the past to the applicant and the child of the marriage.
  (b) The respondent has behaved in an irrational and dangerous manner on occasion.

(c) The applicant and child require protection from the respondent.

(5) The applicant requests an order restraining the depletion of the property of the respondent and for the possession, delivering up, safekeeping and preservation of the property of the respondent pursuant to s. 12 of the Family Law Act, 1986, [or relevant provincial law] on the following grounds:

(6) The applicant requests the leave of the court for an order abridging the time for the service of this notice of motion and filing of the record on the following grounds:

(7) The applicant claims her costs on a solicitor and client basis pursuant to Rule 57.01 (Ontario) [or relevant provincial rule].

THE FOLLOWING DOCUMENTARY EVIDENCE will be used at the hearing of the motion:

(1) Affidavit of the applicant sworn

(2) Financial Statement of the applicant sworn

Date: _____

[Solicitor's name & address]

TO: [Other Party or their
lawyer's name and address]

(iv)   An Affidavit

An affidavit is a written statement of facts made under oath (sworn) and usually accompanies or supports a Notice of Motion. It is witnessed by someone authorized to do so. It is a way of putting evidence of particular matters before the court. Rather than hearing the evidence orally the judge (and the other side) has an opportunity to read the other person's version of what happened. Sometimes the spouses involved sign the affidavit, sometimes another witness does and sometimes even the lawyer signs it. It usually depends on who has the best knowledge on the point in question. The Notice of Motion will describe the court order desired and the affidavit sets out the facts upon which the request is based.

SUPREME COURT OF ONTARIO

BETWEEN:

Petitioner
(wife)

and

Respondent
(husband)

AFFIDAVIT OF SERVICE

I,   , of the City of   , in the
Municipality of   , law clerk in the
office of   , solicitor for   , the Petitioner (wife),
MAKE OATH AND SAY:

1.   I served   , the Respondent (husband)
with the Offer to Settle dated
by sending a facsimile copy by telephone transmission to   ,
to   solicitors for the Respondent (husband).

SWORN BEFORE ME at the City of   )
            in the Municipality of   )
)
    , 1991   )   _____
)
_____   )
A COMMISSIONER, etc.

(v)   The Financial Statement

Much turns on this key statement about the individual's and the family's resources. It is basically an affidavit relating only to financial concerns. It summarizes financial abilities and liabilities. From these statements, which vary from province to province, the courts and the parties determine property division, spousal support, child support and even such issues as possession of the matrimonial home. The following form is from Ontario but the basic theory of dividing net worth is true for all provinces and the territories. For more information see Chapter 6, "Dividing The Family's Property".

FINANCIAL STATEMENT—S.C.O.
(Form 70K under the Rules)
AMENDED JUNE 1, 1986

DYE & DURHAM CO LIMITED—Form No 904

Court file no.

SUPREME COURT OF ONTARIO

ries in
of
ceeding.)

BETWEEN:

and

FINANCIAL STATEMENT

I,..
(Full name of deponent)

of the...of...in the
(City, Town, etc.)

....of...MAKE OATH AND SAY:
(County, Regional Municipality, etc.) / AFFIRM:

    1. Particulars of my financial situation and of all my property are accurately set out below, to the best of my knowledge, information and belief.

ALL INCOME AND MONEY RECEIVED

(Include all income and other money received from all sources, whether taxable or not. Show gross amount here and show deductions on pages 2, 3, 4 & 5. Give current actual amount where known or ascertainable. Where amount cannot be ascertained, give your best estimate. Use weekly, monthly or yearly column as appropriate.)

Category	Weekly	Monthly	Yearly
1. Salary or wages			
2. Bonuses			
3. Fees			
4. Commissions			
5. Family allowance			
6. Unemployment insurance			
7. Workers' compensation			
8. Public assistance			
9. Pension			
10. Dividends			
11. Interest			
12. Rental income			
13. Allowances and support from others			
14. Other (Specify)			
TOTAL	$	(A)$	$

Weekly total $_____ × 4.33 = (B)$_____monthly

Yearly total $_____ ÷ 12 = (C)$_____monthly

GROSS MONTHLY INCOME (A) + (B) + (C) = (D)$_____

Page 2—FINANCIAL STATEMENT
(Form 70K under the Rules)
AMENDED JUNE 1, 1988

DYE & DURHAM CO. LIMITED
Form No. 904 or 914

OTHER BENEFITS

(Show all non-monetary benefits from all sources, such as use of a vehicle or room and board, and include such items as insurance or dental plans or other expenses paid on your behalf. Give your best estimate where you cannot ascertain the actual value.)

Item	Particulars	Monthly Market Value

TOTAL (E) $_____

GROSS MONTHLY INCOME AND BENEFITS (D) + (E)=$_____

ACTUAL AND PROPOSED BUDGETS

	ACTUAL BUDGET for twelve month period from _____, 19___ to_____, 19___ Show actual expenses, or your best estimate where you cannot ascertain actual amount.			PROPOSED BUDGET Show your proposed budget, giving your best estimate where you cannot ascertain actual amount.		
CATEGORY	Weekly	Monthly	Yearly	Weekly	Monthly	Yearly
Housing						
1. Rent				1.		
2. Real property taxes				2.		
3. Mortgage				3.		
4. Common expense charges				4.		
5. Water				5.		
6. Electricity				6.		
7. Natural gas				7.		
8. Fuel oil				8.		
9. Telephone				9.		
10. Cable T.V.				10.		
11. Home insurance				11.		
12. Repairs and maintenance				12.		
13. Gardening and snow removal				13.		
14. Other (Specify)				14.		
Food, Toiletries and Sundries						
15. Groceries				15.		
16. Meals outside home				16.		
17. Toiletries and sundries				17.		
18. Grooming				18.		

Page 3—FINANCIAL STATEMENT
(Form 70K under the Rules)
AMENDED JUNE 1, 1986

DYE & DURHAM CO. LIMITED
Form No. 904 or 914

CATEGORY	ACTUAL BUDGET			PROPOSED BUDGET		
Food Toiletries and Sundries–cont'd.	Weekly	Monthly	Yearly	Weekly	Monthly	Yearly
19. General household supplies				19.		
20. Laundry, dry cleaning				20.		
21. Other (Specify)				21.		
Clothing						
22. Children				22.		
22. Self				23.		
Transportation						
24. Public transit				24.		
25. Taxis, car pools				25.		
26. Car Insurance				26.		
27. Licence				27.		
28. Car maintenance				28.		
29. Gasoline, oil				29.		
30. Parking				30.		
31. Other (Specify)				31.		
Health and Medical						
32. Doctors, chiropractors				32.		
33. Dentist (regular care)				33.		
34. Orthodontist or special dental care				34.		
35. Insurance premiums				35.		
36. Drugs				36.		
37. Other (Specify)				37.		
Deductions from Income						
38. Income tax				38.		
39. Canada Pension Plan				39.		
40. Unemployment insurance				40.		
41. Employer pension				41.		
42. Union or other dues				42.		

Page 4—FINANCIAL STATEMENT
(Form 70K under the Rules)
AMENDED JUNE 1, 1986

DYE & DURHAM CO. LIMITED
Form No. 904 or 914

CATEGORY	ACTUAL BUDGET			PROPOSED BUDGET		
Deductions from Income–cont'd.	Weekly	Monthly	Yearly	Weekly	Monthly	Yearly
43. Group insurance				43.		
44. Credit union loan				44.		
45. Credit union savings				45.		
46. Other (Specify)				46.		
Miscellaneous						
47. Life insurance premiums				47.		
48. Tuition fees, books, etc.				48.		
49. Entertainment				49.		
50. Recreation				50.		
51. Vacation				51.		
52. Gifts				52.		
53. Babysitting, day care				53.		
54. Children's allowances				54.		
55. Children's activities				55.		
56. Support payments				56.		
57. Newspapers, periodicals				57.		
58. Alcohol, tobacco				58.		
59. Charities				59.		
60. Income tax (not deducted at source)				60.		
61. Other (Specify)				61.		
Loan Payments						
62. Banks				62.		
63. Finance companies				63.		
64. Credit unions				64.		
65. Department stores				65.		
66. Other (Specify)				66.		

Page 5—FINANCIAL STATEMENT
(Form 70K under the Rules)
AMENDED JUNE 1, 1986

DYE & DURHAM CO. LIMITED
Form No. 904 or 914

CATEGORY	ACTUAL BUDGET			PROPOSED BUDGET		
	Weekly	Monthly	Yearly	Weekly	Monthly	Yearly
Savings 67. R.R.S.P.				67.		
68. Other (Specify)				68.		
	$	$	$	$	$	$

TOTALS OF ACTUAL BUDGET

Monthly Total $_____

Weekly Total $_____ × 4.33 = $_____

Yearly Total $_____ ÷ 12 = $_____

MONTHLY ACTUAL BUDGET   = (F) $_____

TOTALS OF PROPOSED BUDGET

Monthly Total $_____

Weekly Total $_____ × 4.33 = $_____

Yearly Total $_____ ÷ 12 = $_____

MONTHLY PROPOSED BUDGET   = (G) $_____

SUMMARY OF INCOME AND EXPENSES

Actual

Gross monthly income
(Amount D from page 1) $_____

Subtract Monthly actual budget
(Amount F from page 5)   — $_____

ACTUAL MONTHLY SURPLUS / DEFICIT $_____

Proposed

Gross monthly income
(Amount D from page 1) $_____

Subtract Proposed monthly budget
(Amount G from page 5)   — $_____

PROPOSED MONTHLY SURPLUS / DEFICIT $_____

Page 6— FINANCIAL STATEMENT
(Form 70K under the Rules)
AMENDED JUNE 1, 1988

DYE & DURHAM CO. LIMITED
Form No. 904 or 914

LAND

(Include any interest in land owned on the valuation date, including leasehold interests and mortgages, whether or not you are registered as owner. Include claims to an interest in land, but do not include claims that you are making against your spouse in this or a related proceeding. Show estimated market value of your interest without deducting encumbrances or costs of disposition, and show encumbrances and costs of disposition under Debts and Other Liabilities on page 9.)

Nature and Type of Ownership State percentage interest where relevant.	Nature and Address of Property	Estimated Market Value of Your Interest as of: See instructions above.		
		Date of Marriage	Valuation Date	Date of Statement
	TOTAL $		(H)	

GENERAL HOUSEHOLD ITEMS AND VEHICLES

(Show estimated market value, not cost of replacement for these items owned on the valuation date. Do not deduct encumbrances here, but show encumbrances under Debts and Other Liabilities on page 9.)

Item	Particulars	Estimated Market Value of Your Interest as of: See instructions above.		
		Date of Marriage	Valuation Date	Date of Statement
General household contents excluding special items (a) at matrimonial home(s)				
(b) elsewhere				
Jewellery				
Works of art				
Vehicles and boats				
Other special items				
	TOTAL $		(I)	

Page 1—FINANCIAL STATEMENT
(Form 70K under the Rules)
AMENDED JUNE 1, 1986

DYE & DURHAM CO. LIMITED
Form No. 904 or 914

SAVINGS AND SAVINGS PLANS

(Show items owned on the valuation date by category. Include cash, accounts in financial institutions, registered retirement or other savings plans, deposit receipts, pensions and any other savings.)

Category	Institution	Account Number	Amount as of:		
			Date of Marriage	Valuation Date	Date of Statement
		TOTAL $		(J)	

SECURITIES

(Show items owned on the valuation date by category. Include shares, bonds, warrants, options, debentures, notes and any other securities. Give your best estimate of market value if the items were to be sold on an open market.)

Category	Number	Description	Estimated Market Value as of:		
			Date of Marriage	Valuation Date	Date of Statement
		TOTAL $		(K)	

LIFE AND DISABILITY INSURANCE

(List all policies owned on the valuation date.)

Company and Policy No.	Kind of Policy	Owner	Beneficiary	Face Amount	Cash Surrender Value as of:		
					Date of Marriage	Valuation Date	Date of Statement
				TOTAL $		(L)	

*Page 8—*FINANCIAL STATEMENT
(Form 70K under the Rules)
AMENDED JUNE 1, 1986

DYE & DURHAM CO. LIMITED
Form No. 904 or 914

ACCOUNTS RECEIVABLE

(Give particulars of all debts owing to you on the valuation date, whether arising from business or from personal dealings.)

Particulars	Amount as of:		
	Date of Marriage	Valuation Date	Date of Statement
TOTAL $		(M)	

BUSINESS INTERESTS

(Show any interest in an unincorporated business owned on the valuation date. A controlling interest in an incorporated business may be shown here or under Securities on page 7. Give your best estimate of market value if the business were to be sold on an open market.)

Name of Firm or Company	Interest	Estimated Market Value as of:		
		Date of Marriage	Valuation Date	Date of Statement
TOTAL $			(N)	

OTHER PROPERTY

(Show other property owned on the valuation date by categories. Include property of any kind not shown above. Give your best estimate of market value.)

Category	Particulars	Estimated Market Value as of:		
		Date of Marriage	Valuation Date	Date of Statement
TOTAL $			(O)	

Page 9—FINANCIAL STATEMENT
(Form 70K under the Rules)
AMENDED JUNE 1, 1986

DYE & DURHAM CO. LIMITED
Form No. 904 or 914

DEBTS AND OTHER LIABILITIES

(Show your debts and other liabilities on the valuation date, whether arising from personal or business dealings, by category such as mortgages, charges, liens, notes, credit cards and accounts payable. Include contingent liabilities such as guarantees and indicate that they are contingent.)

Category	Particulars	Amount as of:		
		Date of Marriage	Valuation Date	Date of Statement
	TOTAL $		(P)	

PROPERTY, DEBTS AND OTHER LIABILITIES ON DATE OF MARRIAGE

(Show by category the value of your property and your debts and other liabilities calculated as of the date of your marriage. Do not include the value of a matrimonial home that you owned at the date of marriage.)

Category	Particulars	Value as of date of marriage	
		Assets	Liabilities
	TOTAL $	(Q) $	(R) $

NET VALUE OF PROPERTY OWNED ON DATE OF MARRIAGE (Amount Q Subtract Amount R) = **(S)** $_____

Page 10—FINANCIAL STATEMENT
(Form 70K under the Rules)
AMENDED JUNE 1, 1986

DYE & DURHAM CO LIMITED
Form No. 904 or 914

EXCLUDED PROPERTY

(Show the value by category of property owned on the valuation date that is excluded from the definition of "net family property".)

Category	Particulars	Value on Valuation Date
		TOTAL (T) $

DISPOSAL OF PROPERTY

(Show the value by category of all property that you disposed of during the two years immediately preceding the making of this statement, or during the marriage, whichever period is shorter.)

Category	Particulars	Value
		TOTAL (U) $

Page 11—FINANCIAL STATEMENT
(Form 70K under the Rules)
AMENDED JUNE 1, 1986

DYE & DURHAM CO. LIMITED
Form No. 904 or 914

CALCULATION OF NET FAMILY PROPERTY

Value of all property owned on valuation date (Amounts H,I,J,K,L,M,N and O from pages 6 to 8) $ _____

Subtract value of all deductions (Amounts P and S from page 9) — $ _____

Subtract value of all excluded property (Amount T from page 10) — $ _____

NET FAMILY PROPERTY $ _____

2. The name(s) and address(es) of my employer(s) are:

3. Attached to this affidavit are a copy of my income tax return filed with the Department of National Revenue for the last taxation year, together with all material filed with it, and a copy of any notice of assessment or reassessment that I have received from the Department for that year.

(Delete inapplicable paragraph 4)

4. I do not anticipate any material changes in the information set out above.

(Give particulars:)

4. I anticipate the following material changes in the information set out above:

Sworn before me at the
Affirmed

in the

on _____ 19 ____

_____
Signature of deponent

Commissioner for Taking Affidavits, etc.

(vi) A Separation Agreement

The separation agreement is the most common of the three types of domestic contract (the other two are cohabitation agreements and marriage contracts). All three contracts must be written, signed and witnessed. A separation agreement acknowledges that the parties are living separate and apart and intend to do so from now on. It recites important details about their background, their marriage, children and so on. It then describes, in as much detail as is required, the terms upon which the parties will end their marriage. It can deal with all or only some of the outstanding concerns. It may describe who will have custody and access, who will have which pieces of property, possession of the home on an interim or permanent basis, responsibility for family debts, life insurance and so on. The agreement can be final or interim (temporary). The following example of a separation agreement is not a complete document but shows a selection of typical provisions. Note that the symbol ">" means "insert appropriate information here."

THIS IS A SEPARATION AGREEMENT MADE ON >, 19>.

B E T W E E N:
>(>wife>husband>)

- and -

>(>wife>husband>)

1. <u>INTERPRETATION</u>
    (1) In this Agreement,
        (a) "husband" means >, who is one of the parties to this Agreement, whether or not the husband and the wife are subsequently divorced;
        (b) "wife" means >, who is one of the parties to this Agreement, whether or not the husband and the wife are subsequently divorced;
        (c) "child" means >, born on >, or, >, born on >, both of whom are the children>who is the child> of the husband and the wife;>
        (>) "cohabit" means to live together in a conjugal relationship, whether within or outside marriage;
        (>) "matrimonial home" means the buildings and lot located at >;
        >(>)"cottage" means the buildings and lot called >;
        (>) "Family Law Act" means the Family Law Act, 1986;
        (>) "property" has the meaning given by the Family Law Act;
    (2) An Act of the Legislature or Parliament referred to by name will mean that Act in force at the material time and includes any amendment or any successor Act which replaces it.
    (3) The proper law of this contract shall be the law of Ontario, and this contract shall also be deemed to be valid and enforceable in accordance with the law of any other jurisdiction. The parties

intend all of their affairs and property to be governed by this contract and the law of Ontario.

(4) The parties agree that the contract is valid and enforceable in Ontario and that they intend it to be a domestic contract in accordance with the Family Law Act, and that it is legally binding.

2. BACKGROUND

This Agreement is entered into on the basis of the following, among other facts:

(a) The parties were married >, at>.

>(>) The parties have > child>: >, born on >, and> >, born on >.>

>(>) The parties have no children and none are intended.>

>(>) The parties are living separate and apart from each other since >, and there is no reasonable prospect of their resuming cohabitation.

(>) The parties desire to settle by agreement all their rights and obligations which they have or may have with respect to:

>(i) the custody of, and access to their child>,>

(>) the support of their child>,>

(>) possession, ownership and division of their property; and

(>) support of each other.

3. AGREEMENT

Each party agrees with the other to be bound by the provisions of this Agreement.

4. DOMESTIC CONTRACT

Each party acknowledges that this Agreement is entered into under s. 54 of the Family Law Act and is a domestic contract which prevails over the same matters provided for in the Act or its successor.

5. EFFECTIVE DATE

This Agreement will take effect on the date it is signed by the last of the husband or the wife.

6. LIVING SEPARATE AND APART

The parties will live separate and apart from each other for the rest of their lives.

7. FREEDOM FROM THE OTHER

Neither party will molest, annoy, harass or in any way interfere with the other, or attempt to compel the other to cohabit or live with him or her.

>. CUSTODY AND ACCESS

(1) The wife will have custody of the child>, subject to reasonable access by the husband on reasonable notice to the wife of his intention to exercise such access.>

(>) The husband will have access to the child> as follows:

>

(>) The husband and the wife each acknowledge that it is in the best interests of the child> for > to have frequent contact with > father and to spend time with him. Accordingly, the husband and the wife will each use their best efforts for the child> to have frequent and regular periods of access with the husband consisting of a combination of both daytime and overnight visits appropriate to the needs and stage of development of the child>.

(>) In making plans for access the husband and the wife will give the needs and convenience of the child> primary importance and will give their own needs and convenience only secondary importance.

(>) The parties will keep each other fully informed of all matters touching the interests of the child> and they will confer as often as necessary to resolve any difficulty raised by or on behalf of the child>.

>. CUSTODY AND ACCESS

(>) The child> shall be in the joint custody of the husband and the wife. The child> shall have > primary residence in the home of the >.

(>) The husband and wife each acknowledge that the other is a devoted and loving parent. The > acknowledges that it is essential to the welfare of the child> that > have as close communication and contact with the > as is reasonably possible, commensurate with the best interests of the child>.

(>) The husband and wife agree and undertake that in all matters relating to the custody, maintenance, education and general well being of the child>, the child> best interests and wishes shall at all times be paramount.

(>) The husband and wife shall conscientiously respect the rights of one another regarding the child>. The husband and wife shall continue to instill in the child> respect for both of > parents and grandparents, and neither the husband nor wife shall by any act, omission or innuendo, in any way tend or attempt to alienate the child> from either of them. The child> shall be taught to continue to love and respect both > parents.

(>) The husband and wife shall have the right to communicate with the child> by telephone and letter at all reasonable times, provided that such telephone communication shall not interfere with the private life of either the husband or the wife.

(>) The husband and wife agree that there shall be full disclosure between them in all matters touching the welfare of the child>, and they agree that they shall confer as often as necessary to consider any problem or difficulty or matter requiring consideration touching the welfare of the child>.

(>) The > shall have generous and regular access to the child>. It is acknowledged that the kind, frequency and duration of such access should be established in advance, and made as certain as existing circumstances permit, in order to enable the child>, the husband and the wife to make plans for their day-to-day living.

(>) If special occasions, holidays, excursions or other presently unforeseeable opportunities become available to the child>, neither the husband nor the wife will unreasonably insist that visiting arrangements be adhered to without exception. On the contrary, the husband and the wife shall at all times maintain a reasonable and flexible position respecting the visiting arrangements with the child>, and at all times, the best interests of the child> shall prevail.

(>) In any matter of contention between the husband and the wife which the husband and wife cannot resolve between themselves by mutual agreement, the parties agree to mediate any such disagreements or differences of opinion through a mediator that the parties may hereafter agree upon. If the parties are not able to agree on a mediator or if the mediation is unsuccessful the parties acknowledge that either one of them may bring an application to a court of competent jurisdiction to resolve the outstanding matters between them.

(>) The husband and wife acknowledge that the wife> may wish to change her> residence from the Province of Ontario as a result of remarriage or career opportunities. The husband> acknowledges that provided that the wife> is leaving the Province of Ontario for such reasons he> will not take any action that would prevent the wife> from leaving the Province of Ontario or unduly insist on exercising the access as set out in this agreement in order that the wife> be prevented from changing her residence from the Province of Ontario. The wife> agrees to give the husband> at least sixty (60) days notice of any intention to change her> residence from the Province of Ontario for the reasons set out in this paragraph so that the parties may make alternate arrangements with respect to access to the children.>

>. FINANCIAL PROVISION

(1) Each of the parties,
   (a) is financially independent,
   (b) does not require financial assistance from the other,
   (c) releases the other from all obligations to provide support, interim support, maintenance or interim alimony pursuant to the Family Law Act, or Divorce Act, and
   (d) releases all rights to claim or obtain support, interim support, maintenance or interim alimony pursuant to the Family Law Act, or Divorce Act from the other.

(2) The parties realize that their respective financial circumstances may change in the future by reason of their health, the cost of living, their employment, and otherwise. No such change will give either party the right to claim, support, interim support, maintenance or interim alimony pursuant to the Family Law Act or Divorce Act, from the other.

(3) The parties intend this Agreement to be final as to the issue of

financial support. Both parties are aware and acknowledge that each of them may suffer or enjoy drastic changes in their respective income, assets, and debts, in the cost of living or in their health, or changes of fortune by reason of unforeseen factors. Nevertheless, the husband and the wife agree that under no circumstances will any change, direct or indirect, foreseen or unforeseen, in the circumstances of either of them give either the right to claim an alteration of any of the terms of this Agreement or the terms in any other agreement between them or of the terms of Decree Nisi of Divorce. More particularly, the parties acknowledge that they may be called upon during the rest of their lives to use, either wholly or in part, their capital for their own support and they agree to do so without any recourse to the other party at any time.

(4) The husband and wife each wish to be able to rely upon this Agreement as the final and binding one, a once and for all settlement of all their differences and affairs to avoid ever engaging in further litigation with each other, whether about matters or causes of actions existing now or at any time.

>. FINANCIAL PROVISION

(>) Commencing on the > day of >, 199>, and on the > day of each and every month thereafter, the husband shall pay to the wife for the support of the child>, the sum of > per month <per child>, being a total of > for the support of > children>, until one or more of the following occurs:
   (i)   the child becomes eighteen years old and ceases to be in full-time attendance at an educational institution;
   (ii) the child ceases to reside with the wife;
   (iii) the child becomes twenty-one years old;
   (iv) the child marries; or
   (v) the child dies.

(>) In clause >(ii), "reside" means to live in the home of the wife, and the child does not cease to reside in the home of the wife when the child is temporarily away from home to attend an educational institution, to work at summer employment, or to enjoy a reasonable holiday.

(>) Commencing on the > day of >, 199>, and on the > day of each and every month thereafter, the husband shall pay to the wife for her own support, the sum of > per month, until one or more of the following occurs:
   (i)   the wife remarries or cohabits;
   (ii) the wife dies; or
   (iii) the husband dies.>

>. INDEXING SUPPORT

(1) The amount of support payable under this agreement for the support of:

>(>) the wife; and>
>(>) each> child,

will be increased annually on the anniversary date of the effective date of this agreement by the indexing factor, as defined in subsection 2, for November of the previous year.

(2) The indexing factor for a given month is the percentage change in the Consumer Price Index for Canada for all prices of all items since the same month of the previous year, as published by Statistics Canada.

>. INDEXING SUPPORT

(1) The support payments outlined in paragraph >, shall be increased annually in each year commencing in >, 19>, for so long as child and spousal> support is payable under this Agreement, by an amount equal to the lesser of the> annual percentage increase in the cost of living of the preceding year and the annual percentage increase in the husband's salary>. The increase shall be calculated according to the Consumer Price Index for Canada for prices of all items since the same month of the previous year, as published by Statistics Canada.

(2) The wife shall deliver to the husband a notice in or about the month of >, 19>, with respect to the increase in the child and spousal> support based on the cost of living increase. >If the husband alleges that his increase in salary is less than the said increase in the cost of living he shall provide such evidence of the salary increase to the wife within thirty days of the delivery by the wife of the notice to him. If the husband fails to deliver such evidence to the wife the increase shall be in accordance with the cost of living as set out in paragraph > herein.>

>. WAIVER OF RIGHT TO INDEX SUPPORT PAYMENTS

Each party hereby:
(a) waives any right, and
(b) releases the other from all claims

that he or she has or may have to require that the amounts or any amount payable for support under this Agreement be increased annually, or at any time, by an indexing factor as provided in the Family Law Act, or by any factor or percentage.

>. MATERIAL CHANGE IN CIRCUMSTANCES

(1) The husband and wife intend paragraphs > to be final except for variation in the event of a material change in circumstances. If such change occurs, the husband or wife seeking the variation will give to the other a written notice of the variation he or she is seeking, and the husband and wife will then confer either personally or through their respective solicitors to settle what, if any, variation should be made.

(2) If no agreement has been reached thirty (30) clear days after notice has been given under paragraph >(1), variation relating to custody, access and support of the child> and wife> may be determined at the instance of either the husband or the wife by an application pursuant to the Family Law Act, or the Divorce Act. Any such application by a party shall be deemed to be an application for maintenance or support pursuant to the Family Law Act or the Divorce Act.

>. HEALTH AND MEDICAL EXPENSES

(1) The husband> warrants that he> is maintaining in force for the benefit of the wife> and child> a plan of insurance established under the [provincial] health insurance plan to protect them> against the costs of health services.

(2) The husband> agrees to continue this insurance or equivalent insurance,
>(>) in the case of the wife> until one or more the following occurs:
(i) the marriage is terminated; or
(ii)the wife> cohabits with another man.>
>(>) in the case of each> child so long as he> is obligated by this Agreement to support the child>.

(3) If the husband> fails to maintain this insurance or equivalent insurance, he> will pay the costs of all health services which would have been paid by the insurance.

>. DENTAL AND >ADDITIONAL MEDICAL COVERAGE

The husband> agrees to continue a dental and> medical plan for the benefit of the wife> and child> through his place of employment as long as he is able to obtain coverage for such plans> through such employment, for the wife> until the husband and wife are divorced and> for the child> so long as he> is required to provide for > support under this Agreement.

>. MATRIMONIAL HOME AND CONTENTS

(1) The parties acknowledge that they hold the matrimonial home as joint tenants.

>(>)The parties agree that the wife> may remain in exclusive possession of the matrimonial home until one or more of the following occurs:

(a) five years elapse from the date of this Agreement;
(b) the wife remarries;
(c) the wife cohabits with another man;
(d) the wife ceases to reside on a full time basis in the premises;
(e) the husband and the wife agree in writing to the contrary.

(>) During the period of her> exclusive possession of the matrimonial home, the wife> will be responsible for paying all mortgage payments, taxes, insurance premiums, heating, water and other charges related to the matrimonial home, and will save the husband> harmless from all liability for those payments.

(>) The wife> will keep the matrimonial home fully insured at her> expense to its full replacement value against loss or damage by fire or other perils covered by a standard fire insurance extended coverage or additional perils supplemental contract and will apply any insurance proceeds to reasonable repairs. The insurance will cover both the husband's and the wife's interest in the matrimonial home. If the husband> demands it, the wife> will produce proof of premium payments and of the policy being in force. The husband and the wife will direct the insurer to send notices of premiums to both of them.>

>(>) The parties will bear equally the costs of major repairs to the matrimonial home, but only if the repairs are undertaken with the consent of both parties. No consent will be unreasonably withheld.>

>(>) During the period of her> exclusive possession of the matrimonial home the wife> shall not change the use of the home, shall maintain its "principal residence" status within the meaning of the Income Tax Act, and shall so designate the home (and no other property) pursuant thereto. If the wife> contrary to this agreement sublets the matrimonial home, changes her> use of it, does not maintain its "principal residence" status for tax purposes, or does not designate it (and no other property) as her> principal residence with the result that the husband> becomes liable to pay any tax or penalty under the Income Tax Act, then the wife> agrees to indemnify the husband> with respect to the liability or penalty.>

>(>) When the wife> is no longer entitled to exclusive possession of the matrimonial home, it will immediately be sold. Upon the sale of the matrimonial home the proceeds will be divided equally between the parties. Until the closing date of the sale of the matrimonial home, the wife>may continue to remain in exclusive possession of it. Any difference between the husband and wife on the method in terms of sale shall be resolved under the section of this Agreement providing for the resolution of differences.>

>(>) The husband and wife agree to divide the contents equally between them as they may agree.>

>(>) The husband and wife acknowledge that the contents have been divided between them to their mutual satisfaction and that each is entitled to the contents in his or her possession.>

>. COTTAGE

(1) Each party acknowledges that the cottage was held by the parties as joint tenants until the transfer referred to in subsection (2) was made.

(2) Contemporaneously with the execution of this Agreement, the

parties have transferred the cottage from themselves as joint tenants to the husband> as sole owner.

(3) The wife> waives any right she> has or may have to, or any interest she> has or may have in the cottage, and releases the husband> from any claim she> has or may have to any such right or interest.>

>. PRINCIPAL RESIDENCE DESIGNATION

(1) For the purpose of the "principal residence" designation provided for in the Income Tax Act, the wife> will designate the family residence as her principal residence for the years from the date of acquisition up to and including 1990, and the husband> will designate the cottage as his principal residence for the years from the date of acquisition up to and including 1990.

(2) Both the husband and wife will designate the family residence as their principal residence for each of the years after 1990 to and including the year in which this Agreement is executed.

(3) Neither the husband nor the wife will designate any other residence or property as his or her principal residence in any of the years after 1990 to and including the year in which this Agreement is executed.

>. AUTOMOBILES

> (as may be agreed) (identify vehicle specifically)

>. CANADA PENSION PLAN

> The wife may apply under the Canada Pension Plan for a division of pension credits.> (or)

> Neither the husband nor the wife will apply under the Canada Pension Plan for a division of pension credits after the dissolution of their marriage.>

>. PRIVATE PENSION PLANS

> (as may be agreed)

>. INVESTMENTS AND OTHER SAVINGS

> (as may be agreed)

>. LIFE INSURANCE

(1) Contemporaneously with the execution of this Agreement the husband> has delivered to the wife> <a certified copy of> the following policy> of insurance:

(>) Policy No. > of > Insurance Company having a face value of $>; and>

>(>)Policy No. > of > Insurance Company having a face value of $>.>

(2) The husband> warrants that he has irrevocably designated the

wife> as the sole beneficiary under the above policy> and that he has filed the sigmation with the principal office of the respective insurer> in accordance with the provisions of the Insurance Act. (Ontario)

(3) The husband> will pay all premiums when they become due and will keep the policy> in force for the benefit of the wife as long as he is required to pay support or maintenance for either the wife> or> child.

(4) Upon the happening of any one of the events described in subsection (3), the husband> may deal with the policy> as he deems fit free from any claim by the wife> or her> estate.

(5) The husband> will deliver to the wife>, within 14 days from the date when it is demanded, proof that the policy> is> in good standing. This proof may be demanded at any reasonable time and from time to time.

(6) If the husband> defaults in payment of any premium the wife> may pay the premium and recover from the husband> the amount of the payment together with all costs and expenses that may be incurred in restoring the policy> to good standing.

>. HOUSEHOLD GOODS AND PERSONAL EFFECTS

Each of the parties acknowledges that:

(a) the contents of the matrimonial home, including furniture, furnishings, household goods, silverware, china, glassware, rugs, books, pictures, bric-a-bric and all other household effects have been divided between the parties or have been purchased or the value set off against the value of other property by one of the parties to the satisfaction of each of them;

(b) each has possession of his or her jewellery, clothing and personal effects;

(c) each may dispose of the items possessed by him or her as he or she deems fit.

>. DEBTS AND OBLIGATIONS

(1) Neither party will contract or incur debts or obligations in the name of the other.

(2) If, contrary to subsection (1), either party contracts or incurs debts or obligations in the name of the other, he or she will indemnify the other from all loss or expense that results from or is incidental to the transaction.

>. NO PROPERTY TO BE DIVISIBLE ASSET

No property owned by either party or by them jointly on the effective date of this contract or at any later time is or will be:

(a) family property, or

(b) property subject to division otherwise than according to ownership, under the Family Law Act and the laws of any jurisdiction.

>. ## PART II OF THE FAMILY LAW ACT

Each of the parties releases and discharges all rights and claims he or she has under Part II of the Family Law Act.

>. ## RELEASE AGAINST PROPERTY

Except as provided in this Agreement the husband and the wife each acknowledge and agree that:

(a) all their property has been divided between them to their mutual satisfaction;

(b) each is entitled to property now in his or her possession, free of any claim from the other;

(c) each may dispose of the property they now possess as if they were unmarried;

(d) each releases and discharges all rights and claims relating to property in which the other has or may have an interest, including all rights and claims involving:

   (i)   possession of property;
   (ii) ownership of property;
   (iii) division of property; and
   (iv) compensation for contributions of any kind, or an interest in property for contributions of any kind.

(e) This section is a complete defence to any action brought by either the husband or the wife to assert a claim to any property, wherever situate, in which the other has or had an interest.

>. ## RELEASE AGAINST THE ESTATE OF THE OTHER

Without restricting the other waivers and releases in this contract, and subject to transfers or bequests which may be made, each party

(a) waives all rights and

(b) releases and discharges the other from all claims that he or she has or may in the future acquire under the laws of any jurisdiction, and particularly under the Family Law Act and the Succession Law Reform Act and their successors, entitling him or her upon the death of the other

   (i)   to a division of property owned by the other or to one-half the difference between their net family properties or to any other share of this difference, or to any share of the property of the other;

   (ii) if the other party dies leaving a Will, to elect against taking under the Will in favour of receiving an entitlement equalizing their net family properties, or in favour of any other benefit;

   (iii) if the other party dies intestate, to elect to receive an entitlement in intestacy or to receive an entitlement equalizing their net family property;

   (iv) if the other party dies testate as to some property and intestate as to other property, to elect to take under the Will and to receive an entitlement in intestacy, or to receive an entitlement equalizing their net family properties;

(v) to share in the estate of the other under a distribution in intestacy in any manner whatsoever;

(vi) to receive support as a dependent from the estate of the other in any manner whatsoever; and

(vii) to act as executor or administrator of the estate of the other.

>. GENERAL RELEASE

(1) The husband and wife each accept the provisions of this Agreement in satisfaction of all claims and causes of action each now has including, but not limited to claims and causes of action for custody, child maintenance or child support,> maintenance, support, interim maintenance and interim support, possession of or title to property, or any other claim arising out of the marriage of the husband and wife, EXCEPT for claims and causes of action:

(i) arising under this agreement;

(ii) for a decree of divorce.

(2) Nothing in this Agreement will bar any action or proceeding by either the husband or the wife to enforce any of the terms of this Agreement.

>. ATTRIBUTION

>(>) The parties hereby elect under clause 74(7)(b) of the Income Tax Act that subsection 74(2) (gain or loss deemed that of transferor) of the Income Tax Act will not apply to a disposition of any property that has been transferred between the parties pursuant to this Agreement, or to any property substituted therefor.

(>) Contemporaneously with the execution of this Agreement, the parties have executed in duplicate a separate form of joint election according to Schedule "A" [not actually attached] attached to this Agreement.

(>) Each party authorizes the other to file an executed copy of the form of election completed according to the form in Schedule "A" with his or her return of income for the taxation year in which this Agreement is executed.

(>) The parties will indemnify each other for any tax liability imposed upon one of them by any taxing authority or government, resulting from the transfer of or disposition of property transferred pursuant to the terms of this Agreement.

(>) Specifically the parties agree to indemnify each other with respect to any liability or charge resulting from:

(a) any tax arrears of one enforced as against the property or income of the other;

(b) any attribution of income or capital gains from one to the other after separation.

(>) The parties will not designate any other property as their principal residence except the matrimonial home, for the period up to and including the year of this Agreement.>

>. RESUMPTION OF COHABITATION

If at any future time the parties cohabit as husband and wife for a single period or periods totalling not more than ninety days with reconciliation as the primary purpose of the cohabitation, the provisions contained in this Agreement will not be affected except as provided in this section. If the parties cohabit as husband and wife for a single period or periods totalling not more than ninety days with reconciliation as the primary purpose of the cohabitation, the provisions contained in this Agreement will become void, except that nothing in this section will affect or invalidate any payment, conveyance or act made or done pursuant to the provisions of this Agreement.

>. AGREEMENT TO SURVIVE DIVORCE

If at any future time the parties are divorced, the terms of this Agreement will survive and continue in force.

>. EXECUTION OF OTHER DOCUMENTS

Each of the parties will execute any document and do all further things, at the cost of the other, that are reasonably required from time to time to give effect to the terms and intent of this Agreement.

>. CONTRACT TO PREVAIL

This contract prevails over:
    (a) any matter that is provided for in the Family Law Act [or relevant provincial law], where the contract made provision for such matters;
    (b) any matter provided for in a subsequent domestic contract between one of the parties and another person other than the other party, where the present contract makes provisions for such matters.

>. GOVERNING LAW

This Agreement will be governed by and construed according to the laws of Ontario [or relevant province].

>. GENERAL

    (1) The husband and wife will each execute any document or documents reasonably required from time to time to give effect to the terms and intent of this Agreement.
    (2) The husband and wife each warrant that there are no representations, collateral agreements or conditions affecting this Agreement other than as expressed in this Agreement.

(3) This Agreement may be amended only by a further instrument in writing signed by the husband and by the wife.

(4) The provisions of this Agreement are binding on the respective heirs, executors, administrators or assigns of the husband and the wife.

>. SEVERABILITY

The invalidity or unenforceability of any provision of this Agreement will not affect the validity or enforceability of any other provisions and any invalid provision will be severable.

>. DEFAULT

If either of the parties is in default with respect to the payment of support pursuant to this Agreement, including any provision with respect to indexing of support payments, the other party may register the separation agreement in the [name of relevant Family Court] and the parties hereby consent to this Agreement being registered.>

>. FINANCIAL DISCLOSURE

Each party:

>(>)has fully and completely disclosed to the other the nature, extent and probable value of all his or her significant assets and all his or her significant debts or other liabilities existing at the date of this contract, and in addition to this disclosure,>

>(>)has given all information and particulars about his or her assets and liabilities that have been requested by the other,>

>(>)is satisfied with the information and particulars received from the other, and

>(>)acknowledges that there are no requests for further information or particulars that have not been met to his or her complete satisfaction.

>. INDEPENDENT LEGAL ADVICE

Each of the husband and the wife acknowledges that he or she:

(a) has had independent legal advice;

(b) understands his or her respective rights and obligations under this Agreement;

(c) is signing this Agreement voluntarily; and

(d) believes this Agreement is fair and reasonable and that its provisions are entirely adequate to discharge the present and future responsibilities of the parties and will not result in circumstances unconscionable to either party.

>. LEGAL FEES

The husband will pay the wife's solicitor's fees for the preparation and execution of this Agreement.>

TO EVIDENCE THEIR AGREEMENT, each of the husband and the wife has signed this Agreement under seal before a witness.

SIGNED, SEALED AND DELIVERED)
   in the presence of:)
)
)
)
)

_____)   _____

Witness as to the signature of   ) >
[wife's signature]   )
[wife]   )
)
)
)

_____)   _____

Witness as to the signature of   ) >
[husband's signature]
[husband]

Caution: Please do not attempt to adapt this contract to your situation without the advice of a lawyer. Many of the clauses are alternatives to each other and would not necessarily be applicable to every case. It also has an Ontario emphasis. It is reproduced as an example or guide only.

(vii) A Lawyer's Account for Fees and Disbursements

From time to time throughout the proceedings and particularly at the end of the matter you will receive "the bill." The ones sent from time to time are known as "interim accounts" and the one at the end is known as "the final account." It will describe the lawyer's fees for services and any disbursements paid on your behalf (e.g., $50.00 for issuing a Petition for Divorce). If the account has been prepared properly it should set out the particulars of each thing done—telephone calls, drafting of pleadings, attending at court and legal research. It should indicate whether the work was done by a lawyer, a student or a paralegal. The hours worked on the client's behalf are totalled and multiplied by the appropriate hourly rate (which will vary from lawyer to student to paralegal). The disbursements should be listed and added to the amount to produce a total account for fees and disbursements. The total account should be compared with the retainer. The final account should also be signed by the lawyer and be attached to a final reporting letter describing the final outcome. Interest is often charged on overdue accounts and this should be noted on the bill itself.

LAWYER'S ACCOUNT #1

[Lawyer's Address
and Telephone]

IN ACCOUNT WITH

[NAME OF LAWYER]
Barristers and Solicitors

November 29, 1991
INVOICE NO: 7661
FILE NO:

RE: DIVORCE/LITIGATION —

FOR PROFESSIONAL SERVICES RENDERED THROUGH NOVEMBER
28, 1990

NOV 16/90	CONFERENCE WITH CLIENT	.30	HRS
NOV 16/90	CONFERENCE RE FILE DISCUSSION WITH RE ASSIGNMENT COURT	.10	
NOV 16/90	TELEPHONE CONVERSATION WITH OTHER SIDE TWO TELEPHONE CALLS	.30	
NOV 18/90	REVIEWING CLIENT'S NOTES AND FILE RE PREPARING FOR ASSIGNMENT COURT	.20	
NOV 18/90	REVIEW OF DOCUMENTS INCLUDING WIFE AND HUSBAND'S FINANCIAL STATEMENT AND OTHER DOCUMENTS	.30	
NOV 18/90	CORRESPONDENCE TO HUSBAND'S SOLICITOR	.10	
NOV 19/90	CONFERENCE RE FILE	.10	
NOV 19/90	TELEPHONE CONVERSATION WITH OTHER SIDE RE PRE-TRIAL CONFERENCE	.10	
NOV 19/90	REPRESENTATION IN COURT AT ONTARIO COURT (GENERAL DIVISION) FOR ASSIGNMENT COURT	2.00	
NOV 19/90	TELEPHONE CONVERSATION WITH OTHER SIDE RE PRE-TRIAL CONFERENCE DATE	.20	
NOV 19/90	TELEPHONE CONVERSATION WITH CLIENT RE PRE-TRIAL CONFERENCE DATE	.10	
NOV 20/90	TELEPHONE CONVERSATION WITH CLIENT	.40	

[Lawyer's Address
and Telephone]

IN ACCOUNT WITH

[NAME OF LAWYER]
Barristers and Solicitors

TWO TELEPHONE CALLS RE FINANCIAL
STATEMENT AND PRE-TRIAL
CONFERENCE DATE

TOTAL FOR ALL FEES $ 630.00

LONG DISTANCE TELEPHONE CHARGES	1.63	
LONG DISTANCE TELEPHONE CHARGES	1.76	
PHOTOCOPYING CHARGES	6.30	
FAX MACHINE CHARGE	.75	
POSTAGE	.79	
PHOTOCOPYING CHARGES	.60	
FAX MACHINE CHARGE	.50	
PHOTOCOPYING CHARGES	2.10	
LONG DISTANCE TELEPHONE CHARGES	1.76	
TOTAL DISBURSED		$ 16.19
		$ 646.19
TRANSFERRED FROM TRUST		$ 646.19
TOTAL AMOUNT NOW DUE		$ .00

LAW FIRM

PER: _____

ACCORDING TO SECTION 35 OF THE SOLICITORS ACT
(ONTARIO) 14% PER ANNUM WILL BE CHARGED, ONE
MONTH AFTER STATEMENT IS SENT.

LAWYER'S ACCOUNT #2

[Lawyer's Address
and Telephone]

IN ACCOUNT WITH

[NAME OF LAWYER]
Barristers and Solicitors

November 29, 1990

INVOICE NO: 7690

FILE NO:

RE: CUSTODY LITIGATION:

FOR PROFESSIONAL SERVICES RENDERED THROUGH NOVEMBER 28, 1990

NOV 13/90	DOCUMENT PREPARATION DRAFT CONSENT AND ORDER	.40 HRS
NOV 13/90	TELEPHONE CONVERSATION WITH CLIENT	.20
NOV 14/90	TELEPHONE CONVERSATION WITH CLIENT	.20
NOV 14/90	TELEPHONE CONFERENCE WITH LAWYER	.30
NOV 15/90	TELEPHONE CONFERENCE WITH LAWYER	.20
NOV 16/90	CORRESPONDENCE TO WIFE'S SOLICITOR	.20
NOV 16/90	DRAFTING SEPARATION AGREEMENT INTERIM AGREEMENT	.30
NOV 16/90	TELEPHONE CONVERSATION WITH CLIENT	.20
NOV 19/90	RECEIPT OF CORRES. FROM WIFE'S SOLICITOR	.10
NOV 19/90	RECEIPT OF CORRES. FROM WIFE'S SOLICITOR	.10
NOV 19/90	TELEPHONE CONVERSATION WITH OTHER SIDE TWO TELEPHONE CALLS RE DRAFT INTERIM AGREEMENT	.30
NOV 19/90	TELEPHONE CONVERSATION WITH CLIENT	.10
NOV 19/90	TELEPHONE CONVERSATION WITH CLIENT	.10
NOV 20/90	TELEPHONE CONVERSATION WITH OTHER SIDE RE CANCELLING TRIP	.10
NOV 20/90	TELEPHONE CONVERSATION WITH OTHER SIDE TWO TELEPHONE CALLS RE DRAFT AGREEMENT	.20
NOV 23/90	TELEPHONE CONVERSATION WITH CLIENT	.30
NOV 25/90	DOCUMENT PREPARATION INCLUDING REVIEW OF FILE, REVIEW OF LEGISLATION AND PREPARING NOTICE OF MOTION, AFFIDAVIT AND DRAFT ORDER	1.80
NOV 25/90	CONFERENCE RE FILE WITH RE MOTION	.20
NOV 25/90	TELEPHONE CONVERSATION WITH CLIENT RE COURT PROCEEDINGS	.30
NOV 26/90	DOCUMENT EXECUTION AFFIDAVIT AND EXHIBITS	.30
NOV 26/90	TELEPHONE CONVERSATION WITH CLIENT	.10
NOV 26/90	AMENDING COURT DOCUMENTS	1.20

[Lawyer's Address

                                        and Telephone]

IN ACCOUNT WITH

[NAME OF LAWYER]
Barristers and Solicitors

	AFFIDAVIT, NOTICE OF MOTION AND ORDER	
NOV 26/90	CONFERENCE RE FILE WITH , TWO TIMES	.20 HRS
NOV 26/90	TELEPHONE CONVERSATION RE FILE FOUR TIMES TO COURT HOUSE AND TO RE MOTION	.20
NOV 26/90	TELEPHONE CONVERSATION WITH CLIENT	.10
NOV 27/90	RECEIPT OF CORRES. FROM WIFE'S SOLICITOR	.10
NOV 28/90	DRAFTING CORRESPONDENCE AND AMENDING CORRESPONDENCE	.50

TOTAL FOR ALL FEES	$ 1,500.00
FAX MACHINE CHARGE	2.25
PHOTOCOPYING CHARGES	4.80
FAX MACHINE CHARG	2.25
FAX MACHINE CHARGE	2.00
PHOTOCOPYING CHARGES	7.80
FAX MACHINE CHARGE	1.00
PHOTOCOPYING CHARGES	27.25
FAX MACHINE CHARGE	1.25
FAX MACHINE CHARGE	6.50
POSTAGE	.79
FAX MACHINE CHARGE	1.00
PHOTOCOPYING CHARGES	1.80
TOTAL DISBURSED	$ 58.69
	$ 1,558.69
TRANSFERRED FROM TRUST	$ 1,558.69
TOTAL AMOUNT NOW DUE	$ .00

PER: _____

ACCORDING TO SECTION 35 OF THE SOLICITORS ACT
(ONTARIO) 14% PER ANNUM WILL BE CHARGED, ONE
MONTH AFTER STATEMENT IS SENT.

(viii) Family Law Client History

Many law firms will ask a client to complete a "Family History" Form. This form facilitates the collection of family details and prevents people from overlooking important details. The following is a modified form which you may wish to use as you sort out your own predicament. A completed form would give any lawyer a big head start on behalf of the client.

DATE: _____

FAMILY LAW CLIENT HISTORY

YOUR FULL NAME: _____

YOUR ADDRESS: HOME: _____

                        OFFICE: _____

TELEPHONE: HOME: _____ OFFICE: _____

DATE OF BIRTH: _____ PLACE OF BIRTH: _____

DATE OF MARRIAGE: _____ PLACE OF MARRIAGE: _____

DATE OF SEPARATION: _____

YOUR STATUS BEFORE MARRIAGE: WIFE: _____

                                    HUSBAND: _____

SURNAME OF WIFE AT BIRTH: _____ AT SEPARATION: _____

IF 2ND MARRIAGE FOR EITHER OF YOU GIVE DETAILS OF EARLIER MARRIAGES _____

_____

_____

DOMICILE: _____ WHEN CAME TO CANADA: _____

LENGTH OF RESIDENCE IN PROVINCE: _____

PRIOR RESIDENCES IN LAST YEAR: _____

_____

NAMES OF CHILDREN   DATES OF BIRTH   GRADE AND SCHOOL:

1. _____

2. _____

3. _____

4. _____

SURNAME OF YOUR SPOUSE AT BIRTH: _____

SURNAME OF YOUR SPOUSE AT SEPARATION: _____

SPOUSE'S DATE OF BIRTH: _____

SPOUSE'S PLACE OF BIRTH: _____

NAME, ADDRESS AND PHONE NUMBER OF SPOUSE'S LAWYER: ___

_____

_____

_____

_____

SOCIAL HISTORY OF MARRIAGE:
(Includes courtship, cohabitation date, lifestyle, conduct, present status and counselling details. Complete in detail. Use additional pages as necessary.)

_____
_____
_____
_____

ECONOMIC HISTORY OF MARRIAGE:
(Includes education, financial position before marriage, history of matrimonial homes, net worth of both of you, employment records, fitness for employment, contributions by the spouses to the marriage. Complete in detail. Use additional pages as necessary.)

_____
_____
_____
_____

CUSTODY AND ACCESS:
(The position of you and your spouse, the allegations and expected cross-allegations. Complete in detail. Use additional pages as necessary.)

_____
_____
_____
_____

YOUR IMPRESSION OF THE SITUATION:
(Complete in detail. Use additional pages as necessary.)

_____
_____
_____
_____

WHAT DO YOU WANT?
(Complete in detail. Use additional pages as necessary.)

_____
_____
_____
_____

(ix) A Glossary of Family Law Terms

ACCESS The opportunity to visit with a child. Under the terms of the *Divorce Act, 1985*, a spouse exercising access rights is also entitled to information about the child's health, welfare and education, unless a court orders otherwise.*

ADULTERY Sexual intercourse by a husband or wife with someone of the opposite sex who is not his or her spouse. Adultery is one of the ways marital breakdown can be established.* (Note: A gay or lesbian relationship will not constitute adultery but may constitute mental cruelty.)

ADVERSARIAL SYSTEM Canada's court system is designed to resolve disputes between two opposing parties. The parties present their respective sides of an issue through evidence. The judge acts as an impartial arbiter, weighing the evidence and deciding how the law applies in each specific case.*

AFFIDAVIT A sworn statement, typed and signed by a person involved in a family law matter. It is witnessed by someone, usually a lawyer, and filed in support of a motion.

ALIMONY An old expression used to describe spousal support. Now that you know what it is, don't use it. Call it spousal support.

APPEAL When a person affected by a judge's decision believes that the judge has made a mistake, that person can ask a higher level of court to review the decision. The court reviewing the decision can uphold it, change it or send the matter back to the original court for reconsideration. There are strict time limits on this type of review.*

APPLICATION A court proceeding starts with the filing of certain documents with court officers and the serving of copies of these documents on other persons affected. Details of the material to be included in this application, the document format and the filing fees are determined by provincial and territorial rules of court procedure.*

ARBITRATION A third person is asked to decide a case for two people who cannot agree. This person acts as a "private judge," with rules and procedures made to the liking of the parties involved. It is not mediation. A decision is imposed because the people agree to be bound by whatever the arbitrator decides.

BATTERED To be beaten, harassed or threatened. See Domestic Violence.

BEST INTERESTS TEST This is the overriding consideration in custody and access matters. The court searches for that which will best serve the child's interests.

CHILD The *Divorce Act* defines a "child of the marriage" as a child of both spouses, a child of one of the spouses towards whom the other spouse acts as a parent or a child towards whom both spouses act as a parent. Biological children, adopted children and children looked after by the spouses may all be considered children of the marriage. The custody and support provisions of the divorce law apply to a child of the marriage who is under sixteen years of age or who is over sixteen and remains dependent on his or her parents because of illness, disability or other reasons.*

COHABITATION AGREEMENT A domestic contract signed by a man and woman˙ who are living together or intend to live together but not marry. In it they may provide for ownership and division of property, support and any other matter affecting their relationship except custody of and access to children.

COLLUSION An agreement or conspiracy to fabricate or suppress evidence, or to deceive the court. If evidence to support a divorce application is the result of collusion, the application can be rejected.*

CONDONATION The forgiveness of a matrimonial offence with full knowledge of the circumstances, followed by an acceptance of the offending spouse back into the family. A forgiven offence cannot be revived at a later date as a basis for a divorce. A legal opinion may be necessary to decide if a matrimonial offence has been condoned by the subsequent actions of the other spouse.*

CONNIVANCE The marital misconduct of one spouse caused by, or knowingly, wilfully or recklessly permitted by, the other spouse. Connivance in creating a basis for a divorce application can result in the application being rejected.*

COMMON-LAW SPOUSE Almost all the provinces recognize that some men and women live together without getting married. While the precise definition varies from province to province, it means achieving the status of a spouse for some legal purposes, such as support, in the province.

CONFIDENTIALITY People in certain relationships are protected by law from having to give any evidence in court regarding communications between them. Communications between a lawyer and a client have this special protection. A court-appointed reconciliator also has this protection with regard to communications made in the course of attempting to reconcile spouses.

Most professional associations have ethical guidelines regarding the confidentiality of communications between members and their clients. These guidelines form a very important part of the professional relationship. However, they do not necessarily provide protection from disclosure in court.

The laws regarding the relationship between other professionals and their clients such as clergy and their parishioners, doctors and their patients, vary across the country. These professionals may be called upon to testify in court.*

CONSUMMATION OF A MARRIAGE The "completion" of a marriage by an act of sexual intercourse by a husband and wife after the marriage ceremony.

CONTEMPT OF COURT A method the court uses to control its own process. It is a wilful disobedience of a court order punishable by fine or imprisonment or both.

CONTESTED DIVORCE If either the husband or wife disputes the ground for divorce, or if the spouses are unable to agree on child-care or support arrangements, a court will have to resolve these matters. A hearing will be held and both sides of the dispute will be entitled to present evidence supporting their view. The judge will consider the evidence presented and impose a solution.*

COROLLARY RELIEF Under the terms of the *Divorce Act, 1985*, people involved in a divorce proceeding can ask the court to make supplementary orders pertaining to financial support for a spouse or child, or for the custody of, or access to, a child of the marriage.*

COSTS Sums payable for legal services. When matters are contested in court, a judge has the discretion to order that the losing party pay a portion of the successful party's legal costs.*

CUSTODY Control over a child given to an adult by the court. This control generally includes physical care of the child and the responsibility to make decisions regarding education, religion and health care, and to provide food, clothing and shelter.*

DECREE NISI Under the *Divorce Act* of 1968, the court which allowed a divorce granted a temporary order called a decree nisi. The divorce was not final until at least three months later when the court granted a decree absolute.*

DECREE ABSOLUTE Under the *Divorce Act* of 1968, a divorce only became final when a court granted a decree absolute. A decree absolute could be granted by the court three months after the day on which the court had allowed the divorce action. If the parties agreed not to appeal the divorce decision, and if special circumstances existed, the court could shorten the three-month period.*

DEPENDANT A person who relies on someone else for financial support. In the context of divorce law, may include a spouse or child.*

DESERTION The failure of a husband or wife to live with his or her spouse. It must be a unilateral act carried out against the wishes of the other spouse. Desertion was a ground for divorce under the old divorce legislation. Under the new divorce law, it would be evidence of the separation period.*

DISBURSEMENTS Out-of-pocket expenses incurred in a family law matter, such as the cost of paying for the Petition to be issued at the court office or the cost of paying someone to deliver it to your spouse. It could also be the cost of a family law assessment.

DISCOVERIES A step in legal proceedings where lawyers get to ask the opposing client, under oath, questions about things said in the legal proceedings, especially in affidavits and pleadings. It is done in the presence of a court reporter and a transcript of all questions and answers can be prepared.

DIVORCE The termination of the legal relationship of marriage between a husband and wife.*

DIVORCE CERTIFICATE The actual piece of paper that officially describes the termination of the marriage. It is needed as proof of the divorce in order to get a marriage licence.

DOMESTIC VIOLENCE (OR "WIFE ASSAULT") The intent by the husband to intimidate, either by threat or by use of physical force on the wife's person or property. The purpose of the assault is to control her behaviour by the inducement of fear.

FEES AND DISBURSEMENTS The bill. This is a statement you will receive monthly, periodically or in one lump sum at the end of the proceeding. The fee is for the lawyer's time, which is calculated by multiplying the hourly rate by the number of hours worked on the case. Disbursements are out-of-pocket expenses.

FINAL ORDER An order that is not interim. Interim orders are effective until the end of the trial. The final order is intended to last indefinitely or until changed by the court.

GARNISHEE A legal procedure which allows for the seizure of money owing to a person who has not paid a court-ordered debt. A court may order the debtor's bank, employer, or anyone else who may owe money to the debtor, to pay the money into court to help pay the debt.*

GET A religious divorce necessary for observant Jews. It is needed in addition to a civil divorce in order to dissolve the marriage.

INDEXING To increase the amount of a support order or provision in a separation agreement by a fixed amount each year. The increase is usually tied to changes in the cost of living index. It is also known as a "cost of living allowance" or COLA.

INTERIM ORDERS There may be a considerable period of time between the initial filing of a divorce application and the date on which a court is able to grant a divorce and related support, custody or access orders. On request, a court can make a temporary order for the interim period to stabilize custody or access arrangements or to provide financial support for a spouse or child.*

JOINT PETITION A special form of divorce petition that can be used by two spouses who wish to have an uncontested divorce. It is one request for divorce filed by two people.

JOINT CUSTODY A mother and father can continue to share responsibility for making major decisions which affect their children, regardless of which parent the children actually live with on a day-to-day basis. Such arrangements require a commitment on the part of both former spouses to co-operate for the benefit of the children. Joint custody does not eliminate the obligation of both parents to provide financial support for the children.*

JUDGMENT The final decision by the court on any issues put to it during the trial. The formal piece of paper that describes who has been successful or not and on which issues.

LIMITATIONS Time limits imposed by the laws and rules of court. If certain things are not done (claim support, division of property) then the right to claim is lost unless the court grants special permission.

LITIGATION Resolving a dispute by using the courts and the adversarial process.

MARRIAGE The voluntary union for life of one man and one woman to the exclusion of all others. In Canada, marriage involves a religious or civil ceremony that complies with the procedural requirements of provincial or territorial laws where the marriage takes place.

Marriage creates the legal status of husband and wife and the legal obligations arising from that status.*

MARRIAGE BREAKDOWN The sole ground for legally ending a marriage under the terms of the *Divorce Act, 1985*. Marriage breakdown can be established in three ways: through evidence that one spouse committed adultery; physical or mental cruelty; or that the spouses intentionally lived separate and apart for at least one year.*

MARRIAGE CONTRACT An agreement between a husband and wife outlining the spouses' respective responsibilities and obligations. Some contracts also include agreements as to how property and ongoing obligations will be shared if the marriage breaks down.*

MATRIMONIAL HOME Where the family or legally married couple have resided. Common-law spouses never have them (as recognized in law) because they have no statutory property rights. It is possible to have more than one at a time.

MEDIATION A process by which people in situations of potential conflict attempt to resolve their differences and reach a mutually acceptable agreement.

Neutral third parties, or mediators, can often help the parties retain a focus on the problems to be solved and possible solutions, rather than on areas of personal disagreement.*

MINUTES OF SETTLEMENT A method of settling a case by writing out and having the parties sign an acknowledgment of how they want their problem resolved.

MOTION A request to the court for a particular order pending trial, such as interim custody or support. Filed with an affidavit.

ORDER The court's decision on a matter that it was asked to resolve. See Motion and Affidavit.

PARTIES   The husband and wife, or anybody else who is named in the case before the court and asking for an order of any kind.

PENSION   A fixed sum paid regularly to a person or surviving dependant following his or her retirement. There are both public (Canada Pension Plan) and private (from one's own employer) pensions. Some provinces consider a pension that is not yet being paid at the time of marriage breakdown to be property that must be divided.

PETITION FOR DIVORCE   The formal document by which one person asks the court to dissolve his or her marriage to another and for corollary relief.

PLEADINGS   The typewritten description of each person's claims in a family law matter, which must be prepared in accordance with the province's Rules of Practice.

POSSESSORY RIGHTS   Some provincial family laws give each legally married spouse an equal entitlement to possession of a matrimonial home upon separation. This right exists regardless of actual ownership of the home by one or the other. The court will fix, or the couple will come to an agreement over, the appropriate period of possession. It usually continues for the period leading up to the trial.

PROCEDURE   The technical rules that lawyers must follow to get a case through the civil justice system. They are contained in the province's Rules of Court.

RESTRAINING ORDER   An order that prohibits contact between two spouses and in some cases their children. It can be a blanket prohibition or it can provide for specific contact at specific times and under specific circumstances.

RETAINER   The contract by which you hire a lawyer to take your case. It can also mean the sum of money you give the lawyer to be applied to fees and disbursements.

RULES OF COURT   See Procedure.

SEPARATE   To cease living together as man and wife, possibly under the same roof but usually not. Done with the intention not to live together again.

SEPARATION AGREEMENT   A contract signed by the parties to settle their differences. It can deal with property, custody, access, support and any other matter. A form of domestic contract.

SHARED PARENTING   Another term used instead of custody and access. It describes a sharing of the decision making that usually is given solely to the custodial parent.

SOLICITOR CLIENT PRIVILEGE   The keeping secret of everything you tell your lawyer.

SPOUSAL SUPPORT   An order that one spouse pay the other a sum of money either in a lump sum or periodically for a set period of time or indefinitely.

SPOUSE   The person you married.

STATUTE   A law passed by the legislature of a province or the federal Parliament (e.g., the *Divorce Act, 1985*).

UNCONTESTED DIVORCE If neither the husband nor wife disputes the ground for divorce, and if they are able to reach an agreement regarding child care and financial arrangements, it may be possible to ask a judge to grant a divorce without a lengthy court hearing. In some provinces and territories it may be possible to get a divorce without having to actually appear in court at all.*

VARIATION If the circumstances which justified making a particular support, custody or access order change, a person affected by the order can ask a judge to alter the order to make it fit the new circumstances.*

Note: The definitions in the Glossary which are followed by an asterisk (*) are from a Government of Canada, Department of Justice publication entitled *Divorce Law for Counsellors*. See Chapter 18 for details on how to obtain this very useful public legal education material. In some cases I have made minor modifications to the definitions, but they were otherwise so accurate that it seemed a shame not to repeat them with appropriate credit. All other definitions are of my own concoction.